The Exquisite Corpse

BOOK SERIES

Publishing works from both emerging and established scholars, The Exquisite Corpse book series challenges readers with questions that are often left unasked about the human body. Like the Surrealist's parlour game, for which the series is named, these books present the body in all of its unruly and corporeal glory. *Reading from Behind: A Cultural Analysis of the Anus* is the first book in this series.

For more information, please contact:
Karen May Clark, Acquisitions Editor
University of Regina Press
3737 Wascana Parkway
Regina SK S4S 0A2
Canada
PHONE: 306-585-4664
EMAIL: karen.clark@uregina.ca

*Reading from Behind

A CULTURAL ANALYSIS OF THE ANUS

Jonathan A. Allan

University of Regina Press

Printed and bound in Canada at Friesens.

Cover and text design: Duncan Campbell, University of Regina Press
Copy editor: Dallas Harrison
Proofreader: Kristine Douaud
Index: Patricia Furdek

NOTE: Every possible effort has been made to contact copyright holders. Any copyright holders who could not be reached are urged to contact the publisher.

Library and Archives Canada Cataloguing in Publication
Allan, Jonathan A., author
Reading from behind : a cultural analysis of the anus / Jonathan A. Allan.

Includes bibliographical references and index.
Issued in print and electronic formats.
ISBN 978-0-88977-384-4 (bound).—ISBN 978-0-88977-389-9 (html).
—ISBN 978-0-88977-388-2 (pdf)

1. Anus—Social aspects. 2. Anus. 3. Buttocks—Social aspects.
4. Buttocks. 5. Sex in popular culture. 6. Anus (Psychology). I. Title.

GN298.A55 2016   306.4   C2016-900158-X   C2016-900159-8

10 9 8 7 6 5 4 3 2 1

University of Regina Press, University of Regina
Regina, Saskatchewan, Canada, S4S 0A2
TEL: (306) 585-4758 FAX: (306) 585-4699
U OF R PRESS   WEB: www.uofrpress.ca

We acknowledge the support of the Canada Council for the Arts for our publishing program. We acknowledge the financial support of the Government of Canada. / Nous reconnaissons l'appui financier du gouvernement du Canada. This publication was made possible through Creative Saskatchewan's Creative Industries Production Grant Program.

 Canada Council   Conseil des Arts
for the Arts   du Canada
Canada
creative SASKATCHEWAN

*Contents

Acknowledgements

READING FROM BEHIND IS A BOOK THAT I NEVER SET out to write but was written in large part thanks to peer reviewers who encouraged me to turn an article into a book. As such, from the outset, let me thank David William Foster for encouraging me to turn that article into this book—in many ways, this book could not have happened without his input, queries, comments, and provocations.

I also wish to thank a range of colleagues at Brandon University—for I truly work at one of the most collegial places—who commented on the manuscript, engaged with me, sent me articles, and above all encouraged me: Emily Holland, Corinne Mason, Allison McCulloch, Doug Ramsey, Serena Petrella, David Winter, and Emma Varley. I also wish to thank Brandon University, my institutional home, for supporting my sometimes curious research. I am especially thankful to the late Carol Steele, the Interlibrary Loan Office, and the entire staff of the Brandon University Library for ordering books and articles that helped to facilitate this research. And thanks to my research assistant, Morganna Malyon, for tracking down sources and proofreading.

Beyond Brandon University, I am especially thankful to all my colleagues in Meeting with Your Writing, facilitated by Jo Van Every. Further still, my thanks to Jeannine Pitas (who also translated the poetry), Brendon Wocke, Frank Karioris, Antonio Viselli, Jesse Carlson, Ricky Varghese, Cristina Santos, Rachel Stapleton, Lukasz Wodzynski, and so many others who read and commented on various parts of the manuscript. And thank you to the anonymous peer reviewers; I am grateful for your kind, careful, and inquisitive readings of this text.

As well, I am thankful to audiences at various conferences who listened and responded to early iterations of these chapters, notably the Department of English at Princeton University, which invited me to speak as I was putting together the final edits, but also the Faculty of Arts Speaker Series at Brandon University (organized by Derek Brown and Allison McCulloch), the Canadian Comparative Literature Association, the Canadian Association of Hispanists, the Sexuality Studies Association, the Red River Women's Studies Conference, the American Men's Studies Association, and others.

The original article that inspired this book was published in *Chasqui: Revista de literatura latinoamericana* 43: 2 (2014), and is included, with permission (and revisions), as Chapter 6, "Unlocking Delmira Agustini's 'El Intruso.'" I also want to thank Kent Monkman for permission to include images of two of his paintings in Chapter 5. I also thank Jeannine Pitas for her careful translations of the poetry.

I would be remiss if I failed to note the support of the University of Regina Press, excited about this project from the outset. Bruce Walsh, Director and Publisher, responded to my initial email with interest and generosity, and Karen Clark, Acquisitions Editor, has guided me throughout the entire process, putting up with my numerous questions and offering advice and ideas along the way. Dallas Harrison has been the ideal copy editor, carefully working through each and every sentence, always with a keen eye to find a better way to say something.

On the home front, I am thankful to my family, who encouraged me to keep on writing, even when the writing wasn't happening. And, of course, my gratitude and love goes to Deanna, who has tried, as much as possible, to relieve all of my anxieties about this book.

This research was undertaken, in part, thanks to funding from the Canada Research Chairs Program, for which I am immensely grateful, and I wish to extend sincere thanks to the Canadian government and Canadian taxpayers for supporting the Canada Research Chairs Program. Additionally, I received funding from the Brandon University Research Committee.

No Wrong Doors: An Entryway

In a hole in the ground there lived a hobbit. Not a nasty,
dirty, wet hole, filled with the ends of worms and an
oozy smell, nor a dry, bare, sandy hole with nothing
in it to sit down on or to eat: it was a hobbit-hole, and
that means comfort. —J. R. R. TOLKIEN, *The Hobbit*

READING FROM BEHIND IS A SHORT BOOK ON THE
ROLE of the anus, the rear, the posterior, the behind, the
bottom, the ass in literary theory and cultural criticism.
I have a basic hunch that the ass is more important than
we have cared to admit, or than we have admitted, but only in part.
I will argue that the rear can help us to understand a wide range of
textual expressions and that "reading from behind" can illuminate
literary and cultural texts in new and exciting ways. However, to do
this, we must change our critical postures and anxieties and address
what is arguably the most pressing issue: our discomfort with anal
things, with other people's asses, and with the fact that perhaps the
ass is filled with meaning that we have not yet attended to for any
number of reasons. It's tricky, for despite the apparent discomfort
with, and avoidance of, the anus, it fascinates us. In fact, Christina
Garibaldi boldly writes for MTV *News*, "It's pretty safe to say that

2014 will be remembered as the year of the booty."; Jennifer Lopez gleefully responds that "It's about time. . . . Before we were just considered like heavy, like we weren't 'in shape' or whatever if you had a big butt or something. So now it's kind of nice that people are embracing womanly curves in that way."[1] The ass is everywhere it seems, yet, as Lopez reminds us, "It's about time" that we look at it.

It truly is everywhere, the ass. Consider just a few of the many examples in recent popular culture: the song "Honky Tonk Badonkadonk"; the iconic behinds of Kim Kardashian and, as noted above, Jennifer Lopez; the twerking booty of Miley Cyrus. Farther abroad is Pippa Middleton's famous "derriere," which inspired a "new plastic surgery trend" known as the "Pippa butt lift," as reported by the *International Business Times*.[2] "Fat Bottomed Girls" indeed. Paying attention to a television show such as *The Big Bang Theory* reveals a significant amount of anal humour, ranging from phrases such as "anal autograph" to "colon calling card," both appearing in a single episode.[3] And to take a longer view of culture, to turn to words, we have the saying "Don't be an ass" and the fine word *asshole*, which itself became the subject of philosopher Aaron James's 2012 book *Assholes: A Theory*—a defining and hermeneutic work less about the thing itself and more about the kind of person that one might angrily call an asshole (incidentally, he dedicates the book to his parents).

With only these few examples given but so many available to offer, it seems fair to say that the ass captivates us. And though some might insist that these popular cultural references are simply oddities or passing fads and curiosities, I believe that we need to think deeper about their meanings and how we respond to them. So many of these ideas of the behind, the ways in which we speak and don't speak about the ass, fold into one another, leading me to conclude that the anus is a governing symbol that can and does explain a wide range of phenomena but that we have—for many reasons that run the gamut from the taboo, to the fear of embarrassment, to the practical question of "Who'd fund this research project?"—until now left largely untouched and unread.

I am interested here in why the anus remains covered, hidden away, a site of humiliation and disgust, even though we seem to see the fascination with it everywhere, from popular music to royal weddings. Interesting too is that, while we have had for a long time theories and discussions of the phallus in particular, but also the womb and clitoris, we do not yet have what might be called an "anal theory" or a "methodology of the anus"—a way to read from behind. This book sets out to overturn this failing—to turn theory on its head by asking different questions, using other modes of reading, of thinking, and of critiquing. What would happen, for instance, if we uncovered and revealed the anus and anal dimensions—tunnels, holes, crevices, enemas—in literary, filmic, and visual texts?

I attempt to answer these questions by working through a series of literary and visual materials, some from "high" culture, others from "low" culture, all of which, in one fashion or another, afford a commentary on the anal dimensions of the text. I explore, for example, what it means to think about the writings of Gore Vidal, Annie Proulx, and the popular romance novelist in a way that considers how they represent anal sex. Via close readings, I consider too the result of seriously questioning why the curvaceous butt appears as fascinating, ready to be spanked, pinched, and teased, and why cultural critics have failed to ask this question. And what happens when the anus is freed from its association with male homosexuality? Although male homosexuality has some claim to the anus, what results in considering it *apart* from male homosexuality? What happens when we see the anus as *more* than male homosexuality?

Reading from Behind thus participates and intervenes in a series of discussions ranging from masculinity studies, to queer theory, to literary and cultural analysis. I dwell on the anus, its meanings and signs, in order to deflate, critique, and expand our understandings of it. We shall come to see, by the book's end, that it is a remarkably complex organ, sign, and symbol that appears repeatedly in literature and culture.

* * *

WITH RESPECT TO THE ANUS, "The prevailing social consensus," writes sexologist and therapist Jack Morin, "can still be described as, 'Don't ask, don't tell.'"[4] Reading this assertion, published in 2010, I am struck by how much one thing has changed—the resonance of "Don't ask, don't tell." Yet so much has also not changed. As much as gays and lesbians might not be forced any longer into the closet, the anus—and discussions of it—continue to remain guarded, closeted, limited.[5] We are still anxious about it. It remains taboo. As I began to think about writing *Reading from Behind*, I realized early on in the venture that Morin's words would ring true for many readers, and I imagine that they will remain true for a long time to come. No doubt conversation about it evokes discomfort for many. It is, after all, central to elimination, shit, the abject. But it also entails eroticism, pleasure, affect, sexuality. Still, it makes people extremely uncomfortable, and perhaps nowhere is this more evident than in academic conferences, during the scholarly peer review process, and the like. So, though it is certainly true that postmodern scholars and their philosophies have allowed scholars in general to ask many new questions, other questions still remain unasked, let alone answered. So as much as the anus might well be a valuable area of inquiry, the discomfort persists, the giggles continue, and the dirtiness of the subject matter continues to taint those involved.

Indeed, the more I spoke about these issues at conferences, the more I paid attention to audiences' reactions, the initial uneasiness yet also the curiosity (often what brought people to the lecture), and the kinds of questions asked. Even today I must admit my own embarrassment at times. There was the uncomfortable experience, for example, when an American border agent read my conference paper on "Rectal Reading" in its entirety, presumably because it was a threat to national security (or maybe because it was during a government shutdown and—being a particularly slow and boring time, like constipation itself—the guard had nothing better to do). As I have thought about these experiences evoked by my research and writing, I have become more and more convinced that "most of us still feel somewhat uneasy"[6] with this subject matter. But what causes this uneasiness? Why are we, or at least so many of us, uncomfortable with discussions of the anus?

There is, it must be admitted, "no simple explanation"[7] for any of these issues, and though I might be tempted to try to resolve these problems, tensions, and discomforts I think that it is more productive to dwell on them. Taboos, we might recall, "have an all-encompassing quality" and are "highly resistant to logic [and] scientific inquiry"; the taboo is always a "product of culture."[8] It is certain that we have a number of ideas about the anus and anal things that constitute what I call "anal mythologies." I mean by mythologies what Roland Barthes meant by them: not so much the lofty myths of Zeus and Aphrodite but the practical, daily myths of wine and milk, steak-frites, and astrology. That is, I am interested in the kinds of myths that inform day-to-day life, the stories that we tell about, say, astrology. The ass too is present in popular culture, a quotidian myth informing common-sense ideas and ideals. For example, a "fat ass" can be a desirable thing—"I like big butts," the song declares. But it can also be derogatory, fat-phobic, and implicated in gendered and racialized thought (e.g., Hottentot Venus). An "asshole," though a very useful thing, is not something that we wish to be called, yet we do not wish to be without one. People can be "anal," which is not to say that they are assholes but that they have anal tendencies, such as cleanliness. Being anal bears no relation to being gay, though in popular culture gay men often appear as anal—think of Will in *Will and Grace* or Mitch in *Modern Family*. And even though being anal is not essential to being gay, the anus seems to be, as Jeffrey R. Guss has put it, "the very ground zero of gayness."[9] In this rendering, any man who experiences anal pleasure, especially his own anal pleasure, becomes associated with gayness, and herein lies the rub: when it comes to the anus, a great deal of phobia resides within and around it.

My argument in *Reading from Behind* is that the anus is a remarkably productive and meaningful site of inquiry. The anus, unlike the vagina or the vulva, for instance, is not always the opposite or inverse of the penis, yet it would be difficult to argue that the anus is not rich in meaning. Although the penis is undoubtedly fascinating insofar as it highlights many anxieties, desires, and fears, and though its symbolic form could certainly be the governing figure in an attempt to outline a history of sexuality (as a critic such as Ilan Stavans has argued), I argue that the anus provides an equally provocative site to begin critical analysis. I also ask questions about the nature of literary and cultural criticism, not because I believe these modes of criticism to be in need of revision or correction but because I am committed to opening up new lines of inquiry or repressed lines of inquiry that have hitherto remained largely uninvestigated—sealed tight, so to speak.

Indeed, readings of the texts that I explore in *Reading from Behind* have been incomplete because critics have failed to account for the anus. The anus is an opening to the text that has remained obscured by critical, intellectual, and affective anxieties that have not permitted readers the chance to engage with the other side of textuality. Thus, I argue that though a poem such as Delmira Agustini's "El Intruso" is largely obvious in its meaning—an intruder enters a private space, and an erotic encounter ensues—there is a secondary meaning, another way of reading the text, that demonstrates a complexity that has not been critically imagined. It is this critical work, as a kind of imaginative reading, that motivates *Reading from Behind*. I intend to explore and consider what happens to gender, particularly masculinity, when the anus is incorporated into textual analysis.

Jonathan Branfman and Susan Ekberg Stiritz use this type of questioning to frame their article "Teaching Men's Anal Pleasure: Challenging Gender Norms with 'Prostage' Education." What would it mean, they ask, to think carefully and critically about the intersection of masculinity and anality? They provide an analysis of a letter sent to Dan Savage, the popular sex columnist:

> "Drew" anxiously describes his new found "fetish": anal pleasure. Drew, a 30-year-old, recently "let a girlfriend 'experiment' on my ass. What started out as a kink with her finger has turned into a full-blown fetish with her dildo." Interpreting this "fetish" as a sign he might be gay, Drew "tried masturbating to some gay porn." Although the porn did not excite him, Drew seeks assurance that he can really be straight despite enjoying receptive anal penetration. As he puts it, "I still don't have any desire to be with a man sexually, Dan, but I LOVE having my ass pounded. Does that tip the scale toward homo?"[10]

Drew has become a "frantic epistemologist," to use the language of Adam Phillips.[11] He is urgently trying to figure out what this newfound "fetish" means—as if it *must* mean something. He turns to gay pornography to see if he really is gay; ultimately, he remains uncertain and requires answers to his anxious questions. He turns to Savage and asks, "Does that tip the scale toward homo?" Surely, in practical terms, Drew must be aware of who is giving him this pleasure: a girlfriend. The scene, in basic terms, is heterosexual insofar as it involves a male body and a female body. Indeed, this is the response from Savage: "Once again: If a man and a woman are doing it—whatever it is—it's a heterosexual act."[12] (To be certain, he is correct on the one hand, but on the other he reduces sexuality to a body with a penis and another body with a vagina. It is too reductive; it does not account for the complexities of gender, sexuality, and sex.)

Incidentally, but importantly, an issue that goes entirely untouched in the sexual advice from Savage is the danger of using a sex toy that might not be designed for anal pleasure. The *Archive of Sexual Behaviour* reports, for instance, that "a healthy, 28-year-old man presented to Emergency Services at our hospital because 5 h ago, while he practiced sex with his girlfriend, she introduced a sexual toy (vibrator) across the anal orifice. Due to suction the object stayed in the rectum."[13] Such narratives are all too common if one consults medical journals, and on the Internet one can find numerous stories such as this involving any number of instruments: vegetables, toys, guns.

The issue here is that medical professionals, sexologists, and scholars of gender and sexuality need to do a better job of educating the public about anal sexual health. The average male, it seems, is evidently curious about, if not interested in, anal pleasure, not least because of the elusive "male G spot," highlighted in various examples from popular culture to sex tips from gay men for straight women. Indeed, it is not surprising that renowned psychoanalyst Donald Meltzer wrote in 1966 that "I have been forced also to the recognition that masturbation of the anus is a far more widespread habit than analytical literature to date would imply."[14] Although his article was published decades ago, it seems that concerns remain as "widespread" today as they were then. If this is the case, then surely there is a responsibility to think carefully about anal health and to treat it as seriously as we would any other medical concern. As a policy initiative (not the goal of this book), this would be not about sexual orientation but about anal health and sexual health. Although not wanting to take on the role of a concerned sexologist, I believe that this discussion of the anus needs to include the work of a cultural critic, such as me, working alongside sexologists, medical practitioners, and sex therapists.

The challenge with Drew's story is that it recalls Guss's contention that the anus has become "the very ground zero of gayness." Drew becomes a "frantic epistemologist" not of what the anus means for other people but of what it means for him. It confuses him. He is like the Lacanian hysteric asking, "Am I a man or a woman?"[15] However, his question is less about sex and more about sexuality: Am I straight or gay? Hetero or homo? And the answer it seems, at least for Drew, is found in and through the anus: what it does and what it means to the constitution and essence of sexuality.

The anus, in this rendering, works to define one's sexuality. The problem therefore resides in the fact that "the ultimate 'feminine' that men must reject in order to be regarded or to regard themselves as masculine" is penetrated.[16] Such a perspective, however, does not (for it cannot) "celebrate our own complex, ambiguous bodily sensations."[17] In a sense, *Reading from Behind* proposes that the anus is "complex, ambiguous," and this is what we need to recognize in our critical theories; and we must equally admit that the anus seems to be caught up in a grand narrative: "the very ground zero of gayness." This tension needs to be exposed, explored, and understood. The anus, as we have witnessed briefly here, calls into question masculinity, sexuality, and orientation. Even in a scenario involving a male and a female, the anus seems to disrupt one's claim to a given sexuality and by extension one's gender.

One of the challenges that must be overcome while "reading from behind" is the less than critical imperative that we orient the anus in a particular fashion. Indeed, one of the goals of this study is to decentre the orientation of the anus. This is not to deny that it has an orientation but to claim that its orientation is not the same for everyone. Further, what would happen—if only as a thought experiment—if we privileged the anal dimensions of texts? Can we read for these instances, these moments, and imagine other readings not indebted to a particular orientation or to the obvious prominence of the phallus, a site of difference, and move toward a space of inclusion? What if the ass, the booty, the moneymaker, the *tukhus* were a fully loaded sign endowed with rich and complex meaning much like the numerous nerve endings of the anus? What if we loosened up our critical inquiries, embraced the pleasure of the text, and removed ourselves from the paranoid, sphincter-tightening hermeneutics of suspicion? Indeed, is it possible to find a way to read texts that engage the anus but not fall victim to a hermeneutics of suspicion, a paranoid, anxious, or nervous reading practice, one that always insists on a certain orientation?

I suggest that the solution, as it were, is to take the anus head on, to read from behind. Instead of keeping the anus covered and controlled, we can explore why it matters and how it functions in a given text. We can undertake new readings of works that afford interesting, provocative, and important critiques of how we think about the anus. It is not a matter of displacing the phallus from literary and cultural analysis—or of forgetting the womb and clitoris altogether—but a matter of looking at the other pieces, the other assemblages, and determining if there is not another mode of reading that affords another perspective on the same texts.

* * *

TO THESE ENDS, I DRAW on the work of Eve Kosofsky Sedgwick, especially her essay "Paranoid Reading and Reparative Reading, or, You're So Paranoid, You Probably Think This Essay Is about You," one of her most provocative and challenging essays. Throughout it, Sedgwick challenges "the hypervigilance of the hermeneutics of suspicion—or what she called, following Melanie Klein, the paranoid position—which had become 'nearly synonymous with criticism itself.'"[18] Instead of paranoid reading, Sedgwick imagines "reparative reading" as a mode of critical theory that embraces the "privilege of unknowing"[19] and that provides theorists, readers, and scholars with a way to think about texts that does not always already, even before reading, imagine a potential outcome—a possible reading, indeed, that does not imagine a *potential* as even *necessary*.

Reparative reading embraces the possibility of any number of readings, some of which might be predictable, and others of which might catch us by surprise. Admittedly, all readings have the influence of the reader, and a reader attuned to a given politics or poetics will likely find these meanings in texts. All of the readings in this book, for instance, attend to anal poetics, but I want to stress that I am not foreclosing any other potential reading. My intention is to ask what happens when we do not focus on the governing symbol, the mainstream reading informed by the phallus, and so on. Reparative readers, on the other hand, do not privilege this "paranoid position" and instead "seek new environments of sensation for the objects they study by displacing critical attachments once forced by correction, rejection, and anger with those crafted by affection, gratitude, solidarity, and love."[20]

My argument is that it is important to remove ourselves from, or at least temper, what I see as a paranoid, sphincter-tightening perspective with respect to the anus, its symbolism, and its affects. It is equally imperative, however, that we understand how this paranoia unfolds in Sedgwick's work and how we can work with her invocation of reparative reading or what we might now call reading from behind. Reading from behind, as I hope becomes clear throughout this book, works to diminish, if not negate, the seemingly unquestioned authority of paranoid (critical) reading, but to do so a radical reorientation of the anus and its role in the collective imaginary is required. That is, we must admit, no easy feat. This book works to relieve the burden of paranoia.

For Sedgwick, reading from a reparative position is about "surrender[ing] the knowing, anxious paranoid determination that no horror, however apparently unthinkable, shall ever come to the reader *as new*" and that, "to a reparatively positioned reader, it can seem realistic and necessary to experience surprise."[21] However, as Sedgwick has noted about reparative reading, once "reparative motives . . . become explicit, [they] are inadmissible in paranoid theory both because they are about pleasure ('merely aesthetic') and because they are frankly ameliorative ('merely reformist')."[22] There is something disconcerting about a theoretical position that surrenders the paranoid search for meaning and knowledge in favour of pleasurable surprises. The reparative reading contends that since "there can be terrible surprises . . . there can also be good ones."[23] The reparatively positioned reader "tries to organize the fragments and part-objects she encounters or creates," and thus "the reader has the room to realize that the future may be different from the present."[24] Reparative reading is neither better nor worse than paranoid reading; it simply stands beside paranoid reading. Modes of reading afford different perspectives on given texts, but unlike the paranoid reader, who might work to understand the whole before its parts, the reparative reader imagines that the parts might constitute the whole. The tension between synecdoche and metonymy perhaps becomes crucial here. The reparative reader works from the part to the whole. The paranoid reader, on the other hand, works from the whole to the part and can thus form an argument that is totalizing and essential. Fredric Jameson, for instance, becomes a paranoid reader when he declares in the opening pages of *The Political Unconscious: Narrative as a Socially Symbolic Act* that we must "Always historicize!"—to which Sedgwick responds, "what could have less to do with historicizing than the commanding, atemporal adverb 'always'?"[25] To stress, paranoia is not bad so much as determined. For Sedgwick, there is a remarkable pleasure and privilege in not knowing and unknowing, and in a sense this is precisely what the anal dimensions of texts afford: a constant process of undercutting knowledge because so much of our critical apparatus has been informed by phallocentrism. Although these phallocentric readings might well offer much to the interpretive task of the critic, I am interested in asking at what cost? What is left behind?

In a reparative gesture, Wiegman spends some time thinking about the generation of Sedgwick's essay, noting that it had many lives before its final draft, initially "as many people do not recall . . . as a four page introduction to the 1996 special issue of *Studies in the Novel* under the title 'Queerer than Fiction.'"[26] Indeed, I had not realized this and was compelled to return to one of its earliest manifestations, though much of the reparative impulses in Sedgwick's work are found before this paper. Wiegman further explains that, "when the special issue appeared in book form the following year as *Novel Gazing: Queer Readings in Fiction*, Sedgwick's introduction was thirty-seven pages long and dressed in the provocative title, 'Paranoid Reading and Reparative Reading; or, You're So Paranoid You Probably Think This Introduction Is about You.'" Further still, Wiegman reminds us that the essay "was later revised, though only slightly, and included in her 2003 collection, *Touching Feeling: Affect, Pedagogy, Performativity*."[27] Those familiar with Sedgwick's oeuvre will note that ideas are often recycled, reused, revivified. Jonathan Goldberg, for instance, notes that "Eve treated her own writing as a series of movable modules,"[28] and this is surely the case of "Paranoid Reading and Reparative Reading." I note all of this history because I draw heavily—though not exclusively—on what is understood as the "final" version of the Sedgwick essay, which appears in *Touching Feeling*. I draw on this final version simply because it is the final version; however, as Wiegman observes,

> scholars have largely used [the 2003 version] to date Sedgwick's call for reparative reading, which aligns it with a post 9-11 thinking of paranoid sensibilities in ways that have skewed our understanding of her work's own present, which was profoundly influenced by her disgust with the national fantasy of gay extermination propelled by the health emergency of AIDS and by her personal battle with breast cancer.[29]

Again, this is the final version that we have available to us, and, had Sedgwick lived, we might well have yet another revision of her paper, just as we have various versions of "Shame Theatricality, Queer Performativity: Henry James's *The Art of the Novel*,"[30] which more than "Paranoid Reading and Reparative Reading" is haunted by "post 9-11 thinking," especially since in revisions it explicitly speaks about 9/11.

In thinking about this article, Jackie Stacey notes that Sedgwick rejected "paranoid reading . . . for its diagnostic judgments, its critical sovereignty and delusions of grandeur that find political agency in textual mastery."[31] If one thing is certain, when we read *about* Sedgwick, we read that she is *reparative* and perhaps even paranoid about paranoia. Paranoid becomes "bad"; reparative becomes "good." But when critics rely on this idea, they miss her point. The paranoid and the reparative must "interdigitate,"[32] like lovers' fingers braided together.[33] Nonetheless, we must spend time thinking about both modes of reading.

For Sedgwick, paranoia has become the governing method of critical theory, not least because anything that is not paranoid "has come to seem naïve, pious, or complaisant."[34] Paranoia, as she explains, works to avoid all possible surprises. For example, that the anus and its eroticism could be anything other than gay would largely come as a surprise to a homophobic culture (even though we know how much that culture can celebrate the asses of women). Sedgwick notes that Guy Hocquenghem "has established the paranoid stance as a uniquely privileged one for understanding not . . . homosexuality itself, but rather precisely the mechanisms of homophobic and heterosexist enforcement against it."[35] That is, if we accept that the anus is "the very ground zero of gayness" and that any admission of anal desire, curiosity, or pleasure is attached to this myth, then surely we must acknowledge the anus as a site of paranoia. We want to know about it without knowing about it, we want to imagine every possible outcome, even though we already know that anything involving the anus is gay. We end up in a circular logic, tickling at the rims of the argument.

For Sedgwick, "paranoia is a theory of negative affects."[36] Those "negative affects" or bad feelings become unbearable, consuming, domineering, totalizing. Silvan Tomkins isolates a series of primary affects of which the following are considered to be "negative": distress-anguish, fear-terror, shame-humiliation, contempt-disgust, anger-rage. Within each, we find nuanced expressions of affect, but these affects are constituted—at least by Tomkins—as negative. The list of positive affects is shorter: interest-excitement and enjoyment-joy. Between the positive and the negative is the resetting affect of surprise-startle, and perhaps, in many ways, *Reading from Behind* aims to reset our affect responses to the anus.[37] To complete this task, however, we must also attend to the negative affects that govern the anus.

Negative affects, especially when treated in a more open fashion than the limited scope of Tomkins, are particularly seductive, and queer theory has embraced negative affects with tremendous zeal, so much so that Michael Snediker has rightly cautioned his readers about the seeming celebration of these affects.[38] Scholars have written about the primary affects and subsequently tailored them in more nuanced or particular ways: for example, "gay shame,"[39] "humiliation,"[40] and "ugly feelings" such as paranoia, irritation, anxiety, envy,[41] depression,[42] the bruising passion and feeling of being "black and blue,"[43] and "feeling brown, feeling down."[44] Optimism has become "cruel,"[45] failure has become a "queer art,"[46] and sex has become "unbearable."[47] Although it is true that negative affects are useful modes of thinking through and about queer theory, surely something is lost in this privileging. Nonetheless, each affect is often associated with the anus, a source of shame, anxiety, humiliation, irritation, and so on. One of the frequently repeated words in Morin's *Anal Pleasure and Health* is discomfort, whether it is sexual discomfort, psychic discomfort, hemorrhoids, or painful bowel movements.

Given how "negative" the affects are that inform queer theory—so much so that José Esteban Muñoz writes that, "in queer studies, antiutopianism, more often than not intertwined with antirelationality, has led many scholars to an impasse wherein they cannot see futurity for the life of them"[48]—it is somewhat surprising that the field has yet to develop extended discussions, and more specifically theories, of the anus, the essential relationship between the anus and subjectivity, the anus and theory. One goal of reading from behind, as a critical practice, might be to reclaim negative affects, somehow to make the negative into a positive in a Pollyannaish kind of reparative reading; however, another goal, and the one that I work to adopt, allows us to negotiate our relations to these affects, thinking through the complicated and complex ways in which affect informs idea. Instead of reclaiming the affect, which would necessarily accept the idea as true, I think that it is worthwhile to benefit from the tension, which might well be discomforting. I am not interested in reclaiming discomfort, for example, nor is my goal in *Reading from Behind* to cure readers of anal discomfort. The subject matter of this book is discomforting to many, even shameful, and I am inclined to agree with Sedgwick that these affects might well allow for "new expressive grammars" because they are, or at least seem to be, "uniquely contagious from one person to another." For instance, shame can be "the first . . . and remains a permanent structuring fact of identity," and the affect itself is "powerfully productive," even if we wish it were not.[49]

The challenge that we are confronted with, time and again, especially in queer theory, is the persistence of paranoia, "a negative affect that only ever stimulates and nurtures our fears, concerns, and worries."[50] Its productivity rests on the fact that it is contagious, duplicating, multiplying, never ending, and ultimately, I'd argue, "self-defeating."[51] In thinking about the "duality" of paranoid reading and reparative reading, Ann Cvetkovich explains that "Sedgwick favors the rich nuances and idiosyncrasies of what she calls reparative reading over the programmatic or ideological readings that seek to line up cultural texts as progressive or reactive. Reparative reading is affectively driven, motivated by pleasure and curiosity, and directed toward the textures and tastes, the sensuous feel, of one's objects of study."[52] Instead of this paranoid mode of reading, we might well "read from a reparative position" that would allow and encourage us "to surrender the knowing, anxious paranoid determination that no horror, however apparently unthinkable, shall ever come to the reader *as new*; to a reparatively positioned reader it can seem realistic and necessary to experience surprise."[53] We might well imagine, then, that curiosity alone is a methodological impulse that motivates research, not for the dogmatic reasons of the paranoid position, but for the mere desire to know something else, to know something anew, to experience something else. Simply put, like Sedgwick, I conceive that many of our reading practices—like our daily lives—are informed and governed by affective experiences, resonances, and traces that can be both negative and positive. To treat literary texts, for instance, as somehow free from affect, to treat sexuality in literature as being without literature, is to misread them. As Northrop Frye pointed out, "the criticism of literature can hardly be a simple or one-level activity."[54]

Even when imagining a reparative criticism, we find critics who seem to be nervous. Lassen, for instance, explains that

> Reparation, by contrast, sets out to satisfy another set of affects. Frequently misread as apolitical, anesthetising, or even naïve, its princip[al] aim is to recover psychological resources that assemble relief and comfort in abundance and confer them on the subject that knows how to indulge in such reparative psychological resources or better: that knows how to extract from them the greatest possible benefit.[55]

Another writer of extraordinarily rich reparative talents, Carol Mavor, writes, cautiously, apologetically, that,

> While the term "reparative" is currently (and destructively) used in psychoanalytic *practice* to cure what some practitioners deem as pathological, perverted (the homosexual, the transsexual, et al.), my reparative work embraces the texts and textures of Sedgwick (who has already pulled the threads through the hettles), in order to usurp "reparative" to repair not the gay body so pathologized by psychoanalysis itself but the body of psychoanalysis, so responsible for this initial pathologization.[56]

The very idea of reparative reading renders critics paranoid, anxious, worried. We apologize for it before we have even begun to do it. Muñoz, like Mavor, defers to another critic: "[U]topian readings are aligned with what Sedgwick would call reparative hermeneutics."[57] In each instance, before we even see what reparation might look like, we've set up a defence for our curious method. The utopian, the reparative, the affirmative, the compassionate redescription,[58] perhaps even the loving are not about being less (rigorous, intellectual, and so many other traces of a seemingly Protestant work ethic that renders work serious) but about more, about possibility, about "a sustained seeking of pleasure."[59] Pleasure is not antithetical to work. "The Pleasure of the Text," Roland Barthes writes, "can say: never apologize, never explain."[60]

These impulses toward the utopian, the affirmative, the reparative are indebted to a deep belief in the pleasures—the inherent, absolute, essential, productive pleasures—of the text, the pleasures of life. Reparative reading, according to Erin Murphy and J. Keith Vincent, is "more attuned to the modest pleasures of close reading," and the goal of literary criticism, at least when at its finest in Sedgwick's estimation, knows "how to allow the paranoid and reparative to 'interdigitate.'"[61] The reparative is not and cannot be totalizing, and *Reading from Behind*, though never fully reparative but motivated by the curious method of reparative reading, is committed to the affective responses that the project has elicited over the years. I hope that the writing is playful, joyful, salubrious, slippery, (dis)comforting, and so on, not because I want to tease the reader, but because these affects allow the reader to come to learn once more, to learn anew. Ideally, then, in our literary practice, our daily reading, our classrooms, we would admit and allow for the "sensuous feel"[62] of the objects that we study.

Nishant Shahani in *Queer Retrosexualities: The Politics of Reparative Return* frames reparative modes of thinking and reading as a kind of "flexible circularity" that "enables a move away from the anticipatory observative practices of paranoid reading."[63] The "flexible circularity" of these modes of reading, which oscillate around words, permit a different mode of analysis that is not depth oriented but perhaps (instead?) plays on the surface, able to tickle, titillate, tease. What if we imagined the soft strokes of a lover's hand caressing our skin as a mode of reading? As Barthes writes, "Language is a skin: I rub my language against the other. It is as if I had words instead of fingers, or fingers at the tip of my words."[64] Reparative reading, in no shape or form, is somehow *less* but, as Sedgwick writes, "additive and accretive."[65] I intend *Reading from Behind* to be about the "additive and accretive" in its recalibration of the phallic signifier as totalizing—and remarkably limiting in the construction of the male body and masculinity.

Finally, this book works, then, to intervene in theories of masculinity, which have long espoused the value of the phallus to the meaning of masculinity, how it is performed, and how it can be lost. But to read masculinity in reparative terms is to call into question its own commitment to paranoia. Masculinity is committed to paranoia and fear, which flutter around the potential for masculine failure, the revelation that one is never—and can never be—masculine enough. In this regard, this book aims to provide a return to Michael Kimmel's provocative thesis about masculinity as homophobia and to couple it with the writings of Guy Hocquenghem, Leo Bersani, and Michel Foucault. To study masculinity requires that the field of critical studies of men and masculinities be informed by and committed to a pro-feminist agenda: that is, I see the study of masculinity not as responding to "women's studies" but as learning from and drawing on those insights to explore the complexity of masculinity. Moreover, in this study, I include insights from queer and affect theories to understand the shifting terrain of masculinity, both as a lived concept and as an object of study. Indeed, in what follows, I explore the limits of masculinity when read from behind, particularly the modes through which masculinity can be called into question when our focus is not oriented by and toward the phallus.

✳ ✳ ✳

IN WRITING *Reading from Behind*, which openly challenges a number of assumptions, it became evident that a discussion, however brief, would have to unfold with regard to the choice of texts and the structure of the book. Each chapter, in a sense, is less a part of a cohesive whole and more a part that works toward a whole. I mean that the chapters can be read individually and that the reader does not need to move progressively and linearly to understand the argument that I set forth.

Like many "efforts to reimagine queer history," *Reading from Behind* works to "resist teleology, linearity, causality, and the pose of epistemological mastery in favor of non-identity, plurality, circularity, and the nonsequential narrative."[66] Each chapter presents a mode of reading from behind, and I contend that there are a number of ways of doing this kind of work. The effort behind these chapters is about questioning the limits imposed on the anus as a totalizing sign that in normative spaces is about evacuation and when plea-sured becomes "the very ground zero of gayness." Surely, between these two poles, a great deal can and does happen.

My goal, therefore, is one that disrupts or calls into question the forms that we use when theorizing. I'd rather see each of these chapters as entry points into various kinds of reading from behind. Each chapter is a case study from an anal archive, akin to the queer archives that interest Cvetkovich. In this archive, "objects are not inherently meaningful but are made so through their significance to an audience."[67] However, all of these texts are necessarily meaningful, but the meanings that I read into them are about a specific purpose and an audience for whom this purpose might well prove interesting. These texts all become rich with affective potential—particularly negative affects such as disgust, shame, and humiliation—because they flirt with the taboo, the homoerotic, the queer, and so on. Each text presented itself in discussions that I had with colleagues and scholars about this project. Some texts I knew I wanted to talk about; other texts were happenstance, luck, or treasures found along the way that now form parts of an archive. So the book explores fictional and non-fictional stories of anal sex and loss of virginity and then moves to poems and films that have an entranceway that has not yet been exposed, or that flirt with different modes of anal-ity, different ways of reading through and alongside the anus. Each text offers a way of thinking about the anus that I hope will expose readers to new modes of criticism and reading that enable them to imagine new textual vantages from which to mount critiques.

Chapter 1, "Anal Theory, or Reading from Behind," evaluates existing scholarship on the anus, particularly the works of Tim Dean, Guy Hocquenghem, Kathryn Bond Stockton, and Nguyen Tan Hoang, and questions the limits of these works in light of feminist and queer theory. One of the challenges that *Reading from Behind* exposes is the tension between masculinity and anality, and this chapter brings together a variety of perspectives to understand the limits and what is at stake in thinking about the anus: notably, homophobia and its corollaries, homohysteria and homoparanoia.

Chapter 2 "Orienting Virginity," ponders how virginity is framed and what it might mean to consider the anus when thinking about virginity. As a concept, virginity is defining. The "first time" is an important time. So many novels, short stories, films, comics, nearly every form of representation, accounts for and explores virginity, but what does it mean to think about virginity in terms of gay male sexuality? How does the anus figure in these discussions? What matters more, penetration or being penetrated? Or what if the anus does not matter at all and virginity is about an intimacy that hitherto has been unknown? This chapter draws heavily on Steven G. Underwood's *Gay Men and Anal Eroticism: Tops, Bottoms, and Versatiles*, which contains a series of "testimonial" narratives. Over and over men give their virginal experiences, their first times, and we are left, in a sense, working to figure out their meanings. Of course, the first time is always given meaning through the stories that we tell about it, how we experienced it, what it felt like, and what constituted its loss. In the cases of these narratives, I ask why so much time is spent dwelling on the anus and identity? The anus, as we learn through these narratives, enables the transition from "virgin" to "non-virgin" and, often enough, the transition to a sexual identity politic: no longer a virgin, now a gay man.

Chapter 3, "Topping from the Bottom: Anne Tenino's *Frat Boy and Toppy*," focuses on the popular romance novel, particularly the increasingly popular male-male romance novel. These novels involve two male heroes who fall in love with one another, essentially a gay re-writing of the standard romance novel. However, and remarkably, very little scholarship exists on these complex novels. They are complicated precisely because of what they are doing with gender and sexuality; the erasure of female bodies in these novels presents an interesting challenge for gender theorists, feminist theorists, and queer theorists. Additionally, these novels are written almost exclusively "by women for women." Straight women are the largest producers and consumers of gay male romance novels. There is a great deal happening with gender and sexual politics that needs to be accounted for by literary and cultural critics. Although the romance novel, in many ways, is at the "bottom" of literary studies, I provide a close reading of Anne Tenino's *Frat Boy and Toppy*, which challenges many assumptions about "topping" and "bottoming." Her novel works in particular to deflate the myth of the pathetic, inactive, submissive bottom.

From this vantage point, I turn in Chapter 4 to what is arguably a more "popular" story of love between men, Annie Proulx's *Brokeback Mountain*, later adapted to film by Ang Lee. The film managed to capture the attention of a range of viewers and became one of the most significant love stories to hit the screens, and arguably we have yet to recapture that excitement. Most viewers of the film and readers of the story have focused on questions of sexuality, notably gay male sexuality, but have failed to account for the complexities of those situations, especially in light of a long tradition of homoeroticism in American literature, a tradition documented by F. O. Matthiessen and Leslie Fiedler. As such, this chapter brings together Matthiessen, Fiedler, and queer theory to explore how *Brokeback Mountain* fits into a long tradition of homoeroticism that extends back to *Adventures of Huckleberry Finn* and *Moby-Dick* while also illuminating the queerness of Fiedler and Matthiessen.

In Chapter 5, "Spanking Colonialism," I explore the tensions that arise in the previous chapter, particularly around race and bottoming. What lurks in the background of *Brokeback Mountain* is a question about colonialism and whiteness. In "Spanking Colonialism," I focus on a series of paintings by Kent Monkman that challenges us to think deeply and carefully about race and sexuality and the kinds of assumptions that we might encounter about sexualized ideas of race. Is the anus itself always already racialized? We might well think about what this kind of question means for sexuality studies and queer theory, and I hope to afford a critical analysis of how these images challenge and confront racist and homophobic ideas about gay male sexualities.

Of course, in many ways, *Reading from Behind* can only begin to scratch the surface of the complexity of anality and anal sexualities. In Chapter 6, "Unlocking Delmira Agustini's 'El Intruso,'" I return to one of the most frequently anthologized poems in Latin American literature. This sonnet is largely read in terms of heterosexuality, but I argue that there is another reading made available when the poem is read from behind. In this reading, I show how the poem might well be about anal sexuality, which itself becomes a site of queer sexuality not just for gay men but also, and importantly, for heterosexuality.

In Chapter 7, "Shameful Matrophilia in *Doña Herlinda y su hijo*," I engage readings of what is arguably one of the most important "gay" films from Latin America. The film focuses on a queer utopia made possible by an overbearing mother who does everything to protect her gay son. She builds a home in which he can keep his lover while also presenting to the outside world the image of secure and safe heterosexuality by arranging a heterosexual marriage for her son. But, in constructing this heterosexuality, the film complicates one's expectations of his sexuality because he is the "bottom" in his relationships despite his "macho" appearance. Here I work again to show the ways in which the bottom is not always a position of submission, as so many have imagined it to be. In this chapter, shame becomes a governing affective register through which to think about the bottom. Shame and submission, however, need to be separated precisely because these two notions do not always fold into one another.

In Chapter 8, the final chapter, I turn to Gore Vidal's campy and highly problematic *Myra Breckinridge*, a novel, I argue, that is remarkably anal yet not recognized as such. I highlight the ways in which the ass gives meaning to Vidal's novel while also continuing to work through shame. It seems to me that a great deal of work remains to be done on Vidal's novel precisely because it is so shameful and shaming, both for the characters in the novel and for readers.

These chapters, though they can be read apart from one another, flirt with each other, allude to what is to come, or refer back to what has already come. They privilege an "anal hermeneutic," which I see as a kind of close reading that closely focuses on anal dimensions of texts, whether it be a prominent ass, an exploration of the ass sexually, or hints and reverberations of anal things (an overly tidy person perhaps). As I hope this introduction has outlined, the ass, the anus, the booty, the moneymaker, the *tukhus* is everywhere yet nowhere. We seem to work hard to avoid thinking about the ass, perhaps we are uncomfortable with it, perhaps it causes us shame, or perhaps it is too queer, but it is nonetheless a fascinating site of research that enables us to think about gender and sexuality in new and critical ways.

Anal Theory, or Reading from Behind

MASCULINITY HAS LONG BEEN DEFINED IN TERMS OF the penis/phallus. Annie Potts, for instance, observes that the "penis stands in and up for the man."[1] Indeed, at this point, it seems to be nearly impossible to deny the permanence of the penis to masculinity and our definitions of manhood. In *A Mind of Its Own: A Cultural History of the Penis*, David M. Friedman declares, without hesitation, that "from the beginnings of Western civilization the penis was more than a body part," and he contends that it was "an idea, a conceptual but flesh-and-blood gauge of man's place in the world."[2] Likewise, Mels van Driel notes in *Manhood: The Rise and Fall of the Penis* that it was "worshipped in ancient religions, then demonized by the Church fathers, secularized by the learned anatomists and physiologists, . . . and then for a while subject to psychoanalysis" and that, "after being praised to the skies by psychologists, abused by feminists and shamelessly exploited in pop culture, in the twenty-first century . . . [the penis is] in danger of becoming totally medicalized."[3] Micha Ramakers observes that the penis is "the simplest, oldest and most common way to symbolize male sexuality."[4] Ilan Stavans proposes that one could write a "history of Latin sexuality through the figure of the phallus."[5] The penis and its symbolic form of the phallus have had a lengthy history marred by controversy, but never has the penis been entirely neutered or rendered impotent, despite many attempts to destabilize its power—indeed, it seems that the opposite holds true today in our culture of Viagra, which has once more given rise to the penis. Even discussions of castration, the most literal form of reducing the prominence of the penis, necessarily reinforce the power of the phallus; after all, what could be more tragic, more fear-inducing, more humiliating than the loss of one's manhood, the proof of one's potency?

One of the aims of *Reading from Behind* is to consider how we might go about displacing—though not replacing or destroying—the primacy of the phallus in literary and cultural criticism. Although van Driel notes that the penis has been "abused by feminists," a claim that many men's rights activists would surely agree with, I believe that it is necessary to return to feminist theory, at least briefly, because it has provided some of the most exciting and innovative—though also problematic—critiques of the phallus. I am not writing this as a feminist study but attempting to show how feminism enables some of the questions behind this book. That is, there is both an implicit and an explicit debt to feminism even though the book is more comfortably aligned with queer theory and masculinity studies.

Sandra M. Gilbert and Susan Gubar open their agenda-setting *The Madwoman in the Attic: The Woman Writer and the Nineteenth-Century Literary Imagination* with a question: "[I]s the pen a metaphorical penis?" They contend throughout their volume, and in subsequent works, that "male sexuality . . . is not just analogically but actually the essence of literary power" and that the "poet's pen is in some sense (even more than figuratively) a penis."[6] On the one hand, though there is undoubtedly a critique of phallic power about to unfold in their work, on the other there is an undercutting effect insofar as they need to reify the penis in order to deconstruct it. In a later book, *No Man's Land: The Place of the Woman Writer in the Twentieth Century*, Gilbert and Gubar ask a similar question:

"[I]s a pen a metaphorical pistol?"[7] Their readers will note, of course, the resemblance between their opening questions. And Gilbert and Gubar are not alone, for instance, in thinking of the pen as a penis: Elaine Showalter writes that "the text's author is a father, a progenitor, a procreator, an aesthetic patriarch whose pen is the instrument of his generative power like his penis."[8]

The penis-as-pen has been a productive analogy for feminist critics; however, I am not content that this site of criticism itself is advantageous to a greater project that aims to deconstruct the phallocentric discourse called into question by feminist critics. Indeed, I contend that, by highlighting the symbolic reference, feminist theorists arguably maintain a necessary status quo (even if the ultimate goal is to deconstruct it) insofar as they need something on which to reflect and establish an argument. The object to which feminist critics disagree must be established and affirmed so as to allow for disagreement, deconstruction, and so on. Moreover, it creates the false and highly problematic assumption that all pens are necessarily, essentially, and equally penises, all of them involved in creation. Surely we cannot agree that all penises are the same, have the same function, and are used in the same way. Judith Butler, though not making a critique of the penis proper, makes an important observation about patriarchy and feminist theory in *Gender Trouble: Feminism and the Subversion of Identity*:

> The political assumption that there must be a universal basis for feminism, one which must be found in an identity assumed to exist cross-culturally, often accompanies the notion that the oppression of women has some singular form discernible in the universal or hegemonic structure of patriarchy or masculine domination. The notion of a universal patriarchy has been widely criticized in recent years for its failure to account for the workings of gender oppression in the concrete cultural contexts in which it exists.[9]

What I take from Butler's critique of "universal patriarchy" is a recognition that not all gendered performances/experiences are universally available, nor do they mean the same thing universally.

Thus, as much as we might want to critique the phallic signifier, and especially the penile focus, we would do well to remember that not all penises mean or do the same thing. Indeed, there is a worrying potential in these analogies for the penis to become heteronormative and hegemonic, a false mythology aiming to show that all penises are the same, used in the same way, and mean the same thing. That is, the penis and its penetration, though appearing to be identical across a range of acts, might have significantly different meanings (for everyone involved). Even the theorization of penetration, we must acknowledge, will have radically different implications and meanings for a range of theorists and their readers. It is in this regard that I begin to move away from the pen-as-penis analogy that has been so influential.

But we should take a closer look at Gilbert and Gubar. They argue that male sexuality, which surely includes but is not limited to the phallus, is what motivates and confirms "literary power" and indeed, I would argue, simply put, "power." To read Gilbert and Gubar carefully is to admit that, though they are fundamentally interested in the penis, we must recognize that it is but a part of male sexuality and that the male body is rich in erotic and sexual potential, much like the female body. To be sure, there is nothing wrong with the existing readings of Gilbert and Gubar, but we have not fully recognized the complexity of male sexuality. Gilbert and Gubar are not alone in this perspective. Hélène Cixous, for instance, argues that, "Though masculine sexuality gravitates around the penis, engendering the centralized body (in political anatomy) under the dictatorship of parts, woman does not bring about the same regionalization which serves the couple head/genitals and which is inscribed only within boundaries. Her libido is cosmic, just as her unconscious is worldwide."[10] Likewise, Luce Irigaray suggests that "*Woman has sex organs just about everywhere. She experiences pleasure almost everywhere.* . . . [T]he geography of her pleasure is much more diversified, more multiple in differences, more complex, more subtle than is imagined—in an imaginary [system] centred on one and the same."[11] Each perspective does a disservice to the male body and male sexuality and reduces that body to nothing more than an appendage that totally informs and defines male sexual experience. Although the penis is a synecdoche of the male, a part that can represent the whole, we must be careful to resist the temptation that the penis *is* the man. We must treat cautiously "microcosm-macrocosm relationships"[12] that inform a theory of masculine sexuality through the penis and it alone. We must move beyond the reductive logic that informs this simple version of male sexuality, largely because it excludes any number of erotic potentials that often inform this study, which proposes a new mode of reading, not just of literary texts, but also of culture. We must begin to read from behind, focused on the complexity of male sexuality.

Since we all have an anus, it seems to me that this "private part" contains a utopian potential for a theory of sexuality, gender, sex, desire, and pleasure that is inherently inclusive. The anus is not exclusive, like the penis or the vagina, to one sex, to one type of body. Indeed, even aberrations of the penis and vagina, for instance in cases of intersexuality, are not inherently problematic to the logic of this study, which argues that we must read from *behind*. The anus is a key part of the human body, a remarkably complex organ that has significant symbolic potential, not least because of the numerous ways in which we have desperately tried to keep it repressed. It is also the organ that most makes many of us rather uncomfortable because of its alignment with abjection, dirtiness, shame, and, in our homophobic culture, male homosexuality. This is largely the interest of this study—deflating not just the phallus but also, more particularly, the primacy of homophobia.

Thus, though I am fundamentally interested in critiquing the assumption that the anus is the "essence of homosexuality, the very ground zero of gayness,"[13] it must nevertheless be admitted that this is a perception, an assumption, rooted in seemingly significant historical truth and value. This observation that the anus is gay— rightly or wrongly—does not quite make sense. After all, it seems to be fair enough to suggest the obvious: we all have one. Admittedly, with these statements, I run the risk of "degaying" the very subject that I set out to explore. Leo Bersani cautions that "de-gaying gay-ness can only fortify homophobic oppression; it accomplishes in its own way the principal aim of homophobia: the elimination of gays."[14] My intention here is neither to *erase* homosexuality or gayness nor to suggest that anality, anal eroticism, and anal sexuality are somehow unique to gayness. Anal sexuality is not unique to gay men, as even the most cursory review of the history of sexuality demonstrates. Anal sexuality might well mean very different things in very different scenarios; this is precisely Eve Kosofsky Sedgwick's point in the opening axiomatic claim of *Epistemology of the Closet*: "[E]ven identical genital acts mean very different things to very different people."[15]

What does the ass, the rectum, the anus mean for masculinity, for the male body? How do men, perhaps especially straight men, conceptualize this site of eroticism, especially when it is imagined as somehow being gay? While engaging this question, one might be accused of degaying gayness, but why does gayness become the barometer through which to understand anality? Repeatedly in my research, I found questions on the Internet about whether or not finding the ass to be pleasurable makes a man gay. If this is the measure of gayness, and if calling it into question runs the risk of degaying gayness, then how do we move forward or to a theory of the ass that recognizes that it is neither orienting nor oriented? I am arguing here that, by understanding the complexity of the ass and its various forms, we are making something polyvalent rather than limiting its relevance to a particular group of people. I am not arguing, however, that we must somehow degay the asshole; at times, it might well be gay (though not in David Halperin's surprisingly sexless *How to Be Gay*); at other times, it might not be oriented sexually at all.

Homophobia as a critical concept requires that we recognize not just what it is but also how it works so that we can begin to dissipate its effects and affects. For Eric Anderson, one of the central concepts in understanding homophobia and its changing nature is "homohysteria," which might best be understood as "the need to distance oneself from the spectre of 'the fag.'"[16] Thus, the male subject, in an attempt to avoid being perceived as a fag, will comport himself in such a way that doubt is removed, what Raewyn Connell calls "hegemonic masculinity,"[17] which finds affinities with Michael Kimmel's thesis about masculinity as homophobia. Homophobia became part of, if not entirely necessary to, masculinity and being masculine. The male, to be masculine, must not be homosexual or perceived to be homosexual and thus becomes homophobic, so the logic went. Anderson, in his recent work, argues that this idea has shifted radically since Connell's and Kimmel's theses, particularly in adolescent culture. Homohysteria nonetheless proves to be a useful concept to think about in the framework of *Reading from Behind*, which largely attends to texts that cannot account for the shifts that Anderson explores in his work.[18]

Anderson explains that his career has been "characterized by expanding upon earlier gender theorizing of Connell and her use of hegemony in explicating how homophobia has been central to the polarization of hegemonic, complicit, subordinated, and marginalized masculinity."[19] Anderson sees a radical shift away from homohysteria and toward "inclusive masculinity," which necessarily affords a vision of masculinity that does not align with Connell's thesis. Anderson argues that "homohysteria peaked in the mid-1980s" and that the "reduction of homophobia has meant that today's youth all know that gay men exist, and they likely believe that they exist in higher percentages than they actually do. But significantly, they increasingly do not care."[20] Although it is tempting to embrace Anderson's inclusive masculinity, in which there is decreasing homophobia, I am not convinced by what is arguably an incredibly optimistic vision of masculinity. If it is true that young people "increasingly do not care," then why do we need to continue having discussions about how "it gets better," as Dan Savage would have us tell queer youth?

Anderson contends that a "homohysteric culture necessitates three factors: 1) widespread awareness that homosexuality exists as a static sexual orientation within a given culture; 2) cultural disapproval towards homosexuality (i.e. homonegativity); and 3) disapproval of men's femininity due to association with homosexuality"; he further contends that "all three conditions must be maintained for homohysteria to persist."[21] If the anus becomes a barometer for this discussion, then we must admit that we still live in a homohysteric culture; however, a queer theorist must question Anderson's argument and its requirement of "static sexual orientation" as a governing principle. No sexuality is as static as we'd like to believe.

If we accept that "disapproval of men's femininity" is also a principle of homohysteric culture, then we must surely work through what approval of men's femininity would look like and what it means for misogyny. Male femininity is as much about homophobia as it is about misogyny. A homohysteric culture, following Anderson, would require, I correctively add here, the maintenance of misogyny.

Homohysteria, as a guiding principle, assumes the certainty of the gay man, whereas my study is not as convinced of this hysteria and instead opts to think through homoparanoia, which imagines that every body is always already possibly homosexual and that the homoparanoid person looks for any clue that the subject being gazed at might well be a homosexual.[22] Paranoia and hysteria are surely similar, but the difference, I argue, resides in the subject himself: the hysteric subject asks if he himself might be gay—as the Lacanian hysteric asks, "Am I a man or a woman?"[23]—whereas the paranoid subject worries about homosexuals who might be around him: the homosexual as threat. Mark McCormack explains that "homohysteria is defined as the cultural fear of being homosexualized,"[24] but again this is about the subject himself, the I in the scenario being homosexualized, whereas in homoparanoia it is about the you or he being homosexualized. I want to situate a difference here, not because I am against homohysteria, but because I wish that Anderson and McCormack had dwelt further on hysteria.

Hysteria assumes the public nature of homosexuality, whereas paranoia assumes and depends on a private sexuality that could be made public. This, in a sense, is what Sedgwick means by the "epistemology of the closet," a kind of open secret that could reveal itself at any time, whether by the revealing subject or by the subject revealed. Indeed, this is why the anus is so productive in the study of homophobia, homohysteria, and homoparanoia. The anus, Guy Hocquenghem writes in *Homosexual Desire*, is "so totally yours that you must not use it: keep it to yourself."[25] Proper, well-mannered, couth, respectable people do not talk about the anus, its movements, or its pleasures; if we must talk about it, then we use euphemisms, humour, and so on, which aim to hide our discomfort. Jeffrey Weeks likewise explains in his introduction to Hocquenghem's *Homosexual Desire* that "the anus is *essentially* private."[26] There are no ifs, ands, or buts about it. By keeping it private, we allow for paranoia to thrive. To speak of the anus is to speak of that which must not be spoken of or named, and one is likely to be understood in our homoparanoid culture as being gay when one speaks with any degree of interest and/or authority in the anus, unless, of course, one is a proctologist largely excused from the social mythology about the anus.

Certainly, some scholars have already worked to explore, critique, and consider the anus in a critical light. Hocquenghem's *Homosexual Desire* is a notable work that provides a stunning Marxist critique of the family, the anus, and capitalism, yet it seems to foreshadow what would become one of the most trying times for the ass: the HIV/AIDS crisis. During the height of the crisis, Leo Bersani published what is arguably his most famous essay, "Is the Rectum a Grave?" Together these works form an important site of critique throughout *Reading from Behind*, and analysis of these texts, while beginning here, continues to unfold throughout the project. More recently, Kathryn Bond Stockton wrote *Beautiful Bottom, Beautiful Shame: Where "Black" Meets "Queer,"* which explores the intersection of race and the "bottom," not always anal but also the bottom of a hierarchy, for example. Subsequently, Tim Dean published *Unlimited Intimacy: Reflections on the Subculture of Barebacking*, which provides significant attention to the anus as desirable and desiring. And most recently, as I was completing this book, Nguyen Tan Hoang published *A View from the Bottom: Asian American Masculinity and Sexual Representation*, which, like Stockton's work, turns our attention to the question of race and identity.

Before exploring these works in detail, I will discuss psycho-analysis, particularly Freudian thought, to which all of the above works owe a certain debt. Leonard Shengold, for instance, argues that, though "anal phenomena are familiar to every student of the psyche who works with people," these phenomena have "somehow receded into the background (and I'm using an anal metaphor here) of our theory in recent years."[27] If we agree that the anus and anal phenomena are central to psychoanalysis, then why have these discussions "receded," and should we ask if they have not receded but been repressed?

The history of anality in psychoanalytic thought, for instance, begins with Freud's "Character and Anal Eroticism" (1908), a paper that Freud suggested "will be off-putting enough" in a letter to Karl Abraham.[28] Peter Gay has noted that anal eroticism had been on Freud's mind "as early as 1907 when Freud thought that "excrement, money, and obsessional neurosis [were] somehow intimately linked."[29] From Gay's perspective, this paper "offers both a summing up of ideas long held and a prospect of revisions to come."[30] The importance of the anus is found throughout Freud's work, and even in his late work we still see discussions of anal eroticism; however, as Shengold has noted, this side of psychoanalysis has receded in recent years.

It is from Freud that we get the typology of the anal personality, which refers to people who "are noteworthy for a regular combination of the three following characteristics. They are especially *orderly*, *parsimonious*, and *obstinate*."[31] This characterology is where we get the expression "You're anal," by which we generally mean tightly wound up, orderly (a popularized notion of being obsessive-compulsive), and rather difficult, even obstinate. But "anal eroticism" is not just about the popularized understanding of the anal personality. Freud's paper is innovative because it recognizes the importance—indeed the primacy—of the anus to character.

Freud, as Paul Ricoeur would have it, is interested in the "hermeneutics of suspicion,"[32] and thus every possible "meaning" is explored for excess meaning. The hermeneutics of suspicion, like paranoid reading (to which we have been introduced), demands that every possible meaning be at least named if not altogether explored. In what follows, I briefly pay attention to the development of anality in Freudian thought and in so doing highlight the ways in which negative affect informs this process. That is, by isolating particular examples, we can bring together the ways in which the Freudian anus connects the comedic stereotype of the anal person and how discussions of the anus seem to revolve around a hermeneutics of suspicion that in turn motivates many of the discussions that follow in this book. Although I am reluctant to embrace the hermeneutics of suspicion, I do recognize that the tension between the paranoid and the reparative is productive and enables readers to plunge deeply into the textures of literature. Accordingly, I briefly demonstrate the organization—however surface-level, for the time being—of the Freudian anus.

Freud spends much time thinking about the origins of anality, found in infants "who refuse to empty their bowels when they are put on the pot because they derive a subsidiary pleasure from defecating."[33] In this instant, Freud not only locates the origin of the problem but also why the infant refuses to evacuate the bowels. This refusal, it seems, is as much about control and autonomy as it is seemingly about pleasure. As Freud notes, "we infer that such people are born with a sexual constitution in which the erotogenicity of the anal zone is exceptionally strong."[34] All of this seems to be fairly straightforward. I imagine that few of us are surprised by these assertions today; however, Freud recognizes that his contemporary readers might be less convinced: "I know that no one is prepared to believe in a state of things so long as it appears to be unintelligible and to offer no angle from which an explanation can be attempted."[35] He attempts here to anticipate not only meaning but also doubt. Called into question is knowledge that "appears to be unintelligible" but, as he will demonstrate, is entirely intelligible—everything can and must be known: "[P]aranoia requires that bad news be always already known."[36] The "bad news" for Freud is the possibility that "no one is prepared to believe" even though everyone might well believe this to be true; he imagines a hostile reader who might exist.

In *Three Essays on the Theory of Sexuality* (1905), Freud had already begun to outline a theory of the anus and anality: "One of the clearest signs of subsequent eccentricity or nervousness is to be seen when a baby obstinately refused to empty his bowels when he is put on the pot—that is, when the nurse wants him to—and holds back that function till he chooses to exercise it."[37] We might be reminded here of Lee Edelman's remark on the "fascism of the baby's face"[38] or of Adam Phillips, who speaks of "the beast in the nursery."[39] Freud's infant exerts a great deal of control and derives much pleasure from not performing as expected. Paradoxically, in a sense, the infant does precisely what he has been trained to do when we insist on the primal lesson of potty training. The infant in Freud's example, however, has taken it too far. He has become too "successful" at controlling his bowels and has suddenly become rather anal. Of course, as a footnote in *The Standard Edition* informs us, there is something comical at play:

> "A friend of mine," he told me, "who has read your *Three Essays on the Theory of Sexuality*, was talking about the book. He entirely agreed with it, but there was one passage, which—though of course accepted and understood in its meaning like that of the rest of your book—struck him as so grotesque and comic that he sat down and laughed over it for a quarter of an hour."[40]

The passage in question is the one that I have just noted. Freud, already in *Three Essays on the Theory of Sexuality*, associated anal eroticism with being obstinate, which, of course, "can go over into defiance, to which rage and revengefulness are easily joined."[41]

This anal baby grows up into an anal adult, whom we often see in film and on television and who, like the baby, serves a comedic purpose. We have come to see anality as remarkably humorous even if, at the same time, we find something rather grotesque about it. It is striking that we can speak today of a person being anal and almost divorce this anality from the rectum: that is, it is a personality type and not a reference to the tightness of the rectal passage, wherein the sphincter can control movement. The correlation between the anus and the comic is well established. It is tough not to read Freud as a master comedian, to a certain degree, and we can imagine a reader laughing for a "quarter of an hour." Freud might well have wanted his readers to laugh—if not, then why provide them with the story?

My point here, in a sense, is that we have to treat carefully this "hermeneutics of suspicion," by which we can determine from an infant's bowel movement his subsequent personality. It seems to me that the "diagnosis" of anality is dependent on a scenario in which correlation equals causation. Thus, the diagnosis functions like homoparanoia, a kind of "street-level semiotic science"[42] or what we more commonly call "gaydar." We look for a sign, any sign, that signifies the totality of the subject. For example, there is a tendency to believe that we can locate and isolate anal personalities without needing to know much beyond the three characteristics of anality. Of course, the failure of this "semiotic science" is that it relies on *a* sign rather than a host of symptoms and signs that can be used to corroborate and confirm and therefore provide a diagnosis.

Beyond homoparanoia, or perhaps alongside it, is the presence of negative affect in theories of anality. Although Freud's own writing contains instances of negative affect, consider for instance Owen Berkeley-Hill's "The Psychology of the Anus," in which he notes that "to displace this feeling of displeasure contrary forces (feelings of reaction) such as loathing, shame, etc. are developed. Thus the activity of the anal zone as a component of sexual impulse falls into abeyance."[43] Negative affecting—shame and loathing and the unclear and remarkably far-reaching "etc."—will become essential parts of theories of the anus in psychoanalytic theory.

For the time being, however, we can note a correlation between Berkeley-Hill's theory and A. A. Brill's case study, in which a child feels ashamed "because he broke wind in the classroom" and "recalled [this] under marked emotivity."[44] What we need to note here is how persistent negative affect is in theorizing and thinking about the anus and anality. The anus, its pleasures and its discomforts, must be controlled and ultimately repressed.

Freud's ideas on anality took hold quickly, and by 1913 a number of papers, including Brill's and Berkeley-Hill's, would be published, a trend that would continue throughout the decade. In 1918, the defining study by Ernest Jones appeared, "Anal-Erotic Character Traits," alongside two more papers by Freud, "On Transformations of Instinct as Exemplified in Anal Eroticism" (1917) and "Anal Eroticism and Castration" in *An Infantile Neurosis* (1918, based on a case study from 1914). These three papers bring together homoparanoia and negative affect. Jones begins thus: "Perhaps the most astonishing of all Freud's findings—and certainly the one that has evoked the liveliest incredulity, repugnance, and opposition—was the discovery that certain traits of character may become profoundly modified as a result of anal excitations experienced by the infant in the region of the anal canal."[45] Jones then notes that "everyone on first hearing this statement finds it almost inconceivably grotesque."[46] Once more we note the negative: "incredulity," "repugnance," "opposition," "grotesque," yet Jones notes the genius of Freud. The article itself provides a studious examination of the Freudian claim that anal persons "are especially orderly, parsimonious and obstinate."[47] Upon reading Jones's article, one quickly learns why, perhaps, the anal character is less than favourable and, as I've noted, became a stock character in popular culture, a comedic creation, who, like the gay man (often quite anal; for instance, as already noted, Will in *Will and Grace* or Mitch in *Modern Family*), is easily recognizable and generates a quick laugh. One is tempted to ask, particularly in light of *Modern Family* and *Will and Grace*, what we are genuinely laughing at in these scenarios. Are we recognizing the "anal person" as code for the "anally desiring" person? That is, do we conflate the anal person, who receives (anal) pleasure like the infant from withholding bowel movements, with the gay man?

In Jones's estimation, we are provided with a less than venerable character who is excessively anal, to the point that Jones's pathology begins to flirt with *phobia*. Initially, his descriptions of the anal person are rather innocuous, perhaps even benevolent:

> The most perfect example of all, and one quite pathogno-monic of a marked anal complex, concerns the act of writing letters. There are few people who do not at times find it a nuisance to bring their correspondence up to date, but the type under discussion may show the completest inhibition at the thought of so doing, and most of all when they have the strongest desire, to write a given letter. When they finally succeed in bringing themselves to the task, they perform it with a wonderful thoroughness, giving up to it their whole energy and interest, so that they astonish the long-neglected relatives by producing an excellently written and detailed budget; they despatch epistles rather than write letters in the ordinary sense.[48]

At first glance, we are provided with an all too common person prone to procrastination but when charged with the task overcompensates and produces "excellently written" letters or "epistles."

Rhetorically, Jones makes use of superlatives and excess—"most perfect" or "completest" or "epistles rather than . . . letters"—in his descriptions of anality. For him, the anal character is *excessive*. Adam Phillips has remarked that "nothing makes people more excessive than talking about excess,"[49] and one cannot help but acknowledge this "excess" in Jones's writing on anality. Excess "implies that we know our limits,"[50] and in this regard what we see unfolding here in anal character traits is an attempt to acknowledge these limits and demarcate at what point excess becomes anal. Moreover, these excesses are fundamentally about control and knowledge, much like paranoia. As Phillips notes, "we are so good at spotting excessive behaviour . . . that we must know, or think we know, what just the right amount of these things is."[51] Indeed, this is precisely what is at stake in outlining a theory of paranoia: it is the assumption that we know and that we have imagined all the ways in which we might not know, so that they are now known. It is not that being "orderly, parsimonious and obstinate" is itself the problem, but that these characteristics can and do become excessive in the anal character.

Jones, moreover, provides psychoanalysts, and literary and cultural critics, with important observations on the anal character, and for him "the most interesting one is the tendency to be occupied with the reverse side of various things and situations"[52]—much the approach that *Reading from Behind* takes as a general rule. It is not a matter, as late-nineteenth-century thinkers would have suggested, of homosexuality, inversion, but of taking things from the reverse, from behind. Jones further notes the ways in which various symbolic referents help to establish what might be called a poetics of anality—tunnels, canals, passages—which enables literary and cultural critics to think about openings, entrances, closings, exits, and centres, as well as, most obviously, holes. What do these things mean, and how do they function in textual examples? How are these things used to deploy meaning? Moreover, it is central to my project to recognize that holes can be inherently confusing, ambiguous, and so on because, of course, they seemingly refer to the vaginal opening, the birth canal; yet, as Jones contends, "the child has no knowledge of the vagina, he can only conclude that the baby leaves through the only opening through which he has ever known solid material [to] leave it—namely, the anus."[53] This childish confusion, as it were, hardly seems to be all that childish when we think about the anus and its relationship to masculinity.

Michel Foucault elaborated on the importance of the phallus and phallic penetration to masculinity: "Much more than the body itself, with its different parts, much more than pleasure, with its qualities and intensities, the act of penetration appears as a qualifier of sex acts, with its few variants of position and especially its poles of activity and passivity."[54] In this example, we find that these two poles—active and passive—are highly, constitutionally so, gendered:

> But it should be remarked that in the practice of sexual pleasures two roles and two poles can be clearly distinguished, just as they can be distinguished in reproductive function; these consisted of positional values: that of the subject and that of the object, that of the agent and that of the patient—as Aristotle says, "the female, as female is passive, the male, as male is active."[55]

In this rendering, penetration is essential to the development of the "male, as male," and to surrender the penetrative act in favour of being penetrated is to renounce one's masculinity. Indeed, years later, Leo Bersani highlighted this very claim in his canonical essay "Is the Rectum a Grave?," in which he explains that, for the Greeks, "to be penetrated is to abdicate power."[56] It is this abdication of power, this fear of the loss of power, that motivates so much of the moral taboo, as it were, on anal pleasure. Indeed, this is precisely what is at stake in our homophobic, homohysteric, and homoparanoid culture: the man who refuses his role and embraces his hole.

The penetrated male uses his anus as if he were a woman; he allows his body to be feminized by another. The logic, of course, is reductive, and we need to think carefully about what the "hole" might mean to the "whole" of this discussion. Is there a way around this problem of reductive masculinity, based on exclusion—excluding the anus and excluding the man who uses his anus? I argue that we must think about the complexity of holes, and in so doing we are not preferring one to another, nor are we arguing that they are the same thing; rather, things can and perhaps should be read from behind in light of what is behind.

The complexity of these recent questions has been the subject of much inquiry, especially in the works of Stockton, Dean, Bersani, Fung, and Tan Hoang, especially when coupled with questions of class and race. Stockton's contribution is itself a study of shame and its generative, recuperative power at the "switchpoint" of "black" and "queer." Throughout *Beautiful Bottom, Beautiful Shame*, Stockton works to "understand why certain forms of shame are embraced by blacks and queers, and also black queers, in forceful ways."[57] Her work contributes, in many ways, to what was and what has become a significant interest in queer theory in negative affect. Throughout her project, Stockton draws on the idea of a "switchpoint," which "refer[s] to a point of connection between two signs (or two rather separate connotative fields) where something from one flows towards (is diverted in the direction of) the other, lending its connotative spread and signifying force to the other, illuminating it and intensifying it, but also sometimes shifting it or adulterating it."[58] Her less theoretical example is a train that can move across tracks by way of a movable section of track, or we might think of on-ramps and off-ramps on the highway.

Importantly, Stockton's work calls attention to race, notably blackness, something that earlier writings, such as those of the psychoanalytic school discussed above, failed to do as well as more recent writings, such as Tim Dean's *Unlimited Intimacy*. However, as we learn throughout her opening chapter, Stockton is interested in "shame's synonym, 'debasement,'" which speaks as much to shame as it does to a kind of "lowering." She explains that debasement "also agrees with the physical, material lowering I discuss in reference to the 'bottom': the body's bottom, . . . but also just as centrally the bottom of one's mind, and by economic reference, the lowest end (the bottom, that is) of an economic scale."[59] When we frame anality in these terms, the deep connections to the loaded language of the bottom, we can begin to look outward not only to the varying connections between the ass and a range of hierarchies, dominances, and oppressions but also to the kinds of desires and pleasures about which we are too ashamed to speak. For instance, in thinking about popular romance novels, I will contend that they function as a bottom in which readers are filled with shame and delight, which highlights the slipperiness of affect.

The connections between the anus and the bottom (of a hierarchy) are never that far apart, especially in late capitalism. In his work, Guy Hocquenghem reminds readers that "ours is a phallic society, and the quantity of pleasure is determined in relation to the phallus,"[60] wherein so much of "value," one of Stockton's chief concerns, is determined by what is at the economic top or bottom. For Hocquenghem, this phallic society is determined and overdetermined by a capitalist economic system, which, he argues, is "responsible for the allocation of both absence and presence: the little girl's penis envy, the little boy's castration anxiety."[61] Hocquenghem's argument becomes that "the phallus draws on libidinal energy in the same way that money draws on labour."[62] What would it mean, then, to renounce the phallus and to choose willingly the bottom?

Hocquenghem argues that society is always already phallic and that "social relationships as a whole are constructed according to a hierarchy which reveals the transcendence of the great signifier." Perhaps his argument itself quickly becomes phallic insofar as the phallus, like his argument, becomes totalizing; however, the larger point, for Hocquenghem, is that in our "phallocratic society," since the "phallus is essentially social, the anus is essentially private" and "must be privatised."[63] Everything about the anus must remain sub-limated, hidden, repressed for the success, it seems, not only of the family and heterosexuality but also capitalism writ large. The bottom requires an economic modality through which we can ascribe values of poverty, abjection, and so on, precisely what Stockton sets out to do when she thinks about "anal economies."

In Hocquenghem's work, we find a kind of early anal herme-neutic or desire to read from behind: "The phallus is to be found everywhere, the popularisation of psychoanalysis having made it the common signifier of all social images. But who would think of interpreting Schreber's sun, not as the father phallus, but as a cosmic anus?"[64] This question is similar to many of the questions that *Reading from Behind* asks. What is on the other side, or another side, of the textual encounter? What would it mean to read narratives to which we have grown accustomed from another angle?

In many ways, one of the challenges of this project is that the body of literature available has largely been read from one angle. To read Dean's project as anything other than courageous seems to be almost impossible. His work on barebacking, without doubt, is courageous and innovative, perhaps even paradigm shifting, but it is richly problematic because of the ways in which it fails to tackle, head on, the deep intimacy between barebacking and what Judith Halberstam calls "the resolutely masculinist and white utopias"[65] in which the work—theory and/or sex—unfolds. *Reading from Behind* will not attend to the question of barebacking, mainly because this work has been done by a range of scholars; however, I would be remiss if I did not speak to what I see as troubling aspects of barebacking in general and of Dean's work in particular.

In *Unlimited Intimacy*, for example, Dean squarely locates his study in the urban space of San Francisco, where the subculture of barebacking originated.[66] There are many ways to think about and through barebacking, especially in terms of multiplicity, intersectionality, and what Stockton calls switchpoints, and we would be negligent if we failed to acknowledge these complexities. Indeed, we must do more than merely acknowledge them; we must think carefully and critically about them. And this analysis of *Unlimited Intimacy*, a kind of reading from behind, works to disorient the critical appreciation of the book to think about what it says and does not say about the politics of race, class, ability, and so on. To be fair, *Reading from Behind*, as an intellectual project, will contain its own gaps, and I do not imagine this intervention in Dean's project as anything more than a hope to further the debate.

Imagine how complex this question of complexity becomes when we read Michael Warner's comment about how to respond to the much publicized barebacking trend or phenomenon: "[W]ell, here's one opinion: we could get really shocked and talk about how terrifying it is. This wouldn't do anything for the *poor* fuckers at risk, of course."[67] What does his use of "poor" really mean here? His intended use, one presumes, speaks to the pitiful and pathetic, but it could certainly lend itself to a reading of barebacking that might attend to class-based issues carefully elided by many scholars of barebacking. What does it mean that the shock and terror "wouldn't do anything for the poor fuckers at risk, of course"? What does the "of course" imply? Perhaps those "poor" fuckers simply do not have access to the information of shock and terror. For Stockton, however, "the bias against queer anality (and against its pleasures) oddly speaks to the stigma of people who live at the bottom of an economic scale."[68] How, then, do we negotiate the class politics of Warner's remark? Moreover, we can continue this reading and move outward to postcolonial and queer of colour critiques, which remind us, once more, that queer cultural practices are never really *just* about white *and* gay men.

Reluctantly, perhaps, I note here that words such as *race, class,* and *ability* are carefully glossed over in *Unlimited Intimacy*, because Dean argues—and his argument depends on this assertion—that "subcultural membership does not depend on race, class, age, serostatus, or even sexuality but simply on one's willingness to embrace risk, to give and to take semen. In this respect, bareback culture is *unusually democratic.*"[69] His thesis, in a sense, is too simple precisely because it actively avoids the intersectional politics of what is at stake in his project. I was very impressed by his brave book, but that *bravery* (a word that appears often in reviews[70]) must be accounted for and engaged critically. Dean's bravery is possible not because of the "unusually democratic" nature of barebacking but because of his position within masculinity and neoliberal politics and culture.

To note the problems of research on barebacking is hardly novel, yet it seems that we must continue to do so precisely because so much of the work seems to universalize the subject and fails to account for the multiplicity of identity. When evaluating the work of Dean, Edelman, and Bersani, for instance, Halberstam admits to being "less than enthusiastic about the archives upon which these authors draw and the resolutely masculinist and white utopias they imagine."[71] It is also important here to speak briefly about David Halperin, often positioned alongside Dean, Edelman, and Bersani as a gay male white theorist, who has also been critiqued by Halberstam for failing to account for race. In *What Do Gay Men Want? An Essay on Sex, Risk, and Subjectivity*, for instance, one could fault

Halperin for not attending to race; however, as he explains, "the focus on gay subjectivity is sharpest in the case of white, socially privileged gay men, whose agency and autonomy are not likely to have been compromised by political oppression or external constraint and whose behaviour cannot be explained by other social facts: that is why much of what I will say here will refer to them."[72] I do not intend to excuse Halperin, but I do want to point out that, though many have critiqued him for his elision of race, it seems that he is at least aware of these gaps and thus limits his remarks to gay white men. He hopes, nonetheless, that his ideas will be of value to a larger audience.

Dean's refusal to acknowledge the intersectional politics of his project is once more confirmed in his article "Bareback Time," which appeared in 2011 as a rejoinder to and continuation of *Unlimited Intimacy*. Dean is perhaps even more explicit in this new essay that "to simply pathologize barebackers as irresponsible or self-destructive would be tantamount to refusing the ethical challenge that this new erotic practice poses to us all, *irrespective of gender, sexuality, or sero-status*."[73] What, then, we might ask, is at stake in eliding these questions or even in taking the time to think about them? His entire thesis begs readers to imagine other possibilities in thinking about barebacking—a movement away from the death drive—yet he seemingly works to avoid even the remotest possibility of race in his work.

His work becomes all the more problematic when Dean asserts that "the temporality of HIV has mutated, and that mutation, while it represents a source of relief, even jubilation, represents also an unexpected source of anxiety."[74] This argument is possible only because he fails to imagine HIV/AIDS outside the imaginary of affluent gay men or, again, what Halberstam has called "white utopias."

My point here is not to provide a laundry list of critiques but to suggest that we have to move carefully and cautiously when considering the universality of a presumed subject while still recognizing the specificity of the individual subject. In what follows, I will address Halberstam's "resolutely masculinist and white utopias" in relation to discourses of barebacking and more particularly to the bottom of/in Dean's work.

Dean's negotiation of gender is always committed to the politics of masculinity: "[I]t is not that all men are equal," Dean writes, "but that all men are treated as *men* no matter how often they take it up the butt," and for him "this may be part of bareback subculture's appeal."[75] Unlike Halperin, Dean seems always to be committed to the idea of treating men as men, and, by extension, I suggest that his work is implicated in what Lisa Duggan understands as the "new neoliberal sexual politics" of homonormativity, "a politics that does not contest dominant heteronormative assumptions and institutions, but upholds and sustains them, while promising the possibility of a demobilized gay constituency and a privatized, depoliticized gay culture anchored in domesticity and consumption."[76] Before someone notes that the practice of barebacking constitutes a radical departure from the norm, let's remember that "wanting sex with another man," as Bersani notes, "is not exactly a credential for political radicalism."[77] Dean reinscribes the politics of hegemonic masculinity precisely because he reaffirms, as we shall see, the masculinity of sexuality. He contends that "in bareback subculture being sexually penetrated is a matter of 'taking it like a man,' enduring without complaint any discomfort or temporary loss of status, in order to prove one's masculinity."[78] His bareback culture is thoroughly enmeshed in the politics of what Connell calls "culturally exalted patterns of masculinity."[79] What would it mean, in this scenario, for the barebacker *not* to take it like *a man*? At bottom, we might ask, who is Dean's *man*? The man whom Dean is interested in is certainly not Lee's "castrated boy,"[80] Halperin's gay man,[81] Sedgwick's "effeminate boys,"[82] or Mavor's boyish men,[83] or what Dean calls "überfags," who "administer tips to style-deficient men."[84]

The man whom Dean is interested in is the "sexual bottom," "regularly addressed by his tops in the most derogatory feminine terms (such as 'bitch,' 'pussy,' and 'cunt')," but he assures his readers that "this misogynistic rhetoric does not impugn his masculinity; indeed, masculinity may be bolstered rhetorically by the use of terms that refer pejoratively to the female genitals."[85] The problem is not that the language does not "impugn his masculinity" but that the language itself is committed to what Halberstam has rightly called "resolutely masculinist" ideologies. What Dean fails to recognize is that this is precisely the kind of misogyny and effeminophobia that informs heteronormative and homonormative performances of hegemonic masculinity: this is about the repudiation and renunciation of the feminine.

Dean wants his readers to believe that the subculture represents "shifts in the cultural construction of masculinity,"[86] but where, we might ask, is the shift? The shift is understood as a kind of "paradoxical logic, [in which] one is masculinized rather than feminized by submitting to masculine domination."[87] In a sense, this is nothing more than reaffirming the logic of the top. Over and over, Dean is committed to reaffirming the politics of masculinity, and that politics is only made possible—and can only ever be made possible—by a commitment to hegemonic masculinity. His idea that the subculture is involved in "remasculinizing masochism"[88] is only made possible by his refusal to depart from heteronormativity and a commitment to a flawed and problematic binary indebted to essentialist effeminophobia and misogynistic logic.

There is, bluntly put, no way out of this "paradoxical logic" that Dean has constructed to reassert and reaffirm masculinity. He has worked carefully and meticulously to establish his "masculinist utopia" in which the male body is celebrated, cultures of masculinity are embraced and endorsed, and even the trace of femininity is expelled if not extinguished. But we should not imagine that this is not also deeply enmeshed in racial politics. As Halberstam notes, "the white gay man ultimately pulls himself back from the brink of castration by embracing loss, self-shattering and masochism, but only by detaching it from contaminated and racialized femininity."[89] In many ways, racialized femininity is what lurks in the background of Dean's "paradoxical logic" because it reinforces masculinity, and by extension melds together race and femininity; and one would be, I imagine, hard pressed to understand the erasure of race and femininity as "paradoxical logic."

Take, for instance, Richard Fung's argument that "the vast majority of North American [pornographic] tapes featuring Asians . . . privilege the [white] penis while always assigning the Asian the role of bottom; Asian and anus are conflated."[90] How, then, do we imagine anal sexuality—with or without condoms—outside racial-

ized politics, outside the politics of femininity? Surely we are not
suggesting that the absence of the condom somehow renders the
scenario and concern that Fung articulates as null and void, and
that all subjects in the sexual scene somehow become democratic
citizens of the neoliberal, homonormative, bareback subculture, as
Dean might have us believe. As Nguyen Tan Hoang argues: "[A]
failure to take Asian American masculinity and explicit sexual representation seriously can be attributed to deep anxieties surrounding
Asian American masculinity, which has been historically marked
by feminization and emasculation."[91] Questions of race, in many
ways, produce anxiety, but we must nonetheless continue, even
if admitting our anxieties, to work through them and what these
elisions of race mean for the task at hand.

The challenge that remains is about what happens to the various
switchpoints that surely exist in the sexual scenario, whether it be
anally figured or not. I am not arguing here that one cannot be
masculine and a bottom, for instance (and this will be the subject
of consideration in the chapter on the Mexican film *Doña Herlinda
y su hijo*), or that one must be feminine to be a bottom (a discussion that will unfold throughout *Reading from Behind*). I am left
asking, however, what happens to the feminine bottom in Dean's
Unlimited Intimacy.

The question of femininity, in many ways, especially the feminized position of being penetrated during anal sex, deserves attention,
especially when it collides with questions of race. As Tan Hoang
and others such as Bersani have noted, "in a patriarchal society, to
bottom is akin to being penetrated and dominated *like a woman.*"[92]
But Hocquenghem would be quick to remind his readers that "the
anus is not a substitute for a vagina," after all, for we all know
that "women have one as well as men."[93] As much as critics might
"have challenged the assessments of bottomhood as feminizing and
emasculating by revalorizing the derided anus,"[94] it is important
not merely to rewrite this as nothing more than inverted heterosexuality. Instead, *Reading from Behind* frames the anus as sexual
in and of itself without a commitment to or a desire to essentialize
orientation. Likewise, we must not pretend that somehow there
are not class-based or race-based implications in thinking about

bottomhood, especially when the images and texts considered often speak directly to these concerns, such as those encountered in my readings of *Doña Herlinda y su hijo* and the landscape and pastoral paintings of Toronto-based Cree artist Kent Monkman.

My assumption is not that all anuses are the same (just as I don't believe that all penises are the same) but that there is something to be found in the fact that we all have an anus regardless of race, orientation, ability, sex, sexuality, gender, religion, ethnicity, nationality, and so on, even though, of course, its symbolic function and value might be quite different depending on the context. The universality of the anus is so assured that a writer such as Gabriel García Márquez can sarcastically write, though surely with grains of fear and truth, that, "the day shit is worth money, poor people will be born without an asshole."[95]

Orienting Virginity

THIS CHAPTER BEGINS OUR EXPLORATION OF THE anal archive in terms of what is ostensibly a fairly universal experience: the loss of virginity. However, what does this loss mean when we frame it around the anus? I set out to destabilize some of our notions of virginity loss, framing the anus as a site in and through which one can lose virginity. Although this is not a book about virginity, many of the texts considered in subsequent chapters flirt with or explicitly call attention to ideas about virginity and its loss. The narratives that I consider here, all taken from Steven G. Underwood's *Gay Men and Anal Eroticism: Tops, Bottoms, and Versatiles*, account for the polemics of virginity loss. In a certain regard, each story, which forms a part of his ethnographic study, becomes part of the anal archive developed throughout *Reading from Behind*.

Virginity, whether we like it or not, remains a rite of passage that most of us will undergo; however, the concept remains rooted in ideas about women, purity, and especially the hymen. In her book *Virgin: The Untouched History*, Hanne Blank mentions male virgins only in passing; the same holds true for Anke Bernau's *Virgins: A Cultural History*.[1] Scholarship on male virginity is a nascent area of interest, whereas female virginity has dominated and driven the subject matter.[2] Virginity, we are told, is something about women, and when men do have roles in virginity it is not in *being* virgins but in *taking* virginity from virgins. The concept, thus far, is remarkably indebted to a heteropatriarchal culture that has allowed for male virginity to remain largely unexamined. In this chapter, I turn specifically to the question of how virginity and orientation come together, particularly around questions of gay male sexuality. The question that I ask here is, can a virgin be oriented? Or how does the first time inform orientation?

Michael Amico has suggested that "The trouble is, every lesbian, gay, transgender, bisexual, or questioning youth has a different definition of what it means to be a virgin!" He then asks a series of questions that helps to frame this discussion on virginity, particularly when considered outside the heterosexual paradigm: "How does a gay person lose his or her virginity? What bodily orifices must be penetrated? Is it the giver, receiver, or both who lose their virginity? Do lesbians need a strap-on to get the job done? Do gay men require a penis?"[3] Presumably, the question "How does one lose virginity?" should not be terribly difficult to answer; after all, we have a concept that is a part of our sexual culture. Nevertheless, as Amico's questions demonstrate, when virginity is positioned in the context of queer culture, the governing question of loss is seemingly irresolvable. One obvious problem, however, with his question is its continued insistence on the phallic signifier and penetration, which in the context of non-phallic relations might present a problem. Although many might simply wish to do away with the concept of virginity (i.e., it is a non-thing), the reality for many is that the concept remains important for admission into a sexual culture. Likewise, loss of virginity is a central rite of passage, like marriage, that, for whatever reason, we are taught about and wish to experience. Logically, it might well make sense to dismiss the notion of virginity, but doing so would not get rid of the problem of the "first time."

Gay Men and Anal Eroticism is not an academic study of gay men's experience of anal eroticism but a compilation of first-person narratives based on interviews that Underwood conducted. Indeed, he does very little analytical work with these narratives; instead, he leaves this work for his readers. Scholars in the humanities and social sciences have woefully under-reviewed his book. I imagine that, if this were a scholarly study, social scientists would critique the methodology of acquiring interviewees and likely question the human research ethics at play throughout the book. One problem, for instance, is the eroticization of his subjects when he introduces them to his readers: "Kevin is a strikingly handsome man. . . . I'm struck by his expressive eyes, his vibrant olive skin, and tall athletic physique";[4] another subject, Tom, "never shifts his gaze during our hour-long conversation. I'm a little intimidated by this direct, aggressive attitude, but I also find it refreshing and even seductive";[5] in thinking about a couple whom he intends to interview, Underwood fantasizes about them, imagining them as "a couple of college professors, polite, well educated, and overly concerned with their privacy. I guessed one would be an English professor (probably the younger one, Leonard), and the other a doctor of philosophy."[6] There is a question of subjectivity and ethics at play here that would need to be engaged with if this were positioned as an academic study. Admittedly, there is very little consideration of how it might influence the objectivity of the interview. Nonetheless, despite its flaws, the text provides insights into some perspectives of gay men on anal eroticism (and perhaps we should read the text as but an invitation to do more research). The only review that I could locate was written by Michael Hattersley for *Gay and Lesbian Review*, in which he explains that, "If you enjoy coming-out stories, this book has plenty."[7] Immediately, as a scholar of sexuality and gender, I am struck by the way in which Hattersley privileges orientation, which we generally associate with coming out, wherein one announces sexuality.[8]

I want to be clear from the outset that I am not particularly interested in what constitutes loss of virginity: that is, this chapter will not once and for all answer the question "How does one lose virginity?" (I don't know that there is an answer that would satisfy everyone.) Nor do I hope to advance a virgin identity politic. (I am not even certain what it would constitute.) Instead, I am specifically concerned with the narratives provided in Underwood's book, working with them in their own complexities, and putting confidence in them as literary truth claims, as "textual assertion[s] . . . considered true by the reader."[9] Additionally, I am certain that virginity itself is a myth that has been central to the sexual and erotic imagination for millennia, and I do not see this changing at any point in the near future. Virginity is fundamentally subjective. Virgins know this and often engage in a search for the ultimate limit of virginity, such as popularization of the term "technical virgin," which I doubt is genuinely a new thing so much as a (re)naming.[10] Incidentally, one of the earliest uses of the term "technical virgin" appeared in a 1971 article on "Typologies of Sexual Behavior";[11] the earliest use that I can find in scholarly articles is in 1929 in the *Eugenics Review*,[12] though its meaning today is slightly different; additionally, the term was used in sex research in 1990.[13] Indeed, in 1987, Carol A. Darling and J. Kenneth Davidson proposed the need to "revisit" the concept of technical virginity.[14] All of this is to suggest that for years we have been flirting with the limits of virginity and asking which "act" means that virginity has finally and officially been lost. Accordingly, my study works within the confines of Underwood's book, from which we can make some theories, or working ideas, about orienting virginity.

Virginity remains a relatively understudied area of scholarship on sexuality, particularly when we move beyond the heteronormative, female-centred readings of virginity. It is not that these readings are flawed or bad but that the discussion itself seems to be stuck in neutral. Has the discussion on virginity changed all that much? In 1973, David G. Berger and Morton G. Wenger wrote that "male virginity is a topic that is all but ignored in the sociological literature on sexuality."[15] As I've argued elsewhere, we can find only "the scantest of mentions of male virginity" and that, "even in books that purport to provide histories of virginity, the male virgin is an anomalous category that cannot yet be given a history of his own."[16] Likewise, Sandra L. Caron and Sarah P. Hinman conclude that male virginity is "an area that has been neglected by sex researchers."[17] However, what has remained consistent in the tiny amount of scholarship on male virgins has been the question of shame and stigma. Being a male virgin past late adolescence, it seems, is shameful. In a 1961 paper, for instance, Irving B. Tebor concluded that "virgin men of college age, regardless of their desire or lack of desire to remain virgin, generally do not receive support and acceptance for their virginity from either their peer group or adults, including their parents."[18] In addressing "reel" (cinematic) and "real" virginities, Laura M. Carpenter notes that "*Fast Times* offers a script in which a male virgin's inexperience compounds his shame,"[19] and she suggests that "a man who was ashamed of being a virgin might recall watching many TV shows that depicted virginity as a stigma."[20] In fifty years of scholarly research on male virginity, it seems, there have been few significant changes with regard to the male virgin and his shame. If anything, we might argue, his increased visibility in the popular media has led to an increase in negative affect, especially shame. The male virgin is largely presented in popular media in comedic fashion, and/or he is someone who must be cured of his condition.[21]

If, as we have seen, male virgins are simply not attended to in scholarship, and male virginity is shameful, one can only imagine how much more complicated this becomes when we begin to think about queer virginity. Virginity itself, for men, functions in a fashion akin to "the closet," a concept that I borrow from queer theory, particularly Eve Kosofsky Sedgwick's *Epistemology of the Closet.* "Closetedness," Sedgwick explains, "is a performance initiated as such by the speech act of a silence,"[22] which is why, I argue, declaration and confession are intrinsic to narratives about virginity. In remaining silent—both in spoken word and in physical action—the virgin does not need to do anything in particular to out himself as a virgin. That is, as with the closeted gay man, we are concerned with "a silence that accrues particularity by fits and starts."[23] I think of this as the attempt to put into words yet the failure or incomplete nature of coming out, which requires speech acts that are "strangely specific."[24] I am inclined to agree with Sedgwick here, particularly with her argument that "the fact that silence is rendered as pointed and performative as speech, in relations around the closet, depends on and highlights more broadly the fact that ignorance is as potent and as multiple a thing there as is knowledge."[25] I recognize that I am making a generalizing argument; however, it seems to me that the closet, ostensibly queer, serves well as a model to think about virginity, particularly for men for whom virginity, like a queer sexuality, can be perceived as shameful.

This notion of the closet is doubled when we are talking about queer virgins or what we might even see as "proto-gay."[26] That is, the closet obscures both virginity and a soon-to-be-explored (and perhaps declared and identified) sexuality. In this instance, then, the closet almost seems to contain yet another closet (one thinks here of the expansiveness of the wardrobe in C. S. Lewis's *The Lion, the Witch, and the Wardrobe*). What I will show, particularly by way of examples from Underwood's book, is how often virginity loss is used to determine sexuality: that is, to exit the closet, as it were, requires as much a loss of virginity as a declaration of sexual identity.

Although not wanting to make this question of virginity loss even more complicated (though as we all know sex is complicated), I must recognize the negotiation that unfolds between sexual preference/orientation and identity. That is, though we are largely accustomed to understanding sexuality as functioning as a binary (or perhaps we've moved beyond the binary toward a continuum), gay male sexuality has its own convention that further problematizes—and this is a good thing—the reductive nature of discussions on orientation. We will be challenged here to imagine orientation in a variety of possibilities rather than the reductive two (hetero, homo) or three (hetero, bi, homo) options that have dominated much of the "orientation discussion." In Underwood's book, we are introduced to three "types" of gay men: "tops, bottoms, and versatiles." Consider, for instance, the following: "Not surprisingly, bottoms are judged on an entirely separate scale than tops. They're more severely stigmatized because getting ass-fucked, similar to a woman having vaginal intercourse, is considered feminizing and shameful."[27] The top, of course, is the penetrator, the bottom the penetrated. None of this is particularly surprising, after all; Bersani notes that "To be penetrated is to abdicate power," an idea that extends back to the ancient Greeks.[28] Versatility, however, proves to be "a unique and important feature of male anal sex" because "some men find it liberating; they enjoy the freedom the male body offers to alternately fuck and get fucked. Versatility to them is akin to speaking two different languages."[29] Given that we are presented with three "types" of gay men's sexualities, we can quickly realize that the binary to which we have grown accustomed is hardly sufficient.

All of this says nothing, however, of BDSM (bondage and discipline, dominance and submission, sadomasochism), which Underwood also briefly considers and which surely must further complicate our notions of sexual orientation. Sarah S. G. Frantz argues, for instance, alongside earlier work by Ivo Dominguez (1994), that, "for some, BDSM goes much deeper than what they *do*. For them, BDSM is their primary sexual identity."[30] Accordingly, we should be careful in being reductive with sexual orientation. How we perform our sexualities cannot be one of a select few options but must be understood as remarkably complex because of our numerous erotic and sexual intersections, and perhaps we might better speak in terms of constellations of desire.

I wish to return to the space of the closet and its implications for virginity studies and sexuality studies. The nature of the closet, I think, is not just about the singular announcement from which all secrets are revealed; instead, as Sedgwick notes, "Even at an individual level, there are remarkably few of even the most openly gay people who are not deliberately in the closet with someone personally or economically or institutionally important to them."[31] I am not suggesting that all layers of the closet are the same; after all, I'm not certain that many virgins are persecuted "personally or economically or institutionally," though I can imagine scenarios such as a scholar of sexuality studies who is a virgin. I wish to stress here that virginity, like queerness, requires an utterance. In the examples that we will consider, often enough this utterance is confirmed by way of the closet: the closeted gay man can become uncloseted because of a loss of virginity, an uncloseted gay man still requires the loss of virginity to become a fully fledged gay man, or any other example of identity calculus.

If we accept the importance of the closet, from which one comes out, and if we accept the various identities hidden away in the closet, then we must recognize the importance of the utterance. Jodi McAlister has provided an important term in speaking about these types of narratives: the "virginity loss confessional genre." The confessional narrative necessarily speaks not only to the physical act but also, and perhaps more importantly, to the psychic and affective aspects of the experience. McAlister explains that for Foucault "the confessional thus becomes part of a framework that did not seek to repress sex but to measure and micromanage it."[32] There is much to be gained, of course, by turning to Foucault and his ideas of confession. McAlister and Foucault are correct in asserting that confession is about "measuring and micromanaging sexuality": that is, in the confession one puts into words the sexual acts that might be thought about or acted upon.[33]

Confession as a mode, however, is rich with moral problems as well and, perhaps more provocatively, gendered paradigms. "Male confessional writings," Björn Krondorfer explains, "do not only render men vulnerable but also reinforce and strengthen their identities."[34] We would be remiss if we did not acknowledge the ways in which gender and sex complicate confession; after all, masculinity is remarkably well structured, governed, and regulated. It is hardly surprising, for example, that Krondorfer is interested in "the difficulty of men testifying to themselves truthfully."[35] That said, I want to stress that the confessional narrative need not be just in the space of a religiously sanctioned confession, and we can think here about legal testimony, psychotherapy, diaries, and even, less optimistically, suicide notes.

Above all, the confession as a genre is an important model to consider here, particularly when we attach it to the "epistemology of the closet." Confession, as I understand it, is about putting into words the stories that we want to tell. In the case of coming out, Sedgwick explains, "questions of authority and experience can be the first to arise": "How do you know you're really gay?"[36] Each of the narratives that we will consider answers this question by returning to authority and experience: that is, one can "prove" one's claim to a gay identity by way of a gay sexual act, and one particular act has more currency than others. Indeed, to be the bottom is perhaps the gay act par excellence. It seems that there is a grain of truth to this, at least within the popular imagination:

I was twenty-one years old when I came out to my parents.
The following night my father, who seemed to have taken
the news surprisingly well, came home late and dead drunk.
Reeking of alcohol and cigarettes, he staggered up to me
and blurted out the most appalling question imaginable:
"So, do you take it up the ass? Is that what you *faggots* do?"[37]

Underwood's father, in this moment, spoke—*in vino veritas*—a
"truth" about male homosexuality, which he understood as revolv-
ing around the importance of the anus. Like Sedgwick, I am not
convinced that the anus is indeed essential to gayness; after all, "what
about male desire for a woman's anus—is that anal desire?"[38] Nevertheless, a man's desire to be anally penetrated by a female partner
also—and often—elicits questions about his "true" sexuality. But,
for the purpose of this study, I accept the principle that the anus is
important not only to heterosexual understandings of homosexuality
but also to homosexual understandings of homosexuality: that is,
the anus remains a synecdoche—a part that signifies the whole—of
male homosexuality, rightly or wrongly.

I agree with Underwood, and numerous others, that there is a
fundamental hierarchy that "discriminates" against bottoms, and
tops are seen, in this light, often enough, as "less gay." Various scholars have called into question this ideology;[39] however, we cannot
negate the perspectives outlined in the case studies of Underwood's
book. I propose, as already noted, treating each narrative as a truth
claim. This sample is flawed, though, for it hardly represents a diversity of subjects: that is, a larger study would need to be conducted
with the support of a human research ethics board to make a more
significant contribution regarding sexual orientation and virginity
in the space of the closet.[40] If there is one tangential intention here,
then it is to encourage scholars in the social sciences to return to
questions of virginity and sexual orientation precisely because there
is a great deal at stake for adolescents negotiating the confusing and
complicated terrain of sexual identity.

Although I recognize that many in queer theory would negate
the importance of orientation as a fixed category, I am not yet
certain that such a movement works for everyone, especially since

so many proto-queer and proto-gay children and adolescents are dependent on a term to give sense to themselves (and to give sense to others about their sense of self). I do not think that we are at a point yet where we can abandon orientations beyond a theoretical exercise, and queer theorists need to be careful in failing to consider the privilege of theory versus the real world. Indeed, in abandoning orientation—which might well be a theoretical goal—one has to ask what happens to numerous protections made available by orientation, such as (even if entirely ineffective) laws regarding hate crimes, hate speech, discrimination, and equality. That is, there is a real and political risk in renouncing orientation.

For each of the participants in *Gay Men and Anal Eroticism*, being a bottom carried a stigma or perception because he might feel various negative affects: shame, humiliation, discomfort, and so on. Moreover, each narrative includes not only the confession of being a bottom but also how the confession relates directly back to the declaration of sexual orientation. In a sense, the question that arises, or lurks in the background, in all of these narratives is rather simple: can a virgin be oriented (sexually), which is to say one who lacks sexual experience with an additional person? Or does the sexual act produce, confirm, and/or declare orientation? One is reminded here of Voltaire: "If you try it once, you are a philosopher; if twice, you're a sodomite."[41]

Underwood's book contains five interviews with "bottoms," four with "tops," ten with "versatiles," and two with couples. The book is well balanced yet limited by the small data sample. A general theme in each of the bottom narratives is the reason for being a bottom; two interviewees deferred to Freud (admittedly, a misreading of Freudian thought); others pointed to a lack of paternal influence or an excess of maternal influence; and another noted that, since it was his first sexual experience, it played a significant role, perhaps the determining role, in his sexual preferences.

Aaron's story is about orientation: "I didn't know any gay people when I was in high school. People in my school were unaware of the fact that there might be gay people running around."[42] We know this to be a fairly standard claim of lesbian and gay studies:

"Gay kids still grow up, for the most part, in heterosexual families and in heteronormative culture."[43] Indeed, this is one of the central claims for motivating an identity politics fuelled by an urgency such as Sedgwick's concern with the number of suicides of queer youth at the opening of her essay "Queer and Now." Orientation is not just about a declaration but also about a confession that one is not part of the governing and normative culture. Thus, when Aaron begins his narrative by noting the lack of gay people in his high school, this acts as a confession that establishes a framework within which he must come to terms with his own sexual orientation. He negotiated "very conflicted ideas about what it meant to be gay." He admits, for instance, that "I thought you didn't do certain things until you were with somebody in a committed relationship, blah, blah, blah, anal sex being the biggest. I wasn't going to do that. I *would not* do it. I got such flack for it." Thus, though he might have had sexual experiences, they were, in his own words, "very limited," and this recalls the tension between technical virginity and virginity.[44] Anal sex, like vaginal sex, remains the apex of virginity loss.

Aaron never uses the word *virginity*, however, and his discussion of anal sex as a first time mimics how we think about the loss of virginity: "So after three months we finally did it and I have to admit, I was amazed. It was like, 'Holy shit, I missed out on this all this time? What the hell is wrong with me?' It was sort of a revelation."[45] The first time is marked by a sense of "revelation" and a strange excitement tempered by a sense of guilt and loss. Other narratives are more particular about this, but even as Aaron discusses subsequent partners he returns to his first time:

> When I was much younger I used to wonder what sex was like for women. This was long before I even thought about the fact that I could find out. I read some things in *Cosmo* and all those women's magazines and various books, where women were describing what it was like. They described it in this very emotional and psychological way. Way beyond pure sensation. The sensation of being "filled up." When it finally happened, I remember the very first time distinctly, I

remember thinking, "Oh shit, this is what it feels like!" And it was with Jeff, who was somebody I cared about deeply. There was an emotional aspect to having someone inside of me. I mean that was pretty phenomenal. All that stuff I'd read sort of came flooding back and I'm like, "Ah, this is what they meant."[46]

Aaron's first time becomes, as one of Kate Monro's interviewees suggests, "the blueprint for all subsequent lovers. If you get it right the first time, do you have a better chance of succeeding further down the line?"[47] Worth noting here is how the first time is an important time, which Aaron—and I imagine that this is true for many people—reflects on as a defining moment in terms of his sexuality.

His understanding of his orientation as a bottom is further complicated by the fact that he sees himself as a "power bottom," which, he explains, means "Shut up and lie down. I'll take care of the rest."[48] In other words, though many understand the bottom as a passive position, an abdication of power, Aaron disagrees: "I'm going to engulf you; you are not going to penetrate me. I'm gonna swallow you up whole. You're going to find out who is really in control."[49] This is important to recognize because it reminds us once more that sexuality—as if this needs to be reaffirmed—is never that simple. For Aaron, "being a bottom is very much connected to my self-esteem."[50] Thus, though so much of the discourse on the role of bottoming has been rather negative, for Aaron bottoming is an essential component of his identity. Through anal sex he comes to understand not only his orientation as gay but also how this orientation informs his sexuality and personality. In other words, though the closet might have contained his apparent gayness—even though he never knew gay people—it is through an exploration of the closet's sexuality that Aaron can understand the totality of this orientation.

Lito is the only non-white subject in Underwood's limited sample. Nevertheless, his narrative highlights cultural differences and, like Aaron's narrative, privileging of the anus. Lito admits from the outset that "I discovered in America [how] to be happy with my orientation, you know? Being gay. In Latin America, this is another story."[51] As with the previous narrative, we are provided with a narrative about oral sex before we come to the apex of sexuality, anal sex, which Lito figures as "a higher level of communication" in which "the bottom experience is deeper and more real."[52] At the level of language, I am struck by the ways in which anal sex, particularly bottoming, is figured as superlative (higher, deeper, more real), as though the top's experience and other sexual activities cannot match the "fullness," to borrow Aaron's word, of anal sex.

Lito realized early on that he was "different," and he quickly declares that "I am gay and a bottom. Passive."[53] One theme that becomes clear throughout his narrative is the "difficulty" of anal sex the first time, a failed time, he explains: "[H]e wanted to fuck me, but I was so afraid that it didn't work," and when it did work, with another person, his college roommate, "it was a psychologically enjoyable and deeper experience."[54] This language once more mimics so much of what we know about virginity as a revelatory experience because it is "a magic moment" or provides access to some "deeper experience."[55] Anal sex functions for Lito as a way of affirming sexual orientation because of its deepness, its pleasure, its magic. Even though he might have wished to renounce his orientation, it was through sexuality, we learn, that he came to understand that "it's a wonderful way to love, to be with somebody."[56]

Each of Underwood's interviewees stresses the importance of orientation, which is twofold: homosexual and bottom. This is not to suggest that tops aren't gay, and for them topping is equally central to orientation, and the same holds true for versatiles. However, what is noteworthy and must be acknowledged across these narratives is the centrality of the anus, not just to sexuality, but also to orientation. Max, a top, for instance, was very confused about his sexuality, which his girlfriend helped to clarify: "You're gay. You've got to be with guys."[57] What is striking, however, about the narratives of the tops is their renunciation of anal pleasure and that first times do not figure prominently for them. That is, the first time is not endowed with "a magic moment," as Lito suggested, or the "phenomenal" and "pure sensation" that Aaron suggested. Consider, for instance, Mark's first time: "I definitely didn't fly out of the closet like a lot of other gay men did. For me it was [a] gradual process," and "[s]oon after I had anal sex for the first time. . . . I had some lube and I fucked him. . . . The first time I did it, it was okay."[58] His narrative lacks the richness, shall we say, of the bottom's narrative. Indeed, it seems, at least from this limited sample size, that the bottom is given access to a distinct type of knowledge.

Indeed, to be entirely polemical, this chapter contains, though it is repressed, an important question: how does the male lose his virginity? One wonders, particularly with the ways that bottoming has been described, and even tops seem to agree that bottoming provides access to an additional level of knowledge, whether penetration is not required for a male to lose his virginity. In this regard, if it is true, as Lito suggests, that "the male body is built to fuck as well as to get fucked,"[59] then what happens when males refuse access to their rectums? What many of these narratives demonstrate, and this is important, is that our notions of active/passive are incomplete. There is much work to be done on the desiring anus and the anus as active agent in sexuality, and this research is important not just for gay men. The work is important because it rewrites the primacy and dominance of the phallus, which has governed so much of how we, as a sexual culture, think about sexuality.

The study of male virginity—heterosexual, homosexual, and everything in between—is a necessary component of virginity studies because it affords a more complete vision of this fundamentally complex and exciting identity category. A central advantage of studying male virginity is that it provides us with a better understanding of how virginity has worked and will continue to work. The concept will not go away; however, we can do a better job of understanding its complexities. We can reduce its stigma and negative affect, and I think that, by turning our attention to non-heterosexual, non-female virginities, we can help to reduce the treatment of virginity for heterosexual females. That is, by showing that virginity is not just for females, not just for heterosexuals, we can relieve some of the tension; we can liberate virginity to be less definitive, less authoritative. My position here is more utopian insofar as I believe that virginity is fundamentally inclusive, especially since we are all born with it. In this regard, academics and activists alike should think about what virginity means outside the context of heterosexual females who have rightly or wrongly held a monopoly—imposed as it might be—on it.

Topping from the Bottom:
Anne Tenino's *Frat Boy and Toppy*

IF UNDERWOOD'S GAY MEN AND ANAL EROTICISM OF-
FERS a series of meditations on virginity loss and anal
sexuality,[1] the popular romance novel, particularly the
recent manifestation of the male-male romance novel,
might well offer one of the richest fictional treatments of these
narratives. This genre often goes to extremes to provide an even
more nuanced and complicated view of male virginity loss and
sexual orientation. To be certain, this is a relatively new field of
study that is expansive and remarkably understudied, and it com-
prises a significant number of works that explore the complexities
of sexuality, gender, desire, and eroticism from a range of oriented
and orienting possibilities. In this chapter, I pay attention to one
romance novel, *Frat Boy and Toppy* (2012), by Anne Tenino. I argue
that it is anally centred in its exploration of orientation and thus
affords an interesting textual world in which we can think about
anal eroticism. Popular romance novels remain widely underread
in the literary academy, and this chapter seeks to show that they
are rich with hermeneutic potential.

Lisa Fletcher notes that the popular romance novel is a "massive genre," that the novels "kiss the retail shelves [only] for a brief moment," that "these novels are too numerous and too fast-moving for scholarly research," and that scholars themselves are not fans.[2] If this is the rubric for the study of romance, then many scholars will surely fail at the task, and I myself must admit this failure, for I am literally always reading from behind. I will never manage to keep up with the romance novels that move off the shelves so quickly. I am not a fan-scholar, or an aca-fan, which we understand as a hybrid scholar trained "to recognize and deconstruct media in specific and sometimes brutal ways" but also something of a "rogue reader." Aca-fans "experience tensions in their scholarship that other researchers may not feel, because they have a significant investment in the text." Moreover, the aca-fan will often "encounter discouragement and discrimination because popular media [are] . . . considered frivolous and fandom is not usually cast in positive light."[3] The aca-fan is thus a specific type of scholar who openly identifies as a fan, as Amanda Firestone does ("I am a *Twilight* fan. A Twilighter. A Cullenist. A Twi-hard"), but the aca-fan also identifies as a critical theorist, an intellectual, an academic, and so on ("I am also a feminist scholar").[4] However, I am struck by her inversion of aca and fan. Firestone is initially a "fan" of the *Twilight* saga and subsequently and additionally "a feminist scholar." The tension perhaps lies most obviously in which of the two identities comes first or in which identity manifests its dominance over the reader. What is clear to me, however, is that I am not an aca-fan. Simply put, I read too few romance novels to ever qualify as a fan.

Because I am not an aca-fan or a fan-scholar, I am reading from behind, always trying to catch up, as Kate Thomas might suggest, "too slow, too stupid," but not (or maybe I am) "too soon."[5] If I am "too soon," it is because I have leapt over the debates regarding the place of feminist theory in popular romance studies, and instead I begin with queer theory—but this works only if we accept a history of popular romance and literary theory, a history written by Eric Murphy Selinger and Sarah S. G. Frantz in their luminous introduction to *New Approaches to Popular Romance Fiction*,[6] a history in which feminism is almost always in tension, if not conflict, with popular romance, a history that includes various forms of psychoanalyzing real and imagined readers. My feeling of being "too stupid" is perhaps less about a lack of intelligence or a sense of ignorance, and more about "feeling late" or a sense of being out of sequence.[7] I feel similar to how Thomas imagines herself, "turning up at graduate school" in 1994 (a year after the publication of Eve Kosofsky Sedgwick's *Tendencies*, Judith Butler's *Bodies that Matter*, and Michael Warner's *Fear of a Queer Planet*) "and taking a queer theory class, I felt late. Like a younger, shorter-legged sibling, it seemed to me that I was trotting to catch up, excited but definitely flustered."[8]

But how, then, do we imagine that we can contribute to discussions of importance when so many rubrics seemingly foreclose the possibility of our participation? My contention is that we might simply admit that indeed we will fail but that, in this failure, we can offer another potential for a given field of scholarship. That is, we can intervene in the discussion because we are not necessarily bogged down by its historical baggage, and we can take a long look at the field, noting its high and low points rather than the totality of its imagined historical continuity. This is a kind of reading from behind; I admit that I am beginning not from the forefront of the discussion but from a figurative and temporal behind. In this reading from behind, we still look *forward* to the contributions that we can make from that position.

Reading from behind, as a phrase, as we have witnessed, however, has another meaning, a more provocative meaning. It recognizes that the anus has become the "proletariat of body parts,"[9] and in a similar fashion we might suggest that the popular romance has become, or has been seen as, the bottom of literary studies. Indeed, the romance reader, like the anal subject, is reminded that it is "so totally yours that you must not use it: keep it to yourself."[10] In other words, it—the anus or the romance novel—must remain entirely private. Consider here, for instance, "how much courage it takes for a woman to open a romance novel on an airplane" and that "society does not approve of the reading of romance novels."[11] To admit pleasure—from either a romance novel or an anus—takes "courage," precisely because these things should be beneath us.

Ever the courageous critic, I have begun to wonder what it would mean to read popular romance novels from behind—both as a critic who is not an aca-fan, always looking back at what has not been read, and as a critic who is fundamentally interested in why we have not attended to the anal dimensions of texts. This chapter is therefore a contribution to the task of reading from behind and to the growing interdisciplinary field of popular romance studies. I focus on the ascendant genre of male-male popular romance novels and its uses of the ass, the anus, the behind.

However, it seems important to offer a caveat: although I might well be one of the first critics to study male-male romance novels in a scholarly fashion, I am hardly the leading scholar. Perhaps I have arrived too soon, because this debate, this inquiry, has yet to be developed by aca-fans who can point to the seminal texts, the best texts, the most complex texts. I am conscious here of the argument of Pamela Regis: "[I]dentifying and studying the strongest romance novels will benefit the entire critical enterprise and help us avoid making claims about simplicity and other qualities that critics assign to the romance novel based on an unrepresentative set of study texts."[12] As much as I accept this claim, I worry that, if this is a prerequisite for scholarship in popular romance, very few will ever be in a position to speak with sufficient authority and expertise. Moreover, what happens to the theoretical training necessary to make these claims? Her axiom requires that we be at the top of the field, at least in terms of having read enough to ensure that we are "identifying and studying the strongest romance novels." Regis works to establish a field of popular romance studies and to define what its methodology *should* look like. She puts the "activism" in "aca-fan," for she urges scholars to study the best texts. There are two reasons: first, to show non-romance readers that the texts can be as complex, aesthetically pleasing, and thought provoking as literary fiction; second, to establish a canon for popular romance studies.

Unlike many critics, I cannot claim to have a personal canon from which to work. I work instead from a canon constructed by petitions for advice on what I should read in regard to my intellectual project of reading from behind. I cannot make any claims for the texts that I study as being "the strongest romance novels." Indeed, ever the postmodern critic, or the Frygian critic (for I might be too soon or too late on this one), I am not certain of the place of value judgments in literary criticism and scholarship. Like Northrop Frye, I recognize, "just as any scholar in any field would have," that our "canons of greater or less importance are related to the conditions of [our] specific research, not directly related to the literary qualities of [our] material."[13] Accordingly, in this chapter I read from behind the subgenre of male-male romance novels, with a particular focus on Tenino's *Frat Boy and Toppy*, and I make no claim for its place on any given canon; the text is merely interesting to me given "the conditions of [my] specific research."[14]

Novels featuring the development of a love story between men have quickly become a recognized subgenre in popular romance. Indeed, the *Globe and Mail* has profiled the subgenre, declaring that "man-on-man romantic fiction . . . has taken a significant bite out of one of publishing's biggest markets." "Even Harlequin—the most profitable and old-fashioned romance fiction house in the world—has recently started to publish same-sex love stories via the company's digital imprint, Carina Press," which caused Erastes, a "47-year-old British author," to exclaim that, "Now that [Harlequin] has started a gay romance line, my prayers have been answered."[15] Nevertheless, as Sarah S. G. Frantz admits, male-male romance "is still growing as a genre," and "it's had and continues to have growing pains, but it's maturing quickly."[16] Although I am inclined to believe that any popular genre is worthy of scholarly consideration (in spite of its flaws), I am pleased that Frantz admits that the genre is still undergoing "growing pains" though "maturing quickly." In the same spirit, I imagine and accept that the scholarly study of male-male romance novels, like that of popular romance novels, will also have growing pains (and this study, of course, is no exception).

A central growing pain, as it were, that has informed much of the popular criticism (the blogosphere, book reviews, etc.) is that the male-male romance novel is largely (at least mythically so) written by heterosexual women for women. Admittedly, these women are often involved in LGBT political activism and/or self-define in a queer fashion. Nevertheless, the criticism follows that gay men, by and large, are not writing these novels about themselves. In other words, their voices and experiences have been appropriated by those who have very little or no experience as gay men. I am not inclined to embrace this critique, for it seems to me to be a quick reduction that works to invalidate the creative enterprises of these authors, and, as Dan Brown's protagonist quips in *Angels and Demons*, "One does not need to have cancer to analyze its symptoms."[17] Further still, if this is a requirement, then who is permitted to study these narratives?

The second growing pain has been the assumption that, since the genre involves gay men, it somehow negates gender politics common to the heterosexual relationship. This, of course, is fallacious. Gender does not stop at the edge of sex identity. Being male is rife with the complexity of gender. Indeed, if anything, these romance novels are rich with the complexity of gender, carefully negotiating the tension between "essential" and "biological" arguments and the poststructural, feminist, and queer arguments about gender as performance. The genre is filled with various forms of gender presentation, from the campy queen, to the alpha male, to the butch bottom, to the gay-for-you hero, and so on; however, one of the genre's growing pains might well be its continued interest in what we might call "hegemonic masculinity," a kind of traditional, white, cis-gendered, masculine corporeality. All of these gender presentations and performances are contributions to the diversity of gendered experiences.

One additional and tangential challenge to the previous critique confronted by the genre is a tendency toward misogyny, wherein female voices are erased altogether or women are presented as being nearly monstrous (e.g., the horrible, overbearing mother), entirely vapid, or manic pixie dream girls. These novels almost always, so the criticism goes, fail the Bechdel Test, which requires that two women in the given text talk to one another about something other than a man. In this regard, there is a need to be careful in arguing that somehow these romances avoid the politics of gender by erasing women and not recognizing that this is a question of gender and politics. It seems to be resoundingly clear that the male-male romance novel is never without gender politics and that perhaps, unlike the heterosexual romance, it can explore these politics in new or different fashions. Even in its most masculine form, say a novel that excludes women altogether, the gender negotiations between men are worthy of consideration.

I acknowledge these growing pains because it seems to me that they must be recognized in academic scholarship (though there are certainly additional growing pains that could and should be addressed by scholars). The male-male romance novel is not without its problems, and readers are often quick to point them out; however, we would be remiss if we adopted these criticisms as reasons not to study this type of novel or to dismiss it altogether. By framing the concerns in terms of growing pains, we admit that the genre is working to understand itself, its limits, and its problems. I also note these concerns because I do not wish to appear oblivious to them, especially when they are not the focus of this chapter; however, I believe that the chapter implicitly highlights their faults.

The opening words of *Frat Boy and Toppy* privilege the ass: "One of Brad's frat brothers bent over naked in the locker room showers early one Thursday morning, and he thought, 'I'd tap that.'"[18] Immediately, a reader's attention is focused, like Brad's, on the frat brother, who happens to be bending over in the shower, and especially on his ass. For Brad, this moment becomes a "paradigm shift," the moment in which after "years trying to avoid the 'G' word . . . denial was suddenly circling the drain."[19] The clincher of this novel is that Brad is coming to terms with his gay identity (not an uncommon narrative trope in male-male romance novels), and it is the ass of his frat brother that helps to confirm this identity. In other words, the frat brother's rear becomes "the essence of homosexuality, the very ground zero of gayness."[20] The ass, not the phallus, is what causes Brad to ask questions about his sexuality.

This important moment shifts our critical attention and the types of questions that we might ask. Although so much of critical theory has argued for the symbolic importance of the phallus, in *Frat Boy and Toppy* the ass does much of the symbolic work. Indeed, as reluctant as we might be to accept the centrality of the ass to gayness, it seems that the rule holds true, at least in the context of this work. The "paradigm shift" that Brad thinks about is twofold in a sense: first, it is about his sexuality; second, it shifts how we, as scholars, think about eroticism and sexuality. In other words, and I want to stress this, the focus is not on the phallus but on the anus. However, it is also not about the destruction or dismissal of the phallus. This is a paradigmatic shift in critical theories of gender and sexuality precisely because it recalibrates "the erotic monopoly traditionally held by the genitals."[21] The anus is remarkably rich with hermeneutic potential, and critical theory has done a disservice to its complexity by privileging the phallic referent. I will argue that much of *Frat Boy and Toppy* is anally focused.

Tenino's novel recognizes and celebrates, I would argue, the complexity of the anus and its eroticism. That is, the anus is not a substitute for or an addition to sex; rather, it has a sexuality of its own. In her work, Eve Kosofsky Sedgwick "encourages us to learn the ways of a sphincter and to differentiate the potentially erotic experience of the buttocks, the asshole, and to think about the arse as a composite muscle, surface and hole, cavity and receptacle." More explicitly, Jason Edwards explains, "Sedgwick encourages us to imagine our buttocks slapped and beaten, our assholes tickled pink, wiped, rimmed, fingered, fisted, penetrated, receptive and embracing."[22] Reading from behind thus embraces the Sedgwickian paradigm in which we need to think carefully and closely about a range of erotic experiences which in many ways are on full display in the popular romance novel, which at bottom is an exploration of the tensions between human sexuality and the affective resonances of love. *Frat Boy and Toppy* attempts to explore these experiences and tensions throughout its narrative.

Frat Boy and Toppy is not the first to do this. Various male-male romance novels, one could argue, are interested in exploring the complexity of anal eroticism; for instance, Heidi Cullinan's *Dirty Laundry* could also contribute to this discussion.[23] Heterosexual romances also explore anal eroticism. The back cover of *Beyond Heaving Bosoms: The Smart Bitches' Guide to Romance Novels* asks, "is anal really the new oral?" Raelene Gorlinsky explains:

[A]t a writer conference about two years ago, the editor panel was discussing this topic. One of the New York editors said "Anal is the new oral." That's an example of how readers have become "acclimatized" to the sex due to the

popularity of erotic romance. Oral sex in romance novels
was uncommon and titillating five or six years ago, [and]
now it is standard and very vanilla. In fact, anal has become
common in e-pubbed erotic romance for quite a while now
and is becoming more so in New York print erotic romance;
it is no longer at all shocking or considered excessively hot.[24]

Tellingly, by 2010 anal sex had found its way into a Harlequin romance, *Private Sessions*, by Tori Carrington.[25] Readers are encouraged
to "learn" the complexity of anal eroticism, and not just as a mere
inversion of heterosexual romance, as if the anus were a substitute
vagina. More importantly, as will become clear, the introduction of
anal eroticism also challenges how we think about gender scripts,
one of the common criticisms of the genre.

The central axiom of this project is that the anus is worthy of study
because it is complex, not quite as simple as it might seem, and in
many ways (often curious ways) the popular romance novel plays
with these complexities. Jack Morin observes that the anus contains
"a vast array of tiny blood vessels and nerved endings, making it one
of the body's most sensitive zones."[26] This observation is echoed, of
course, by Sedgwick's writings on the anus. It is remarkably complex
and sensitive and, if a second axiom is to be offered, highly affective.
We likely have "a wide range of negative ideas and feelings about [the]
anus."[27] These two axioms inform much of the practice of reading
from behind, the goals being recognition of both the complexity of
the organ and its affect and understanding of why we have disre-
garded this "most sensitive [of] zones."[28] This point is highlighted
toward the close of *Frat Boy and Toppy*, after Brad has embraced his
homosexuality and come out of the metaphorical closet to a number
of people. During one instance of coming out, Brad explains to a frat
brother, "Your anus is one of the most sensitive parts of your body.
It's more sensitive than a lot of your dick."[29] Ensuring that the anus
is more than just a body part, acknowledging its complex nature, is
central to reading from behind, even if this particular example seems
to be heavy-handed and didactic. Throughout *Frat Boy and Toppy*,
readers are encouraged to think about anal eroticism, particularly
its relation to sexual identity.

It is important to know, from the outset, that Brad is a jock and frat boy with "high, prominent" cheekbones,[30] "beautiful musculature,"[31] "a nice set of arms," and evidently quite a "view from behind."[32] He is "almost Native American looking," has "blue eyes" and "a darker ring around the iris,"[33] and is "macho."[34] In a sense, Brad represents a masculine ideal, a macho or, in the parlance of romance, an alpha male. Indeed, his nickname in the fraternity is "alpha dawg."[35]

The popular romance novel eroticizes the Indigenous body—and this critique might well extend to non-white bodies in general. This problem, what might be understood as a racist ideology, is found throughout the history of the popular romance novel. Robin Harders, for instance, observes that "one of the most popular and enduring romantic captivity scenarios is that made famous in Edith Hull's 1919 novel *The Sheik*, in which the beautiful 'civilized' heroine is captivated, body, soul, and heart, by the 'wild' desert-living sheik."[36] I note this historical tradition not to absolve it but to point out that there is much research to be done on the popular romance novel, particularly on the eroticization of the body of the other, and in romance the male body is often the site of otherness, which becomes all the more othered when race, for instance, is incorporated. The consideration of race in *Frat Boy and Toppy* is based on suppositions and assumptions; Brad might not be Indigenous, but he is "Native American looking," whatever that might be. The narrative assumes, moreover, that all readers will know what that is.[37]

Brad's alpha, macho qualities are important to recognize because they function as a sort of narrative conceit. As readers, we are led to believe that Brad is powerful, assertive, controlling—after all, he has the "beautiful musculature" of a jock. He has "spectacular masculinity"; "every aspect of his being, whether his body, his face, or his general demeanour[,] is informed by the purity of his maleness."[38] Readers of romance know that the hero is defined in terms of this purity, that he is strong, virile, almost excessive in perfection, representing a hyperbolic ideal of the male body. Admittedly, this glorification of the body is changing, particularly as conceptions of masculinity change; however, readers familiar with the genre will understand this representation of masculinity as the embodiment of maleness.

This masculinity is inherently enmeshed in how readers imagine the anus and its sexuality; moreover, it contributes to a larger discussion on anal sexuality in general. Bersani's understanding of anal penetration as an abdication of power is informed by Foucault's work in the second volume of *The History of Sexuality*, which explores the sexual behaviour of the ancient Greeks, wherein "Passivity was always disliked, and for an adult to be suspected of it was especially serious."[39] The Greeks, as articulated by Foucault, constructed a sexual system in which each partner had a prescribed role, that of *erastes* or *eromenos*, which can be described as "active" and "passive" (as Foucault does by citing K. J. Dover). Indeed, we find this very model in *Frat Boy and Toppy*: "[I]n ancient Greece," Sebastian, a teaching assistant in Greek history, explains, "[t]he older guy was the *erastes* and the young guy was his *eromenos*. I'm Brad's *erastes*."[40] The point of interest for the reader is that while Brad is given "spectacular masculinity" he is also very interested in anal pleasure, being passive and receptive. In other words, "the rectum is the grave in which the masculine ideal (an ideal shared—differently—by men *and* women) of proud subjectivity is buried."[41] It is hardly surprising, in a sense, that a reviewer such as Frantz applauds this in her review of *Frat Boy and Toppy*: "Big bad football player Brad is a bottom and LOVES it."[42] Tenino inverts the model of "spectacular masculinity" and everything that it entails. This inversion, moreover, challenges the reader's expectations of such masculinity.

Tenino carefully deconstructs many of the myths surrounding anal desire and anal sexuality in queer culture, notably because she presents not the seemingly passive Sebastian but Brad as the bottom. Throughout the narrative, we have indications that Brad is interested in receiving anal pleasure and that he has a complicated relationship with the ass. His first indication, as noted, that he might be gay—or at least bi—is when he finds himself in fantasy for his "bent over" frat brother. But as he begins to explore his sexuality, when he "start[s] checking out gay porn, he [i]s a little surprised to always find himself identifying with the guy getting fucked."[43] He acknowledges that these images make "his asshole twitch and the muscle in his butt contract"[44] and that he has a fundamental desire to experience those feelings beyond the virtual interface. The initial solution to this desire is masturbatory. With "the hairbrush with the perfect handle,"[45] Brad heads to the bathroom and takes the necessary time "working it into himself,"[46] and as we might expect he shudders, shivers, and nearly moans with it.[47] This "first time" with the hairbrush reveals just how "sensitive" the anus is, and he feels "each one of those rings slip past his sphincter, and every time one stretche[s] him wider . . . he [feels] it zing up his spine."[48]

The first time that Brad pleasures his anus seems to evoke some of the ideas common to anal sex, at least in theoretical terms, that it is a kind of self-shattering. For Bersani, self-shattering "disrupts the ego's coherence and dissolves its boundaries" and is about "the joy of self-dissolution."[49] In other words, more mundane words, things begin to fall apart, not necessarily in an irresolvable fashion, but one's "solid" or "established" identity begins to come undone, for instance Brad's uncertainty about his sexuality. His exterior and performed heterosexuality is thus called into question, its coherence is disrupted, and the boundaries of the heteronormative ideal begin to dissolve in favour of the *jouissance* of "self-dissolution." Of course, in this instance, this self-shattering is fully at the hands of Brad. He is not shattering because of another body penetrating his body but because he is curious about the limits of his own pleasures. The narrative's language is about "something . . . blooming inside of him,"[50] which I contend is akin to Bersani's shattering insofar as it is about recognition. Although Brad's sexuality has always been a site of confusion, it has now become necessary for this confusion to resolve itself (a flawed idea that imagines sexuality has a teleological endpoint, but the romance novel depends on the teleological, whether it be sexually or happily ever after and wedded bliss). The sexual confusion, however, is squarely situated in anal desire and what to do with this "most sensitive" part of the body.[51] Through these masturbatory explorations with the hairbrush, Brad can confirm his identity: "*I'm so gay.*"[52] Of course, anal masturbation can hardly qualify as gay in any identifying or essential sense. At best, this masturbatory exploration indicates that one finds oneself endlessly pleasing and pleasurable.

This self-shattering is more fully felt when Brad has sex with Sebastian for the first time, which also happens to be his first time with another man. Virginity has long been central to the romance novel, almost an archetype essential to the genre. One needs only recall how Ann Snitow suggested that the heroine's virginity is "a given"[53] when summarizing the genre in the 1970s through a handful of novels.[54] Yet we have seen, in recent years, a renewed interest in virginity in the form of the virgin hero, and this discussion is particularly prevalent in the male-male romance novel, especially when the trope at hand is coming to terms with one's orientation. The loss of virginity in *Frat Boy and Toppy* is as much about self-shattering as it is a confirmation of orientation for Brad.

When readers are introduced to Brad, he is a "gay virgin" since he has not had "'sex' with a same-sex partner";[55] however, he has had significant experiences with opposite-sex partners, a point that he laments on various occasions, noting that he was an "asshole" to these previous partners.[56] In this context, an asshole is a "repugnant person" who "allows himself to enjoy special advantages in interpersonal relations out of an entrenched sense of entitlement"[57] and not a desiring, sexual asshole.[58] I note this, however briefly, because the novel oscillates between both uses of the word *asshole*.

Returning to the task at hand, as obvious as this surely seems, "Virgins can have a variety of sexual orientations,"[59] even though the bulk of scholarship—though this is changing—is about heterosexual virginity. The first time is an important time not least because of what it confirms (or helps to clarify), and this is precisely the case in *Frat Boy and Toppy*. Virginity loss is not just about the first time but also about what it means in the context of sexuality and uses of the body.

Brad, in many ways, is virginal with regard to his orientation, not just because he has yet to have sex with a man, but also because he has not learned "how to be gay," as David M. Halperin might have it.[60] Sebastian asks, "So, I guess the only question left is, are you top, bottom, or verse?" Brad is uncertain what "verse" means.[61] For the *cognoscenti*, the terms "top," "bottom," and "verse" ("versatile") refer to orientation, the position that one takes during anal sex. This kind of language is part of what one must learn; it is part of "a conscious identity, a common culture, a particular outlook on the world, a shared sense of self, an awareness of belonging to a specific social group, and a distinctive sensibility or subjectivity."[62] Learning how to be gay is not exclusive to gay men, after all, for "Women have written brilliantly about gay male culture. (So have a few straight men)."[63] To which I am tempted to respond, "We try." When Sebastian calls on the identities of *erastes* and *eromenos*, there is an implicit pedagogy at play, and of course this is further admitted because Sebastian acts as a teaching assistant in Brad's course. The pedagogical scene, the eros of pedagogy, is manifested in various ways.

Much of the erotic exploration with Sebastian plays with common notions about anal sex. Readers are reminded of Brad's "virgin ass," which might "clench up tighter than a nun" if confronted with "a huge dick."[64] His anxiety here is a sort of psychic anal spasm, the "involuntary contractions of the anal sphincter muscles."[65] I suggest that this is psychically bound because thus far Brad has merely been thinking about, in a paranoid fashion, what might happen. He anticipates what could happen the first time, and of course this is part of the excitement of it. Every first time is entirely new, nothing can be known before it happens, yet everything can be imagined. The anal spasm is a type of paranoia that "block[s] anal enjoyment" in an almost protective gesture.[66]

Throughout this opening sex scene, Brad is always positioned as someone ready and willing to learn how to be gay, but that does not mean that the scene is devoid of panic, anxiety, and paranoia. The scene begins with Sebastian "push[ing] gently against Brad's hole."[67] Indeed, we are told that he explores Brad's anus "a lot more carefully than Brad had been [doing] himself."[68] The care here is important because it is seemingly as much about his hole as the whole of his identity. We might well admit that there is an "ethics of pleasure" here,[69] a genuine concern if not love (both *caritas* and *eros*) for his partner: "[E]verything slowed down from frantic and desperate to slow and intense."[70] This is not violent sex but sex in which the partners in the eroticism are not equals. Over and over again, we are told about the care taken: "Not slow or fast. Careful. Working his way deeper. Trying to read Brad's face."[71]

Following the sexual episode, we are once more privy to a focused narrative on the reactions of Brad: "Everything looked different inside his head. . . . He floated, feeling so fucking good and, just, high."[72] Indeed, in thinking about sex with women, he acknowledges that sex with men is "so much better than he'd thought," and only now has "he got to actually feel skin for the first time."[73] I want to be careful here, for this is not about condomless sex but about ecstasy, "the joy of self-dissolution."

After this initial episode, Brad begins to understand his sexuality and its complexities. In various scenes, he is introduced to new pleasures of the anus. Sebastian declares, for instance, that "I'm going to teach you all about rimming," which leaves Brad "clutching the sheets and sweating into them."[74] At the end of this episode, Sebastian, ever the teacher, says, "You're going to learn how to have a beautiful, *active* ass, Bradley."[75] I highlight this passage because once more it is a renegotiation, or "paradigm shift,"[76] of the ass and its pleasures. For Sebastian, there is an attempt to rewrite the symbolic potential of the ass, not just as "the proletariat of body parts,"[77] not just as something that must remain passive and private, but also as something desired and desiring.

Through these erotic episodes, Brad learns how to be gay and can ultimately declare to friends and ex-lovers, "Oh yeah, I'm gay."[78] At the novel's close, he comes out to his frat brothers, who have a hard time believing that he is willing to abdicate his endowed masculinity, to allow his body to be penetrated. One of the frat brothers exclaims, "You can't be gay. . . . You're too macho!"[79] Another friend is stunned and asks, "You *bottom*?"[80] For one reason or another, "it pissed him off . . . that they would just figure, since he was the jock and Sebastian was the brain, that Brad must be fucking him."[81] Indeed, this is the same thing that pleases a reviewer such as Frantz. The popular imagination presumes that, since Brad is the very vision of masculinity, surely he would be a top; however, Tenino's narrative openly and carefully explores what it means to bottom. And, as readers learn (as does Brad), there is a great deal of pleasure to be found in the anus.

If there is a lesson here, it is that there is a great deal to be learned from the bottom: Brad comes to understand himself, and his earlier confusion is washed away. Tenino's narrative works, in many ways, to reclaim the role of the bottom. Although "bottoms are judged on an entirely separate scale than tops," and are "more severely stigmatized because getting ass-fucked . . . is considered feminizing and shameful,"[82] a novel such as *Frat Boy and Toppy* works to debunk so many of these myths. More importantly, being a bottom is not always about the abdication of power, as Foucault and Bersani might have it; after all, Brad receives a great deal of pleasure from "engulfing"[83] Sebastian. Tenino's narrative celebrates the complexity of the anus, not just a hole to be penetrated but also an access point to Brad's sexuality and confirmation of it. Nevertheless, though the narrative allows for versatility in anal pleasure,[84] it never fully explores this potential. That is, both Brad and Sebastian are oriented, and essentially so, as bottom and top. Accordingly, the novel's unanswered questions revolve around Sebastian's own relationship to anal pleasure and the complexity of the anus. His pleasures, it must be admitted, are fundamentally phallic. However, I am not certain that, to borrow a quaint term, this is the "authorial intent"; instead, I imagine that the author is interested in challenging the idea that the bottom is passive, receptive, and inactive. The anal poetics at play throughout *Frat Boy and Toppy* thus seemingly serve a political purpose: that is, the rubric by which we assume that masculinity cannot be passive is fallacious, and the anus is not merely a site for shameful pleasure. The anus affords Brad a clarity that was obscured by anal repression. Nevertheless, one cannot help but admit that many questions remain about Sebastian's own negotiation of anal pleasure and the seeming insistence on a binary of tops and bottoms, with an excluded or absent versatility.

Cautiously, however, it is important to note that reading from behind the male-male romance novel requires a larger and more sustained study if we are to make assumptions about the subgenre. *Frat Boy and Toppy*, arguably, is more interested in the bottom than it is in the top or the versatile male. However, other male-male romance novels have made use of versatility, or the inversion of roles, as the key to living happily ever after, akin to the declaration of love. Future research might well attend to these questions and address the various critiques of the romance novel, which lament, for instance, the appropriation of gay male voices or the problems of gender politics. This contribution is but an initial scholarly study of the male-male romance novel, and hopefully future work will explore many of the complicated, fascinating, and contradictory aspects of the genre.

As much as we privilege the top, the powerful, and the upper echelon of any hierarchy, there is still a great deal happening at the bottom that is rich and complex and needs to be considered. In a sense, one might well read Tenino's narrative allegorically to speak about the very nature of popular romance studies. Critics might well lament the fact that the romance novel remains understudied, but like the anus it is merely a matter of needing to uncover the potential power of being (at) the bottom. The ass, like the romance novel, is not nearly as simple as we might imagine; instead, it is complex, complicated, and rife with symbolic and hermeneutic potential. Instead of lamenting the fact that popular romance is not at the top of the literary stock market, we might well celebrate its place at the bottom. Likewise, at least for me, by admitting that one is "too slow, too stupid, too late," perhaps there is a recognition of never fully understanding the polemics of not being at the top. By reading from behind, we can privilege another side of the text, another side of literary history, another side of sexuality. The phallus, undoubtedly, remains iconic, but perhaps we can turn our attention to the phallic understudy. At bottom, we might say, we have much to learn from an ass.

CHAPTER 4

Orienting *Brokeback Mountain*

Things are in the saddle,
And ride mankind.
—RALPH WALDO EMERSON,
"Ode to William H. Channing"

ANNIE PROULX'S BROKEBACK MOUNTAIN (1997, PUB-
lished as a stand-alone book in 2005) and especially its
film adaptation by Ang Lee in 2005 have been widely
studied and analyzed by academics. Several academic
journals devoted significant portions of individual issues to *Brokeback
Mountain*; for example, *GLQ: A Journal of Lesbian and Gay Studies*
included essays on the film by Corey K. Creekmur, John Howard,
Dana Luciano, Martin F. Manalansan IV, Dwight A. McBride, and
Michael Cobb, who famously referred to the film as a "Christmas
gift for conservative Christians."[1] Likewise, *Film Quarterly* included
a series of essays, as did the *Journal of Men's Studies*, which attended
to the particular issues of masculinity and men in the film. *Brokeback
Mountain* struck a nerve, and for some time it was a part of the
cultural zeitgeist. David M. Halperin, for instance, explains that "it
was the case for many years that gay men looking for partners on
the Internet would attach the poster from *Brokeback Mountain* to

their profiles,"[2] and Oprah Winfrey seemingly endorsed the film when she "hosted the cast for a pre-Academy Awards" event.[3] The film was, and to a certain degree remains, a poignant moment in the history of American culture.

The question of orientation has haunted and bothered a great deal of the scholarship on *Brokeback Mountain*. Sheila J. Nayar, for example, declares that "*Brokeback* cannot rightly be scrutinized as a gay film or a film about gays."[4] Richard N. Pitt speaks instead about the enigma of bisexuality:

> Because the bisexuality of these characters is practically ignored by the media, no flurry of news articles or maga-zine examinations of the "white bisexual" phenomenon followed the movie's premiere. Instead the movie served as a catalyst for discussions about societal pressures that cause homosexual men to remain in the closet, a set of discussions that had none of the pejorative tone that followed society's introduction to black bisexuality.[5]

D. A. Miller insists that it is "the idea of homosexuality that is hot in *Brokeback Mountain*" rather than the homosexuality itself.[6] Extraordinarily, perhaps (for I do want to be tentative here), Clif-ton Snider suggests that, "If Ennis and Jack were born gay, that means they fit an *archetypal gay persona*" in his Jungian-inspired article.[7] Curiously enough, this is not the only debate surround-ing orientation. Some critics speak about the problem of generic orientation. Elaine Showalter, though not entering into a specific debate, sees Proulx's version as a "kind of grim fairytale."[8] David Wilbern returns our attention to the pastoral by suggesting that the film exhibits a pastoral style, as does Ginger Jones.[9] Nayar also calls the film a "heteronormative tragedy."[10] Erika Spohrer asks if *Brokeback Mountain* can really be seen as a "gay cowboy movie."[11] And Harry Brod further complicates her question when he argues that "They're bi shepherds, not gay cowboys."[12] Indeed, B. Ruby Rich would include the film in *New Queer Cinema*, though she argues that "*Brokeback Mountain* has blown it all wide open, collapsing the borders and creating something entirely new in the process."[13]

Rich, like so many others, seems to be uncertain about the genre of the film. Orientation in *Brokeback Mountain* scholarship thus remains hotly contested, but what motivates this discussion? Why do viewers—why do we—care about the various configurations of orientation contained in the film?

In a certain regard, all of the confusion over *Brokeback Mountain*, the film or the short story, arises because it is something of an open secret, a secret that everyone already knows. After all, even Willie Nelson has covered Ned Sublette's song "Cowboys Are Frequently, Secretly Fond of Each Other." Since the early writings on American literature, particularly those of Newton Arvin, F. O. Matthiessen, and especially Leslie Fiedler, homoeroticism, which I understand here as a queering of eroticism, has been on the radars of readers and literary critics alike. Admittedly, eroticism itself was certainly considered prior to these critics. In her 1927 study *The Frontier in American Literature*, Lucy Lockwood Hazard writes that, "with all the much boasted and much berated modern frankness of speech concerning sexual matters, the flapper or the Freudian would blush to read aloud certain passages in the chronicles of the godly fathers of New England."[14] It would be quite a treat to see how a critic such as Hazard would respond to *Brokeback Mountain*. As we shall see, a critic such as Fiedler, however, might be enchanted by, if not enamoured with, Proulx's tale.

Erotic tensions are central to the American literary imagination, and Matthiessen and Fiedler often highlight homoerotic tensions. Indeed, I argue in this chapter that *Brokeback Mountain* is part of a long tradition of homoerotic tension that runs rampant throughout American narratives, and this fact is troubling to the contemporary reader and/or viewer of *Brokeback Mountain*. In other words, contra earlier critics, *Brokeback Mountain* is not terribly "new" or "novel" so much as yet another artifact in the expansive archive of America's queerness. What *Brokeback Mountain* did was swing the closet doors wide open and highlight in no uncertain terms the radical queerness of American literature.

I want to begin this exploration of *Brokeback Mountain* by returning to the early critics of the American novel, particularly Arvin, Matthiessen, and Fiedler. What I hope to do in this chapter, beyond reading from behind, is position them as theorists doing queer work without ever admitting it or conceptualizing it as such. There is no doubt that, in varying ways, they participate in a homophobic culture, but beyond the superficial reading, I contend, is a theory of American sexuality that recognizes the complexity of the singular notion of sexuality. That is, their work struggles to understand sexualities that do not correspond to, and simply cannot correspond to, a heteronormative ideal. These critics thus work to understand an erotic relationship without naming it as gay, queer, homosexual, and so on. I argue that their work, especially when positioned alongside each other, can help us to understand the complexity of a work such as *Brokeback Mountain*, which has been caught up in many debates about its "orientations." Moreover, I hope to show that *Brokeback Mountain* fits comfortably into the literary histories that these early critics of American literature tracked.

To begin, though Matthiessen and Fiedler have fallen out of favour (as has Arvin, whom I will briefly consider), their intellectual successes and influences cannot be denied. William Calin, for instance, argues that Matthiessen "helped launch and define an entire professional field" and that, more particularly, he "launched the idea that five writers—Ralph Waldo Emerson, Henry David Thoreau, Nathaniel Hawthorne, Herman Melville, and Walt Whitman—are worthy of the most rigorous intellectual scrutiny."[15] Calin is prone, perhaps, to hyperbolic affirmation (he calls Northrop Frye "the last great humanist and the first major theoretician"[16]), but in this case it is difficult to disagree with his claim. Likewise, Fiedler suggests that "The success of *The American Renaissance* [sic] has been immense; it has given name and shape to new courses in American literature, and has had an impact outside of our own country unequalled by any other single study."[17]

In recent years, as is so often the case, we have nonetheless witnessed a renewed interest in Matthiessen's *American Renaissance: Art and Expression in the Age of Emerson and Whitman* and particularly what it does not do. Eric Cheyfitz, for instance, argues that "*American Renaissance* was not Matthiessen's book. For not only did he repress his politics in its production; he repressed his sexuality, and this in a book that is centrally concerned with questions of embodiment."[18] To be fair, Cheyfitz admits that there was a "social and professional danger" in admitting to homosexuality.[19] Indeed, if one reads Northrop Frye's diary entry on Matthiessen's suicide, one of the very few times that Frye mentions Matthiessen, one cannot help but note a tinge of homophobia: "On the way home today the MacGillivrays told us that F. O. Matthiessen of Harvard had committed suicide. He said it was the state of the world, which is hardly possible: there are too many other better reasons."[20] What these "better reasons" for suicide might be are never enumerated. Nevertheless, Cheyfitz opines, "was it necessary to discuss Whitman's homoeroticism, when he does so in passing, within the context of the 'pathological' and the 'regressive'?"[21] Cheyfitz criticizes the following passage from *American Renaissance*:

> Readers with a distaste for loosely defined mysticism have plenty of grounds for objection in the way the poet's belief in divine inspiration is clothed in imagery that obscures all distinctions between body and soul by portraying the soul as merely the sexual agent. Moreover, in the passivity of the poet's body *there is a quality vaguely pathological and homosexual.* This is in keeping with the *regressive, infantile fluidity, imaginatively polyperverse,* which breaks down *all mature barriers,* a little further on in "Song of Myself," to declare that he is "maternal as well as paternal, a child as well as a man." Nevertheless, this fluidity of sexual sympathy made possible Whitman's fallow receptivity to life.[22]

As will become apparent throughout this chapter, I believe it imperative that some reparative work be done with a critic like Matthiessen, who contributes, I think, not to a gay literary practice but to a queer one. Unlike many critics, Matthiessen is essentializing neither the body and the soul of the poet nor the poet himself. It is not Whitman, for instance, who is homosexual, pathological, and regressive but a poetic style. There is a great deal of work that can be done with the rather utopian phrase "fluidity of sexual sympathy," and I aim in this chapter to work with these moments, not to walk around or evade homophobia but to read these texts anew, from a perspective informed by queer theory through the example of *Brokeback Mountain.*

In a similar line of questioning of *American Renaissance*, Jay Grossman notes that "the word 'Calamus' does not appear anywhere," which causes him to ask, "How shall we think through this absent word, which marks the absence in *American Renaissance* of any sustained discussion of Whitman's most overtly homoerotic lyrics, especially when considered in light of another 'fact' we 'know' about Matthiessen, that he was himself 'homosexual' and shared more than twenty years of his life with another man, the painter Russell Cheney?"[23] I admit that it is possible to be frustrated by "this absent word," but I lament the assumption that since Matthiessen was homosexual, somehow that would influence and affect every word written by him. Nevertheless, like Grossman and Cheyfitz, I cannot help but admit the homophobic implications involved in this absence.

Critiquing Matthiessen, however, for an apparent internalized homophobia seems to be of interest for any number of reasons, but these reasons, I believe, are ultimately unsatisfying. Such perspectives might well leave a reader with a "distaste for loosely defined" psycho-imposed biographical criticism.[24] It must be admitted that his homophobia, as it were, would certainly be more accepted than his homosexuality. As Arthur Redding has noted, this is likely more than just homophobia, and by the time of his death Matthiessen was "in the midst of repeated subpoenaed appearances before the House Un-American Activities Committee,"[25] a sentiment echoed by Kenneth Boulding: "I date the beginning of the Cold War, the real beginning for people like myself[,] from the moment Matthiessen's body hit the sidewalk outside Boston Garden."[26]

It is worth recalling here that Newton Arvin's *Whitman* (1938) called attention to Whitman's homosexuality, as noted both by the critic and by other critics. Arvin was charged, by 1960, with being a "lewd person," and "within a month [of being charged] Arvin had been forcibly 'retired' from Smith and committed to a state mental hospital."[27] Although the events are not inherently connected, the analysis of homoerotic content surely could not have helped his cause, even though he won the National Book Award in 1951 for his biography of Herman Melville. Nevertheless, it is worth noting how Arvin positions Whitman. "Homosexuality is only one of the eccentricities or pathologies that may give a particular bias to a writer's work," Arvin explains, along with "the sense of impotence, the feeling of inferiority, an abnormal horror of psychology, the delusion of persecution."[28] Arvin's position does not embrace a gay identity politic, and "what really interests us in Whitman is *not that he was a homosexual*, but that, unlike the vast majority of inverts, even of those creatively gifted, he chose to translate and sublimate his strange, anomalous emotional experience into a political, a constructive, a democratic program."[29] My intention here is nothing more than a desire to highlight the fact that various critics were cautiously treating Whitman's homoeroticism and homosexuality and that two of them were ultimately victims of homophobia.[30]

However, as with Matthiessen, I am equally interested in the reparative potential of these early writings. Arvin, for instance, seems to me to highlight a problem that Eve Kosofsky Sedgwick elaborates in her *Epistemology of the Closet*. Arvin writes that

> The line that can be drawn between the normal and the abnormal, though a real one, is at best an uncertain and somewhat arbitrary line, drawn rather for practical convenience than for the sake of absolute distinctions, and it is one of the profoundest lessons of modern mental science that the extremist abnormalities are only exaggerations, distortions, unhealthy over-growth of the most normal traits and tendencies.[31]

I cannot help but think of the ways in which Sedgwick destablizes binaristic thought in the opening sections of *Epistemology of the Closet* and more particularly her remarkably obvious yet nevertheless surprising first axiom: "People are different from each other."[32] But even in all of the psychologizing that unfolds, Arvin declares that "Whitman was no mere invert, no mere 'case': he remained to the end, in almost every real and visible sense, a sweet and sane human being."[33] This, it must be admitted, is a departure from *American*

Renaissance, but it seems to be essential to recognize the complexity of homophobia and homosexuality in these early histories.

Returning to Matthiessen, another approach is to ask, as Travis M. Foster does, "What are the traces, consequences, and effects of Matthiessen's homosexuality on and for his scholarship? How might those effects in turn have wound their way into a genealogy of modern literary criticism and American studies?"[34] I want to be cautious here because I do not want to appear to be endorsing a branch of biographical criticism; instead of endowing Matthiessen's sexuality with too much power, I propose that we focus on his so-called homophobia, readily available to us in the text, just as we will when we deal with Fiedler's homophobia. Through the text, we can explore these issues and how they might inform our contemporary readings of these authors and their works as well as how they might inform contemporary readings of the authors whom they study and the authors whom we might study, who fall beyond Matthiessen's or Fiedler's scope.

Truthfully, it seems that some critics have gone out of their way to blame Matthiessen for what is tantamount to a failure of activism: that is, because he was a homosexual, he should have done more. Redding notes that "By nearly every critic who considers him, Matthiessen is judged a failure, sometimes noble, sometimes tragic, but a failure nonetheless, on a personal, political, sexual, and aesthetic level."[35] One might well be reminded of Quentin Crisp's quip, "If at first you don't succeed, failure may be your style,"[36] or indeed Judith Halberstam's project of "the queer art of failure."[37] Like Redding, however, I am troubled by this perception and thus return to Matthiessen—perhaps I am on the wrong side of literary history. But it seems to me that there is much left to be said about Matthiessen and Arvin, particularly with regard to reclaiming their role in the development of American literary studies and criticism and how they might still be influential today.

Although I believe it imperative that we are aware of this historical narrative, I want to introduce the third theorist, Leslie Fiedler, whom I intend to position alongside Matthiessen and Arvin in a reading of *Brokeback Mountain*. Fiedler, like his counterparts, calls to attention the question of sexuality and eroticism in American literary culture, even though today we might lament and bemoan the various homophobias found in these writings. To be clear, though these critics might be homophobic, their homophobias function differently: Matthiessen's, for instance, is fundamentally internalized, whereas Fiedler's is externalized. One might go so far as to suggest that Fiedler is flamboyantly heterosexual since he insists on announcing it: "In one sense, [*Love and Death in the American Novel*] has been essentially present from the moment I read aloud to my two sons (then five and seven) for their first time *Huckleberry Finn*, and saw all at once what it has taken me so long to get down."[38] Although I am not suggesting that children confirm heterosexuality, I am suggesting that they are often the hallmark signifier of one's heterosexual activity. An anonymous reviewer for *Daedalus* goes a bit further, noting that in this moment "the case [has] been made for Fiedler's own mature heterosexual genitality,"[39] even though, of course, as we shall see, *Huckleberry Finn* is one of the many texts that corroborate his thesis about "innocent homosexuality," which many now see as a homophobic thesis.

The idea of innocent homosexuality appears initially in Fiedler's 1948 essay "Come Back to the Raft Ag'in, Huck Honey!" (published in *Partisan Review*) and is developed later in *Love and Death in the American Novel*. In his essay, while considering *Moby-Dick* and *Huckleberry Finn*, Fiedler suggests that "Of the infantile, homoerotic aspects of these stories we are, though vaguely, aware."[40] I admit from the outset that the idea of homosexuality as immature and heterosexuality as mature is problematic. This I cannot and will not dispute. But I want to return to Fiedler's thesis precisely because the analyses are so indebted to a theory of homosexuality in a time well before the rise of gay and lesbian studies and queer theory. If this chapter does anything for Fiedler, it is reparative, creating "new spaces that affirm queer political possibilities" and that "might have something to do with a dominant grammar of the time that is in need of urgent critique."[41] Although I am not compelled by the need for an "urgent critique," I am convinced that there is a queer possibility in Fiedler (just as there is in Arvin and Matthiessen).

Fiedler suggests that "There could be no apter image to preside over the birth of our literature: the evocation of delicate homosexuality, fleeing from gross female assault and haunted by the incest taboo."[42] We can admit from the outset that the discourse is problematic, but let us work through the possibilities contained in *Love and Death in the American Novel*. Fiedler argues that it is "maturity above all that the American writer fears, and marriage seems its essential sign."[43] The marriage plot, of course, is central in fiction, but for Fiedler marriage means the end of one's immaturity, one's boyhood. I am utterly enthralled with how prescient his theory is in relation to the development of queer theory. He explains that "marriage also means an acceptance of the status of father."[44] Although I imagine that Lee Edelman might shiver at my positioning him alongside Fiedler, is this not precisely what Edelman cautions when he speaks of "reproductive futurism" "blindly committed to the figure of the Child"?[45]

Tangentially, it is worth noting that queer theorists have also engaged in critiques of marriage. One thinks here of the work of Jack Halberstam, Lisa Duggan, and Michael Warner, to name but a few. But we also find the same questioning in the work of Matthiessen, who also seemed to be bemused by marriage. Consider the following from a letter between Matthiessen and his partner, Cheney: "Marriage! What a strange word to be applied to two men! Can't you hear the hell-hounds of society baying full pursuit behind us? But that's just the point. We are beyond society. We've said thank you very much, and stepped outside and closed the door."[46] I refer to this because it seems that Matthiessen is very much ahead of his time; not only does he confirm Fiedler's thesis, but also his ideas could almost be part of the contemporary debates surrounding gay marriage.

Let us return to Fiedler's innocent homosexuality and to the problems involved in this discourse. Fiedler suggests that the American does not "see himself as the swaggering son of the continental imagination, the adulterer who is every cuckolded husband [and] humiliates his father and revenges his mother." Instead, he argues that, "To our writers, for whom courtly love is something learned about in school, extra-marital passion seems not only an offense against the mother, but also, like marriage itself, a disclaimer of childhood: a way of smuggling adult responsibility and guilt in through the back door."[47] I cannot help but smile at his invocation of "the back door" while arguing for a notion of "delicate homosexuality" (a point to which we shall return). What is important, however, for the time being, is the juxtaposition of boyhood and marriage, necessarily a responsibility to procreate. To marry is to renounce one's boyishness. And not to marry but to engage in adulterous behaviour is equally problematic. It is a kind of theft, a cheat, a pursuit of mischief. I cannot help but wonder about Fiedler's thesis and our culture's effeminophobia, "our culture's pervasive fear of effeminate boys,"[48] those who refuse to grow up.

Fiedler's argument relies on a general anxiety about heterosexuality. Moreover, Fiedler renounces the possibility that a marriage plot could ever lead to happiness. He notes that "There is finally no heterosexual solution which the American psyche finds completely satisfactory," and he therefore asks, "Is there not, our writers ask over and over again, a sentimental relationship at once erotic and immaculate, a union which commits its participants neither to society nor sin—and yet one which is able to symbolize the union of ego and id, the thinking self with its rejected impulses?"[49] The answer, of course, is to be found in the boyish charms of American fiction, or what we will come to know as innocent homosexuality, "today's fishing trip with the boys, tomorrow's escape to the ball park or the poker game."[50] In his earlier essay on *Huckleberry Finn*, the same imagery is used: "The existence of overt homosexuality threatens to compromise an essential aspect of American sentimental life: the camaraderie of the locker room and the ball park, the good fellowship of the poker game and fishing trip, a kind of passionless passion, at once gross and delicate, homoerotic in the boy's sense, possessing an innocence above suspicion."[51] The queerness of this is not found in the environment itself, for instance the locker room; rather, contained within this space is the possibility that the homoerotic could be "overt." Homosexuality haunts "the camaraderie of the locker room." Sedgwick, of course, later refines these ideas in her magisterial *Between Men: English Literature and Male Homosocial Desire*, wherein she locates and considers the tension and affinity between homosociality and homosexuality.[52] Curiously, *Love and Death in the American Novel* is remarkably absent from her study. We should not be surprised, however, that both Sedgwick and Fiedler find Henry James a rather provocative and exciting author for their individual theses. Fiedler writes that "James is basically, hopelessly innocent, an innocent voyeur, which is to say, a child!"[53] For Fiedler, James, called a "minor writer" by Richard Chase,[54] a reviewer of Fiedler's book, is fully committed to innocent homosexuality. Sedgwick goes further than Fiedler, but both remain indebted to a theory of homosexuality when considering James, comfortably situated today in the canon of American literature.

When readers begin to think about innocent homosexuality, they quickly encounter any number of examples from American literature. *Moby-Dick* immediately comes to mind "Upon waking the next morning about daylight," Ishmael explains, "I found Queequeg's arms thrown around me in the most loving and affectionate manner. You had almost thought I had been his wife."[55] Another novel that comes to mind, to which I will devote some attention, is *Huckleberry Finn*. Both, we might say, are among the greatest American novels, situated at the centre of any canon of American literature. Critics might argue over which of the two is genuinely the greatest novel of American literature. Nevertheless, they are defining novels of the American tradition. It is with *Huckleberry Finn* that Fiedler can begin to hypothesize in his 1948 article, and the novel becomes fully known to him, as noted above, when he reads it aloud to his sons (one wonders about their innocent homosexuality and his relation to it). Fiedler argues that "there is an archetype, a model story, appearing and reappearing in a score of guises, haunting almost all of our major writers of fiction."[56] That archetype is found in *Moby-Dick*, in which the hero finds marriage "intolerable," and "only through a pure wedding of male to male could he project an engagement with life which did not betray the self,"[57] which, of course, is an incredibly narcissistic project.

Fiedler almost seems to be surprised by his thesis: "What is hard to understand at first is why middle-class readers were not appalled at the implications of the homoerotic fable, opposed as it is to almost everything in which middle-class society pretends to believe."[58] Yet these homoerotic tones were not entirely unnoticed. Rufus Wilmot Griswold speaks of "that horrible sin not to be mentioned among

Christians" in his review of Whitman's 1855 *Leaves of Grass*,[59] which often eroticizes the male body. To take but one example, "I see a beautiful gigantic swimmer swimming naked through the eddies of the sea, / His brown hair lies close and even to his head.... [H]e strikes out with courageous arms.... [H]e urges himself with his legs."[60] One can only imagine the confusion of innocent homosexuality at play here, a confusion, I believe, that continues today. One is equally tempted to ask if it is all that surprising that, by the 1990s, we began to see a contained interest in queer sexuality with the introduction of queer television, consumed largely by heterosexual audiences that embrace an idea of innocent homosexuality, that is, a neutered or asexual homosexuality. How much of innocent homosexuality has really changed?

Nevertheless, though his thesis has plenty of queer potential, by the time of the revised edition Fiedler thinks it necessary to add the following footnote:

> "Homoerotic" is a word of which I was never very fond, and which I like even less now. But I wanted it to be quite clear that I was not attributing sodomy to certain literary characters or their authors, and so I avoided when I could the more disturbing word "homosexual." All my care has done little good, however, since what I have to say on this score has been at once the best remembered and most grossly misunderstood section of my book.[61]

I am reluctant to suggest that Fiedler protests too much here, because I do not think that he advances a homophobic politic the way that other critics have when considering Whitman, Melville, and Twain. To provide but one example, K. C. Glover writes that

> Starting at the dawn of the sixties the most pressing topic relating to his life became Melville's sexuality. The most notable contribution to this line of scholarship came from Leslie Fiedler with his *Love and Death in the American Novel*. His psychoanalytic look into Melville's work looked to find overt, covert, and latent homosexuality throughout. In our

time the emphasis is still on Melville's sexuality, most notably his supposed homosexuality. Any questioning of this has led some to say, like Rictor Norton, that any attempt to dissuade others of Melville's homosexuality is homophobia and that Melville himself was "confused" and "closeted."[62]

Indeed, Glover proves *why* Fiedler felt the need for the footnote; so many readers of Fiedler have simply misread or misunderstood *Love and Death in the American Novel*. To correct Glover, at no point does Fiedler suggest that Melville was homosexual; instead, he highlights the importance of innocent homosexuality in *Moby-Dick*. The author and the work are two separate entities, a point noted by Arvin (who also spoke of a certain queerness in Melville's work in his biography *Herman Melville*[63]). Nevertheless, I think that it is important to spend some time thinking about this footnote beyond its apparent need, a need that continues, as evidenced by Glover's misguided reading of both Melville and Fiedler.

In today's theoretical jargon, the two sons to whom Fiedler read might been seen as proto-queer kids. But the larger point is that this footnote contributes to many readings that have understood his work as *homophobic*. He clearly worries that readers might think that "characters or their authors" might be homosexual, but then what does it say about the author, who writes about the characters, or authors who, some readers believe, might now be homosexual? In other words, his homophobia is a worry about a reader thinking "takes one to know one." I cannot help but wonder if this is what motivated a comment made by Fiedler in 1982: "What the larger audience believes, however, is that Fiedler (whoever the hell he is!) once claimed that Mark Twain's Huck and Jim (whom everyone know[s] from movies and television) were a pair of faggots buggering each other as they drifted down the Mississippi."[64] I am taken aback by his comment, I am even more surprised that it made it into print, yet I cannot help but note that this is precisely the way in which Glover understands Fiedler's thesis.

More to the point, however, is that we must insist that for Fiedler the homoerotic is essential to the development of the American novel. He notes, over and over again, that "in all classic American books we have been examining, there are hints of such a love."[65] The American novel, or at least the classic American novel, is endowed with a homoeroticism in some cases "buried deep beneath the ken of the authors themselves, in others moving just beneath the transparent surface."[66] Fiedler himself seems to be terribly enamoured with and horrified by his own thesis—it is a shocking revelation. He insists that he does not mean sodomy, yet he just as quickly acknowledges that

> In our native mythology, the tie between male and male is not only considered innocent, it is taken for the very symbol of innocence itself; for it is imagined as the only institutional bond in a paradisal world in which there are no (heterosexual) marriages or giving in marriage. Paradisal, however, means for hard-headed Americans not quite real; and there is, in fact, a certain sense of make-believe in almost all portrayals of holy marriage of males, set as they typically are in the past, the wilderness, or at sea—that is to say, in worlds familiar to most readers in dreams.[67]

What is essential for Fiedler—and this is the point that we must recognize because it demonstrates why *Brokeback Mountain* was so provocative—is that homosexuality is always innocent, also paradisal in the novels studied in *Love and Death in the American Novel*. This is important because our access to Eden is dependent on a prelapsarian, which is to say innocent or naive, consciousness. His argument about innocence is not therefore, I would contend, exclusively about guilty versus innocent in a juridical sense, but about a more Blakean innocence, one that has yet to be corrupted. As Fiedler explains in an interview, "innocence is a state, but you only know it when you're expelled from it. Adam didn't know he was in the Garden until he was outside the Garden."[68] Indeed, part of this, the part that is most liberating, is the idea that there was a time before we knew about sexuality and its sinfulness. This, I think, is what Fiedler is arguing for.

Innocent homosexuality, therefore, in our reparative reading, is not about overcoming homosexuality or about a maturation out of homosexuality, but about a time when one is not concerned with, bothered by, or fearful of homosexual sexuality and eroticism. One is reminded of Proust's "search for lost time." Indeed, this homoerotic tension runs through much of Sedgwick's work on homosocial desire: the problem, the fear, is that it could always become *homosexual* desire. The fear that something might become gay is more terrifying than the actual homosexuality. Fiedler is interested in "a world of male companions and sport, an anti-civilization, simple and joyous, whose presiding genius is that scarcely articulate arch-buddy, 'good, old Bill.'"[69] Thus, unlike a critic such as Christopher Looby,[70] I am not certain that the "innocent" of "innocent homosexuality" affirms the need for and existence of a "guilty homosexuality" (wherein innocence and guilt form a binary in a legal or judicial sense), but instead innocence is positioned as a naïveté, ignorance, unawareness.

Innocent homosexuality, then, as Marjorie Garber writes of Matthiessen's readings of Hawthorne and Melville, is a kind of "aesthetics of the hint, the indirect insinuation or covert admission, [which] was the only way Melville or Hawthorne could approach the articulation of a difficult truth."[71] The "hint" does not confirm homosexuality; instead, it flirts with a possibility thereof. It is telling, of course, that innocent homosexuality, so often about the "aesthetics of the hint," is so committed to a "paranoid reading," wherein we become "frantic epistemologists, second only to paranoiacs (and analysts) as readers of signs and wonders."[72] In our contemporary parlance, we might see innocent homosexuality as a proto-bromance: that is, it absolutely flirts with and hints at an erotic potential, but that eroticism must remain covert.

The bromance, John Alberti explains, is often found in "romance comedies centred on confused homosocial/homoerotic relationships between putatively straight male characters."[73] The bromance, like innocent homosexuality, is divorced from maturity, though, unlike innocent homosexuality, the bromance as a genre might ultimately be about the process of maturation. For instance, in these romantic comedies, the male "claims of sexual mastery are subjected to endless ridicule," and "male sexuality is the real mysterious Other for these characters, a source of inexplicable desire and humiliation and an aspect of identity that renders them almost useless as functioning members of society."[74] In a certain regard, it is hardly surprising that Alberti should focus, in part, on *The 40-Year-Old Virgin*, a romantic comedy that is perhaps the apex of sexual immaturity and often enough "read" as an indication of the hero's apparent homosexuality (in a simplistic logic that failure to perform heterosexually is indicative of homosexuality). A central quality of the bromance, Elizabeth Chen notes, is that it is "non-sexual"[75] even though it is fundamentally caught up in an erotic game of tug-of-war. More particularly, Chen argues that "Only heterosexuals can have a bromance." However, part of this is "the phenomenon of 'straight panic,' in which individuals experience anxiety about how others perceive their sexuality, and thus feel the need to reassert their heterosexuality."[76] This definition, particularly the invocation of "straight panic," seems to have much in common with Fiedler's anxiety about his use of the homoerotic.

All of this is to suggest that perhaps Fiedler's thesis of innocent homosexuality, though disputed and perhaps even discredited, carries weight in our times of bromance. Is the bromance just a renaming of innocent homosexuality insofar as it is fundamentally a site in which eroticism is teased, hinted at, and flirted with but in which a threshold must never be crossed? Indeed, I argue that this is precisely why *Brokeback Mountain* created such a storm. In what follows, I argue that the "problem" with *Brokeback Mountain* is that it reveals a few too many ghosts haunting the American imaginary and that, unlike earlier texts that flirted with the threshold of innocent homosexuality, Proulx and Lee force us to confront a homosexuality that is always already present in these novels. That is, the innocence that we demand and recognize is a willful innocence that we have imposed on these novels. Moreover, this is precisely why so many critics have questioned the sexual orientation of the heroes of *Brokeback Mountain*. Indeed, the problem is not orientation at all but the ways in which innocent homosexuality, homophobia, and compulsory heterosexuality align with one another in American literary culture.

Brokeback Mountain is not the first novel in American literary history to explore openly male homosexuality. Indeed, it is not surprising that Fiedler's book appeared shortly after Gore Vidal's seminal *The City and the Pillar* (1948), which opens with a nearly archetypal presentation of innocent homosexuality:

> Naked, Jim joined Bob at the water's edge. The warm breeze on his bare skin made him feel suddenly free and curiously powerful, like a dreamer who is aware that he is dreaming.
>
> Bob looked at him thoughtfully, "You got a good tan. I sure look white. Hey!" He pointed at the water. Below the dark green surface, Jim could see the blunt slow-moving shape of a catfish. Then, suddenly, he was falling and there was a rush of water in his ears. Bob had pushed him in. Choking he came to the surface. With a rapid movement, Jim grabbed Bob's leg and pulled him in. Grappling, they turned and twisted in the water, making the pond foam. As they wrestled, Jim took pleasure in the physical contact. So, apparently, did Bob. Not until both were exhausted did they stop.[77]

Vidal's scene hints at Twain's equally innocent scenes in *Adventures of Huckleberry Finn*, wherein Jim and Huck swim together, like Bob and Jim (who, like Jim in Twain's novel, happens to be the darker of the two), or chat about the daily events and stories of their lives in the pleasure of raw nakedness. There is a great deal of innocence in these moments: "[W]e slid into the river and had a swim," or,

> Soon as it was night, out we shoved; when we got her out to about the middle, we let her alone, and let her float wherever the current wanted her to; then we lit the pipes, and dangled our legs in the water and talked about all kinds of things—we was always naked, day and night, whenever the mosquitoes would let us—the new clothes Buck's folks made for me was too good to be comfortable, and besides I didn't go much on clothes, nohow.[78]

We have here two competing examples in which we can locate without too much difficulty the tension of innocent homosexuality. There is no sexual action unfolding, yet we cannot help but notice a hint of eroticism in both scenes. Incidentally, nakedness also appears in Twain's *The Adventures of Tom Sawyer*, and once more we see innocent homosexuality:

> After breakfast they went whooping and prancing out on the bar, and chased each other round and round, shedding clothes as they went, until they were naked, and then continued the frolic far away up the shoal water of the bar, against the stiff current, which latter tripped their legs from under them from time to time and greatly increased the fun. And now and then they stooped in a group and splashed water in each other's faces with their palms, gradually approaching each other, with averted faces to avoid the strangling sprays, and finally gripping and struggling till the best man ducked his neighbor, and then they all went under in a tangle of white legs and arms and came up blowing, sputtering, laughing, and gasping for breath at one and the same time.
>
> When they were well exhausted, they would run out and sprawl on the dry, hot sand, and lie there and cover themselves up with it, and by and by break for the water again and go through the original performance once more. Finally it occurred to them that their naked skin represented flesh-colored "tights" very fairly; so they drew a ring in the sand and had a circus—with three clowns in it, for none would yield this proudest post to his neighbor.[79]

Vidal's scene might have much in common with both of these scenes, not only because of the nudity, but also because of the imagery.[80] In Vidal's novel, we are also presented with playful nudity and rest: "Not until both were exhausted did they stop. For the rest of the day they swam, caught frogs, sunned themselves, wrestled."[81] I highlight these three texts here precisely because they all exhibit—in varying degrees—what Fiedler understands as innocent homosexuality. These episodes can be found throughout American literature, particularly during the nineteenth century, and I believe that it is imperative that we recognize this history as we consider *Brokeback Mountain*.

I do not believe that it is a stretch of the imagination to position *Brokeback Mountain* as a central text, nearly canonical at this point, in twentieth-century American literature. Unlike earlier critics of the novel and the film (it seems that the bulk of scholarship is on the film), I am interested in positioning *Brokeback Mountain* in relation to Fiedler and Matthiessen, to whom, I believe, we owe a certain debt, particularly those of us who work in gender studies and American literature. One might be so bold as to suggest that Fiedler and Matthiessen are proto-queer theorists, writing queer theory long before it would become a critical methodology for literary analysis.

In orienting *Brokeback Mountain*, I want to begin with the problem of genre before moving to sexuality, for it seems to me that there are fundamental questions about the genre of *Brokeback Mountain*. It is fairly straightforward, a short story, but the debate is more particular: what kind of short story is it? Ian Scott Todd, for instance, speaks of the film version as holding an "ambiguous position in relation to the Western genre."[82] Leigh Boucher and Sarah Pinto call the film "Ang Lee's big gay tragic historical love story."[83] As noted above, some have framed the tale as a kind of fairy tale, a subject that Fiedler was considering at the end of his scholarly career, and as a tragedy, which, we might suggest, is really at the heart of his project. My point here in highlighting the question of genre is straightforward; nearly every instance of generic trouble finds its discussion in Fiedler's work. After all, what could be a more problematic question for a genre to contain than "the failure of American culture to accept mature heterosexual love as the matrix of life, value, sensibility, and imagination"?[84] The real success of *Brokeback Mountain* is quite simply that it cannot be pigeonholed; in this way, like *Moby-Dick* and *Huckleberry Finn*, it defies the limits of genre.

I want to begin by admitting that I am somewhat stunned by the near absence of Fiedler in criticism on *Brokeback Mountain*. But, of course, like so many before him, he has fallen out of favour among the literary establishment because of his apparent homophobia, documented above. Nevertheless, I remain committed to a reparative reading of *Love and Death in the American Novel* that finds, I believe, its apotheosis in my reading of *Brokeback Mountain*. As far as I can tell, Mark John Isola is one of the few critics to ask, "What [is] this tradition [Fiedler's thesis] doing in Proulx's writing?"[85] Yet that question remains suggestively unanswered; Isola focuses instead on "fluid textuality" and the many instances in which fluids are mentioned throughout the narrative. Unlike Isola, I am not terribly surprised that Fiedler's thesis should work its way into Proulx's story: if anything, her story is an argument for historical continuity.

There can be no doubt that the film and the short story are remarkably different. The story itself is relatively short, whereas the film is and feels long at just over two hours. Adaptation, of course, is not a perfect science, and we would be misguided if we insisted on textual fidelity in our adaptations. In this regard, I follow Linda Hutcheon's theory of adaptation. Hutcheon argues that "An adaptation's double nature does not mean, however, that proximity or fidelity to the adapted text should be the criterion of judgment or focus of analysis." She also cautions that "the morally loaded discourse of fidelity is based on the implied assumption that adapters aim simply to reproduce the adapted text," and we should see adaptation as "repetition without replication."[86] I am convinced by Hutcheon's argument and thus, though I recognize that the two texts are autonomous and different, I am not interested in entering into a debate about which is better or if Lee was faithful to Proulx's text. Moreover, such an exercise would contribute little to this chapter.

Matthew Bolton, in his article "The Ethics of Alterity: Adapting Queerness in *Brokeback Mountain*," highlights the problem of adaptation and fidelity: "Unlike Proulx, instead of leading with difference, Lee's film defers it until a quarter of the way through the film, when an explicit sex scene finally confirms *Brokeback Mountain*'s queerness for its audience."[87] His observation is to the point, but the film viewer, even before viewing the film, has already been told that it is a queer film. The central difference is the placement of the queer orientation of the narrative:

> [T]he implied audience of *Brokeback Mountain* spends half
> an hour with Ennis and Jack before they are made aware,
> along with the characters, of the true nature of their rela-

tionship. Although the narrative progression is roughly the same, this is a substantially different temporal investment even from the *New Yorker* version [of Proulx's story]; readers of this "Brokeback Mountain" arrive at Jack and Ennis' first sex scene at the bottom of the story's second page—hardly the thirty minutes cinematic audiences will spend with these characters before uncovering their sexuality.[88]

Lee's film perhaps allows for a development of our queer and paranoid curiosity, which, it seems, is unavailable to readers of Proulx's story. But is this an issue of genre? That is, Proulx's short story is not afforded the expansive time of either the film or the novel as a formal structure. If we consider Fiedler's thesis, then so much of his argument is devoted to novels, often long novels such as *Moby-Dick*.

Lee's film facilitates Fiedler's thesis about innocent homosexuality, precisely because we have sufficient time to become curious, paranoid, or discomforted by what unfolds on the screen. As Fiedler explains, "There is an almost hysterical note to our insistence that the love of male and male does not compete with heterosexual passion but complement it."[89] The hysterical note is developed through the thirty or forty opening minutes of the film. This "hysterical note" is what Sedgwick might call a kind of "unknowing,"[90] which is to say "a problem about . . . obstinate sexual incomprehension."[91] Lee's *Brokeback Mountain*, at least its first quarter, like Fiedler's *Love and Death in the American Novel*, thrives on what Sedgwick calls the "privilege of unknowing."[92] In this space of unknowing, we become "frantic epistemologists," as Adam Phillips has suggested,[93] seeking out meaning. This unknown meaning is precisely what innocent homosexuality is about—an inability to know the contents of the relation. Although it is certainly true that Lee's adaptation allows for an incremental and delayed development of this unknowing, I would also contend that the short story—within its own convention—contains brief moments of innocent homosexuality (at least for the reader). I am not alone, as already noted, in recognizing this potential.

Although I am not prepared to advance this argument, one cannot help but note that for Fiedler the genre almost always already contains this innocent homosexuality. In this regard, even before reading the genre, I might already have a feeling about what might unfold. For Wolfgang Iser, this is called "advance retrospection," wherein, "during the process of reading, there is an active interweaving of anticipation and retrospection, which on a second reading may turn into a kind of advance retrospection."[94] That is, the reader aware of the formula, two American men together in the wilderness, can anticipate the action that will unfold. The clues and cues are already there even if he or she has yet to read the given work.[95]

If we were to read *Brokeback Mountain* not as a rereading or a second reading, but as another reading in American literature, we can perhaps anticipate the innocent homosexuality unfolding. Both the film and the short story are rich with anticipation precisely because they are part of an already established tradition of innocent homosexuality. Consider, for instance, how Ishmael and Queequeg interact throughout the opening sequence—the opening quarter—of *Moby-Dick*. I have already cited the first time the two sleep together, but consider a chapter such as "A Bosom Friend," in which Ishmael explores their intimacy. He once more highlights "the affectionate arm I had found thrown over me upon waking in the morning," but he develops this further:

> He seemed to take to me quite as naturally and unbiddenly as I to him; and when our smoke was over, he pressed his forehead against mine, clasped me around the waist, and said that henceforth we were married; meaning, in his country's phrase, that we were bosom friends; he would gladly die for me, if need should be. In a countryman, this sudden flame of friendship would have seemed far too premature, a thing to be much distrusted; but in this simple savage those old rules would not apply.[96]

This is precisely Fiedler's innocent homosexuality, marked by a "hierogamos," a marriage, "the elopement of good companions."[97] This marriage seems to be central to the opening of *Moby-Dick*: "[I] kissed his nose; and that done, we undressed and went to bed, at peace with our own consciousness and all the world. But we did not go to sleep without some little chat."[98] If we, as readers, are versed in American literature, is it not possible that we might engage in a pseudo–advance retrospection informed not by a second reading but by a reading aware of earlier texts?

Likewise, a reader familiar with *Huckleberry Finn* or *Tom Sawyer* might recognize the implicit innocent homosexuality that seems to be foreshadowed in *Brokeback Mountain*. However, perhaps that reader will assume that Proulx challenges, confronts, and ultimately disregards the possibility of innocent homosexuality. Her narrative, unlike those of Twain and Melville, who flirt with the homoerotic, is ostensibly homoerotic *and* homosexual. When I first began to think seriously about Fiedler and Proulx, I was struck by what seemed like a Bloomian gesture of misreading, unlike Glover's poor reading. Harold Bloom suggests that misreading is "a corrective movement . . . which implies the precursor poem went accurately up to a certain point, but then should have swerved, precisely in the direction the new poem moves."[99] Thus, while Fiedler speaks about innocent homosexuality, Proulx would privilege homosexuality.

If we return to the question of sexual orientation in *Brokeback Mountain*, it seems to be obvious, at first glance, not only do we confront homoerotic potential, but also this erotic tension is fundamentally crossed. That is, the homoerotic potential finds its apex, as it were, in the "very ground zero of gayness"[100]: the anus. Jack and Ennis do not flirt with erotic tension, they do not hint at it, nor do they merely tease each other (and the reader); indeed, quite the contrary is the case.

> "Jesus Christ, quit hammerin and get over here. Bedroll's big enough," said Jack in an irritable sleep-clogged voice. It was big enough, warm enough, and in a little while they deepened their intimacy considerably. Ennis ran full-throttle on all roads whether fence mending or money spending, and he wanted none of it when Jack seized his left hand and brought it to his erect cock. Ennis jerked his hand away as though he'd touched fire, got to his knees, unbuckled his belt, shoved his pants down, hauled Jack onto all fours and, with the help of the clear slick and a little spit, entered him, nothing he'd done before but no instruction manual

needed. They went at it in silence except for a few sharp intakes of breath and Jack's choked "gun's going *off*," then out, down, and asleep.[101]

The scene contains none of the regular tensions of eroticism; there is no flirting, no foreplay, no continual deferral until an eventual breaking down of erotic resistance. Like Ennis, we quickly enter into the heart of the matter. The film is perhaps less graphic in its depiction (one presumes that ratings might have informed this decision), but readers *know* what is happening. My point, however, is that in this moment we, as readers, recognize that the innocence has been lost, not because of the action involved as though we are pious and moral readers, but because a knowledge has been acquired.

It seems—and I want to stress that this is about appearance—that Fiedler's thesis has lost credibility, for surely we would not call Jack and Ennis's homosexuality innocent. After all, they have gone *too far*, they have reached, in the eloquent phrase of Mark J. Blechner, "the darkest continent."[102] By most accounts, because Jack and Ennis enter into this nether region, this "darkest continent," we now have to attend to the question of their sexual orientation. I would argue, the vast majority of interpretations of this work have focused almost exclusively on the fact that they engage in anal sex. But is this enough to "orient" Jack and Ennis as gay, by and large the governing opinion?

To problematize this further, I argue that there are times when a focus on the anus misses the point. The insistence on the anus, as the marker of orientation, fails to recognize its complexity and is a homophobic gesture that I believe needs to be unpacked. It is phobic not in terms of fearing or hating homosexuals but because it insists that there can only ever be one way that one gains access to orientation, made possible through the anus. A close reading of *Brokeback Mountain*, both the film and the novel, will demonstrate that what is really at play for Ennis is "anal desire."

After he descends Brokeback Mountain, he marries Alma Beers and has her "pregnant by mid-January,"[103] which we knew was going to happen. This was what we expected. This is, of course, in Fiedler's terms, the end of innocence. But there is something else happening. Indeed, there is another anal scene between Alma and Ennis,

> slipping his hand up her blouse sleeve and stirring the silky armpit hair, then easing her down, fingers moving up her ribs to the jelly breast, over the round belly and knee up into the wet gap all the way to the north pole or the equator depending on which way you thought you were sailing, working at it until she shuddered and bucked against his hand and *he rolled her over, did quickly what she hated.*[104]

Ennis, we can say, desires the anus—any anus. We might well read this scene as yet another affirmation of his homosexuality: that is, the anus becomes the locus through which he expresses desire. In such a rendering, we would imagine that Alma's ass becomes a conduit through which Ennis can play, once more, with Jack's ass. But we need to think carefully about what it means to ask, is Alma's ass a substitute for the *real* thing?

I am not convinced by this argument; however, the rise of being on the "down low" in queer of colour critique, particularly queer black studies, does give us reason to think about what this kind of anality might involve. Jeffrey Q. McCune Jr. explains that "men who often disidentify with traditional descriptors of sexuality (gay, bisexual, etc.) have been referred to and refer to themselves as 'men on the down low.'"[105] Moreover, as McCune argues, "the term 'down low' (DL) has come to be understood as describing a group of problematic black men who sleep with other men while having relationships with wives/girlfriends."[106] To a certain extent, we might imagine that Ennis is on the down low, even though he is not black, but this does not account for his anal desire with Alma. And there is a desire for anal sex that is not necessarily gay—there is a slippery slope at play in the kind of logic that would sustain this reading; simply put, even in the confines of heterosexuality, the man can become gay because of his anal desire. Such a reading, I imagine, relies on "the fiction of identity," "accessed with relative ease by most majoritarian subjects."[107]

Perhaps, however, another aspect of McCune's explanation that might be worth considering is the idea of disidentifying. Throughout *Reading from Behind*, I have been reluctant to imagine that somehow the ass, anal sex, and the rectum are always already gay. After all, as Sedgwick rightly asks, "what about male desire for a woman's anus—is that anal desire?"[108] This might well be the question that we ought to ask of *Brokeback Mountain* and this particular scene: what about Ennis's desire for Alma's anus—is that anal desire? We would not presume, by any stretch of the imagination, that because Ennis desires Alma's ass he is homosexual or bisexual, so why does the anus become this governing symbol? I am not negating that what Ennis and Jack do appears to be homosexual, but I am reluctant to accept the totalizing argument that appears in so much scholarship; after all, this might well be about disidentification, "a survival strategy that works within and outside [the] dominant public sphere simultaneously."[109] And it is this simultaneity, the kind of interdigitation of orientations, that interests me: his anal desire is not so much orienting as it is a desire for the anus, which might or might not be oriented. In other words, we might return to another Sedgwickian question: "[I]s the rectum straight?"[110]

The former reading, the one that would insist on homosexuality and Alma's ass as a substitute, fails to account for the complexity of the ass. I am reminded here, once more, of Guy Hocquenghem's remark that "the anus is not a substitute for the vagina."[111] I am reluctant to endorse a reading that insists on the gayness of Ennis precisely because I am not sufficiently convinced by that reading's insistence on an identifying process that might or might not be part of the subject's own sense of self. Moreover, I am reluctant not because I dispute homosexuality but because it negates the complexity of not only the anus but also sexuality writ large. More to the point, there is an intellectual dishonesty at play when we treat a work so superficially, and it renders a work far less complex than it really is.

This is why I return to the earlier critics Matthiessen, Arvin, and Fiedler. They were, we can admit, homophobic in varying ways, but their homophobia was about a range of sexualities that does not correspond to the heteronormative ideal. Fiedler's thesis is no more wrong than the critical thesis about Ennis and Jack's homosexuality.

I argue that his thesis, in spite of its homophobia, is rather liberating because it allows for a range of sexualities, whereas the scholarship on *Brokeback Mountain* generally—though not always—offers but one sexual orientation for the heroes that is absolute and essential: homosexual.

Brokeback Mountain is not, as we might assume, a corrective gesture, but it continues to affirm Fiedler's thesis about innocent homosexuality. It is innocent homosexuality precisely because it can only ever exist in a utopian space removed from society. That is, *Brokeback Mountain* is not about a "permanent removal from society . . . but an outing, a long excursion,"[112] like the fishing trips that Jack and Ennis take. What readers find in *Brokeback Mountain* is a boyish charm in which innocent homosexuality can thrive, even when we read that "'I'm not no queer,' and Jack jumped in with 'Me neither.'"[113] This moment affirms Fiedler's thesis precisely because it is about unknowing, a refusal to identify, a radically utopian gesture made available only through innocent homosexuality. Throughout the film, afforded the luxury of time and space, we see Jack and Ennis frolicking together in nature, fully ensconced in hierogamos. I think here, for instance, of the scene in which Jack and Ennis swim naked. This is a scene repeated in the history of American literature, the boyish charm of water splashing alongside the naked body, the roughhousing of Vidal's *The City and the Pillar*, or the chitchatting of the naked bodies together in *Huckleberry Finn* or *Moby-Dick*. Fiedler explains that these novels contain "a long line of heroes in flight from women and home."[114] Moreover, "the reader feels that he is being asked to recreate in fantasy a place to which neither he nor the author can ever return—the 'home' to which the American writer complains he cannot go back."[115] The point is this: it is only during "an outing, a long excursion," that any of this is possible.[116] As readers, we, like the characters whom we read about, embark on a long trip in which we too are invited to think about our own sexualities, and how oppressed we are by sexualities, wherein one perception suddenly orients us.

To read *Love and Death in the American Novel* today, well over fifty years since its publication, is to confront a text that seemingly is remarkably homophobic; however, when positioned alongside one of the most successful "gay" films in history, Fiedler's text challenges us to think more deeply and more critically about that film and its reception. What is remarkable about *Love and Death in the American Novel* is not that it elaborates a theory of innocent homosexuality, which many critics find problematic, but that it elaborates a theory resolutely not dependent on a reductive and limited and essentializing understanding of homosexuality. I would go so far as to suggest that innocent homosexuality is rather remarkably complex, a complexity sadly lost in criticism of *Brokeback Mountain*. The question that we might ask today is this: if Jack and Ennis did not have anal sex, would they still be gay, or would we, once more, see yet another example in a long line of examples of innocent homosexuality?

This is precisely the point: even though Jack and Ennis explore innocent homosexuality, and perhaps go further than readers are comfortable with (which explains why we respond so viscerally to it), they nevertheless are married to women, reproduce, raise children, and so on. The reparative potential of innocent homosexuality is perhaps found in its queerness, a queerness that we today advocate—a desire to recognize that orientation is limiting. Orientation has become a "chronic, now endemic crisis,"[117] and for this reason we should embrace queerness, "the open mesh of possibilities, gaps, overlaps, dissonances and resonances, lapses and excesses of meaning when the constituent elements of anyone's gender, anyone's sexuality aren't made (or *can't be* made) to signify monolithically."[118]

CHAPTER 5
Spanking Colonialism

It can't be helped;
It must be done.
So down with your breeches
And out with your bum.
—JAMES JOYCE, *A Portrait of the Artist as a Young Man*

I BEGIN THIS CHAPTER WITH A FRAMING DEVICE, Richard Amory's *Song of the Loon* (1966), one of the earliest successful gay pulp novels. As the back-cover copy reads, the novel tells the story of "a lusty gay frontier romance . . . of Ephraim MacIver, a nineteenth-century outdoorsman, and his travels through the American wilderness, where he meets a number of men who share with him stories, wisdom, and intimate encounters."[1] *Song of the Loon* remains a somewhat underread book. My own copy is yet to be read as deeply as I might wish because of a certain amount of discomfort that I feel as I read this book. I glossed over the discomforting narrative instead of reading it closely. The book is ostensibly queer, but its queerness is uncomfortable. Actually, I am uncomfortable with its racial politics, its colonialist and primitivist implications, and its eroticization of the Indigenous body. It is not that I doubt the veracity of an erotic Indigenous body, but that I am discomforted by how the Indigenous body is eroticized for the pleasure of the settler in the narrative and more than likely the settler-reader, to whom I want to pay some attention, along with the equally problematic settler-author.

The discomfort is perhaps prefigured by the opening words of the novel, which appear, in the reprint published by Arsenal Pulp Press, before the book has even begun. I quote this section in full:

> The author wishes it clearly understood that he has, unfortunately, never known or heard of a single Indian even remotely resembling, for instance, Singing Heron or Tlasohkah or Bear-who-dreams. He has taken certain very European characters from the novels of Jorge de Montemayor and Gaspar Gil Polo, painted them a gay aesthetic red, and transplanted them to the American wilderness. Anyone who wishes to read other intentions into these characterizations is willfully misunderstanding the nature of the pastoral genre, and is fervently urged not to do so. The same might be said of those who love to point out anachronisms and factual improbabilities.[2]

Having read this book a few years ago, set it aside, and now returned to it, I can see why it has discomforted me as a reader—and perhaps even why I have been reluctant to attend to what are arguably the most pressing issues in Canadian cultural studies. Looking back at this paragraph, I can see now why I have been so troubled. For one thing, the book starts out by telling me that it is not for me (after all, I probably am guilty of reading "other intentions" into it). As a reader, I think "That might well be what you think your book is doing, but let me show you what your text is actually doing." To speak of an author's intentions is about as accepted an intellectual enterprise as to speak about his biography to explain those intentions. There is, to wit, something of a "whiteman-splaining" unfolding here.[3] Amory tells his readers what he is doing before they have even read a single word of *Song of the Loon*. He is a paranoid author. He knows that readers might protest his treatment of the Indigenous body, but he explains that this is because of "the nature

of the pastoral genre," which the reader "willfully misunderstand[s]"
if he or she chooses to focus on "a gay aesthetic" painted *red*. But
is there another way to read this book? It eroticizes the Indigenous
body explicitly for the pleasure and titillation of the settler-reader.
The author is interested in *whitewashing* a historical narrative that
might or might not have truth in history (it *could* have happened,
I suppose) so as to enable a kind of erotic fiction that negates—or
at least explains itself as doing so—the racial politics of this novel.

Amory, however, is not alone in this kind of whitewashing;
literary critics, especially those writing in the popular press, do the
same. They wilfully attempt to erase the problematic nature of this
text, yet that nature can be very productive for us—as readers—to
think about, especially when negotiating the nature of eroticism in
colonized spaces. In his "Reflections on *Song of the Loon* at Forty,"
Ian Mozdzen comments thus: "Sensuous noble savages that you
encounter often offer revelry, wisdom, peace, even medicine-visions,"
and *Song of the Loon* is a "charming, delightfully queer pastoral."[4]
Maybe I am alone, but I am struck by how "pastoral" has become
a code that (wilfully) obfuscates the complexity of settler and Indigenous relations. It is as if we are supposed to believe that, since
the novel is pastoral, somehow it is excused of its racist implications. Mozdzen is not alone in privileging the pastoral genre; Ken
Furtado explains that "The story itself is a pastoral, consciously
patterned after a popular 16th century Spanish novel."[5] Not to
be snide, but were the Spanish not involved in one of the largest
colonial projects in human history during the sixteenth century?
And what are the implications of ignoring the colonialist project
in favour of the pleasures of the reader (whoever he or she might
be)? Accordingly, then, how can we separate the historical realities
of that moment from its literary production? That is, how do we
separate the narrated history from the authorial history and vice
versa? What does it mean to imagine historical fiction as existing between histories, that of the author and that of the literary
creation? I am postmodern enough to think that the "political
unconscious" is not just a product of postmodernism and so-called
late capitalism. All texts reflect the social and political unconscious
of their given time.

All of this says nothing, however, of the fact that, in reflecting on *Song of the Loon*, Mozdzen encourages his reader to "Don your loincloth and explore, push outward! 'Your penis lengthens—let it swing!'"[6] How can we not recognize—even in all of its pastoral glory—the colonialist implications of this novel and its reception? How do we negate the fact that Mozdzen emphasizes and privileges, as is so often the case, the phallus "push[ing] outward"? Toward what is this lengthened penis pushing and swinging? Even though *Song of the Loon* might be cluttered with "ugly feelings,"[7] the bulk of which are caused by the ugliness of the subject matter, the purple prose wishes to whitewash the redness of its colonial project.

Although *Song of the Loon* is not the kind of text that my colleague wanted me to consider, I could not get this example out of my mind. But there had to be another example to consider, another textual world less implicated in a project of simply reducing bodies to erotic objects for the pleasure of settler-colonialism. Accordingly, I do wish to pair it alongside and in fundamental tension with a series of landscape paintings by Toronto-based Cree artist Kent Monkman, "one of Canada's most celebrated contemporary multidisciplinary artists."[8] Margot Francis describes these images as exploring "the relationship between Eros and the conquest of Indigenous peoples, this time through the cheeky appropriation of the genre of landscape painting," and the particular "paintings explore homoerotic connections between Indians and cowboys in risky vignettes that reverse the dynamic thrust of traditional narratives."[9] Daniel Heath Justice, Bethany Schneider, and Mark Rifkin, in their description of Monkman's *Heaven and Earth*, echo Francis; they describe it as "revers[ing the] perceived power dynamic, repositioning the familiar status of Native bodies (often those of women) as submissive victims of the colonial erotic to assertive and enthusiastic agents of unashamed sexual subjectivity while also intimating the penetrability of white male bodies."[10] The perception that power can be inverted or reversed is important to the interpretation of Monkman's work, yet I wonder if there is not something else happening in these images. In reversing the power dynamics, we are called to pay attention to the dynamics of sexuality, the complications of race, and the critiques of power, particularly when it is erotically charged.

Monkman's paintings, in a sense, are "difficult" images, not because they require one to strain to understand the concept, but because they provoke affective and intellectual responses that work to destabilize and critique how we think about normativity, eroticism, and power, especially when figured in hegemonic and hierarchical terms. The paintings often seem to "flip" the narratives to which we have grown accustomed. Moreover, they challenge the scholar versed in critical theory to think deeply about the content as much as the form. These paintings trigger responses. Consider here, for instance, Monkman's *Cree Master 1* (2002; see Image 5.1).

We are presented with an idyllic image of the Canadian west. We see a rather standard image, one that echoes typical thematics in Canadian art. Although, as Northrop Frye might say, "What you will not see is a typically Canadian landscape: no such place exists,"[11] the image is distinctly Canadian. Hints of the Group of Seven are present. As we absorb this image, suddenly our eyes are drawn to

5.1 *Cree Master 1 (2002)*

the bottom right-hand corner, where an erotic image appears. An Indigenous man is spanking a Mountie. The Mountie is over the lap of the Indigenous man, his ass slapped pink. The Mountie gazes into the calm waters, which surely reflect his face to him as he is spanked repeatedly.

How are we to interpret *Cree Master 1*? Like critics of *Song of the Loon*, we could simply call this work pastoral and absolve it of its provocations, but this is not likely what Monkman wishes us to do, nor do I think that we should absolve the pastoral of its colonial implications. Although we might well appreciate the pastoral elements of work, we must still continue to recognize how these aesthetics are nonetheless political. To argue that these elements are *just pastoral* is to shut down dialogue, affect, and engagement with the work.

In an interview, Monkman explains that "when I make these paintings I'm not necessarily repeating history, but I'm nudging people toward seeing that there are these big missing narratives," and more authoritatively he declares that "I think a lot of people fled society for the frontier not just to have sex, or same-sex relationships, but to escape oppressive societal norms."[12] Monkman challenges viewers to think carefully and critically not only about his paintings but also about some of the larger historical narratives that form the consciousness of the nation. For Shirley J. Madill, Monkman engages in "intelligent mischief," which "takes on significant political and social importance in light of today's discourse on the subject of the colonization of Aboriginal sexuality and the homophobia that originated from Christian European imperialism."[13] But Monkman's "intelligent mischief" works both ways.

The image, in a sense, highlights so many fantasies of the Canadian west. Margaret Atwood writes that "The West, or the wilderness, is in Canadian fiction much more likely to come through as a place of exile," unlike the American vision of the west as "something to be conquered and claimed." But Atwood continues and observes that

> there are the settlers, come from the old country with their European artefacts, building their walls within which they hope to recreate that old country; they don't have to *really*

fight because the Mounties are there, the rules of the game are set up already, the flag is flying. No outlaws or lawless men for Canada; if one appears, the Mounties always get their man.[14]

Likewise, Jennifer Reid suggests, "the myth narrative associated with the force traditionally involved the image of Mounties pacifying savage Indians in order to render the West secure for Canadian colonization."[15] The Mounties, in essence, have "become a national symbol."[16] Nevertheless, as with so many symbols, there is another possible reading, perhaps many possible readings.

In Monkman's painting, of course, we are confronted by the figure of the outlaw, of whom Atwood speaks, and the rule-enforcing Mountie, but clearly that narrative has been rewritten, inverted, and, of course, queered. The Mounties are so often represented in Canadian cultural texts as enforcing law and order, but in the Monkman painting the Mountie is the one being disciplined. Without doubt, we are presented with an inversion of the myth of the Canadian west, the Mounties, and even, though to a lesser degree, the Indigenous person. But I want to think carefully about what else we might find in this image. After all, it is ripe with pleasure.

The riskiness of this image is that we might be tempted to respond quickly to it. We might laugh. We might feel discomforted. We might smile. We might feel disoriented. But we should temper this sense of immediacy. We should work against an immediate reaction; instead, I propose that we look at this painting slowly. Let it sit there; let it affect us. I imagine here close reading as a kind of queerness, as Elizabeth Freeman suggests, for "to close read is to linger, to dally, to take pleasure in tarrying, and to hold out that these activities can allow us to look both hard and askance at the norm."[17] Close reading is a kind of erotic engagement with literary and visual texts that enables us to move slowly through the density of the words or images. In what follows, I suggest that spanking is important to interpreting the painting but also "a theory of its own."[18] This painting encourages us to think about the mechanics of spanking, the aesthetics of that experience, the long pleasures and pains, the quick taps, the slow repetitions involved in achieving the pinkest of asses. A pensive interpretation of this image ought to reflect the slowness of spanking, matched by the stillness of the waters, which the Mountie gazes upon as he is slowly and methodically spanked.

Rebecca F. Plante notes that "The history of spanking . . . is an old and venerable one." To be clear, we are considering here spanking that involves "emotional and sexual gratification of either or both parties."[19] In other words, we are not concerned with the corporal punishment—even though, of course, there is a correlation between the two, as Freud notes in his 1919 essay "A Child Is Being Beaten." In his work on the beating fantasy, he notes that it arises in "early childhood" and in some cases is "retained for auto-erotic satisfaction" in later life.[20] Our interest is thus less in the disciplinary consequences of early childhood and more in the satisfaction found later. Hence, I wish to consider the pleasure located in *Cree Master 1* made possible through spanking. More particularly, I am arguing here that in this scene, as with other paintings by Monkman, the "meaning is unclear,"[21] and I hope to afford but one possible reading of these paintings.

In thinking about spanking as theory, I turn to Eve Kosofsky Sedgwick, for whom spanking is the "idea of potentially queer rhythms," which aligns "childhood spanking" with "her early childhood attraction to two-beat lines."[22] Sedgwick's most detailed meditation on spanking appears in "A Poem Is Being Written," which, of course, "obviously means to associate the shifty passive voice of a famous title of Freud's."[23] I suggest here that reading *Cree Master 1* as a disciplinary scene is superficial; we need to read more deeply into the poetics of pleasure. That is, though there is undoubtedly a correlation between spanking and disciplining, we must also recognize that the Mountie does not seem to be terribly displeased with the spanking.

Sedgwick has urged her readers to think about sexuality in new and exciting ways that move beyond the primacy of the phallus. One of her important lessons, Jason Edwards explains, was that she "repeatedly, perversely insists on the ass's potential pleasure-giving and -receiving properties."[24] Like Sedgwick, I insist on this pleasure, not because I believe that we all must engage in such pleasure, but because we must recognize that it is there as a possibility, contained in Monkman's painting, and to ignore this possibility is to minimize the value of his painting. Spanking therefore needs to be considered carefully in relation to a variety of discourses, not just those that invert the colonial negotiation of power.

In what follows, I think about things such as speed of spanking, rhythm, and ritual, in addition to the more immediately available negotiation of power, which I imagine is intimately linked not only to pleasure but also to affect. In "A Poem Is Being Written," Sedgwick recalls that "the two most rhythmic things that happened to me [as a child] were spanking and poetry," and she draws to our attention rhythm, beat (as in two-beat poetry), pulse, blow, hammering.[25] Each word calls attention to the sound of spanking, matched by the repetition of the event. Equally important to Monkman's painting is Sedgwick's question, reflecting on her own spankings as a child: "Did this imaginative contraction happen once or over and over again?"[26] This question embodies one of the primary concerns available to the viewer of Monkman's painting: the Mountie's ass has not been spanked just "once" but "over and over again." Rhythm and repetition are important to this scene. The repeated spanks, one imagines, punctuate the silence, the staccato of palm meeting cheek, piercing the calm air, in which we see not even a bird to make noise. The only noise, we might imagine, then, is that of repeated spanks.

What likely most discomforts, in a sense, is the ritual quality of this image, coupled with what is ostensibly a humiliating scene. The scene is humiliating because it is about a "topsy-turvy regime, from high to low, from exalted to degraded, from secure to insecure."[27] In this painting, a great deal is happening insofar as topping from the bottom has become methodological and hermeneutic—we are reading from behind. In thinking about spanking, Sedgwick speaks of "a careful orchestration of spontaneity and pageantry, 'simply' over the parental lap."[28] Spontaneous yet a pageant, this is what seems to unfold in Monkman's painting; as viewers, we witness a pageant of spanking. Sedgwick's language highlights a tension between the private and public aspects of the spanking scene, especially when we begin to think about witnessing the humiliating scene. Colleen

Lamos, in an article on flagellation and flogging in James Joyce's *A Portrait of the Artist as a Young Man*, provides a similar scenario: "Such scenes demonstrate that flogging was a collective act—indeed, a theatre of punishment—in which the offender's shame and the spectators' fearful excitement mingled. For the boys who watched this drama were themselves likely to have been subjected to the same treatment, their own abjection lending added pleasure to their schoolmate's abasement."[29] In thinking about spanking, we see words such as *orchestration, pageantry, theatre, collective act, drama,* and *scene.* These are chiefly visual and performative words that cue our attention as viewers to the scene in which we "hear" the thick whacks of spanking. But, still further, the scene in question is without witnesses; instead, we, as viewers, become witnesses.

In our role as witnesses, we are confronted by negative affect, humiliation, and shame. Spanking is shameful in a number of ways: (1) we are shamed when our spanking is witnessed; (2) we are usually spanked for shameful reasons; (3) if we enjoy our spanking, then the enjoyment, like the spanking, becomes shameful (and I think that the fullness of that shame is important). Silvan Tomkins notes that "shame is the affect of indignity, of defeat, of transgression, and of alienation."[30]

Tomkins suggests that the shamed person will drop "his eyes, his eyelids, his head, and sometimes the whole upper part of his body."[31] I am reluctant to read too much into the physicality of shame, but it does seem that the Mountie has dropped not only his breeches but also his head. More to the point, however, is how we as viewers negotiate not only the shamefulness of the scene but also our enjoyment—or lack thereof—from the scene. Indeed, as viewers, we might feel a sense of humiliation, which "involves a triangle: (1) the victim, (2) the abuser, and (3) the witness."[32] Although I am reluctant to adopt the language of abuse and victim, I am interested in adopting the idea of witnessing and what it means to view a scene such as that of the spanked Mountie.

As viewers of Monkman's painting, we witness the spanking, similar in a way to how Jack and Ennis are observed by the boss in *Brokeback Mountain.* The challenge that we face is rather simple: how are we to respond? Indeed, this sense of unknowing is perhaps

5.2 *Ceci n'est pas une pipe (2001)*

what is most troubling for the viewer—the painting of an embarrassing and humiliating scene has done its work once more, and we have been equally humiliated in describing the work as "unclear."[33] Perhaps, we might say, Monkman's spanking has extended to his viewers. Our glee in viewing this scene is matched by our having been outwitted; our discomfort is that our role in colonialism has been called to attention; our shame results from being witnesses to a lengthy history that has only begun to tinge our historical consciousness.

This lack of clarity that Francis locates in Monkman's painting *Ceci n'est pas une pipe* (2001; see Image 5.2), and that I have located above, is not because Monkman lacks direction but because these paintings are difficult. Like Francis, I want to dwell on this painting, but my intentions here are to highlight a rereading of this painting and *Cree Master 1* in an attempt to think deeply and carefully about the anal images and poetics of Monkman's work.

In her analysis of this painting, Francis wonders "is this rape or an erotic fantasy?"[34] One is tempted, however, to imagine if her question cannot be rephrased as a "both/and" scenario. After all, why must one exclude the other? Although not wanting to negate the traumas of rape, especially in a society such as ours, slowly coming to terms with its culture of rape, I want to stress that this scenario seems to play, once more, with theories of sexuality: popular, academic, scientific. The image itself, like *Cree Master 1*, is provocative. Francis describes the painting as "a benign landscape with an expanse of puffy white clouds and invitingly blue sky," and "our eye is drawn . . . to the foreground of the painting, where a cowboy is bending over a fallen tree trunk, and an Indian dressed only in a loincloth is grasping him firmly from behind."[35] Initially, when I began to think about this project, this was the image that grabbed my attention, for many of the reasons that Francis identifies. Like her, I agree that the "meaning is unclear," and I am enamoured with her treatment of the painting in her smart book. She notes that in the painting are "several elements" suggesting

> that the cowboy may welcome the brave's advances. First, the cowboy's gun seems to have been carefully set aside just to the right of the kneeling man, well within reach if he wanted to put an end to the encounter. And, second, the posture, as he swivels around to look at the brave, indicates considerable fascination, as well as alarm, as he offers his (attractive) butt to the dashing brave behind him.[36]

This painting is a standard inversion of the roles played by the Indigenous person and the settler. But *what if* this is not what is happening? *What if* there is yet another way to read this painting, one that recognizes and dwells on the initial uncertain meaning? *What if* we accept the painting as unclear? *What if* we are humiliated and shamed by its lack of clarity, which makes it difficult for us to understand? *What if* we have to struggle for meaning?

Jane Gallop, for instance, speaks of anecdotal theory as "drag[ging] theory into a scene where it must struggle for mastery" and says "theory must contend with what threatens its mastery."[37] Francis does not negotiate anecdotal theory, and neither does this chapter, but I am interested in the negotiation of "mastery" and threats to it. Indeed, ever the queer theorist, I am tempted to ask, Are we, with all of our theoretical and intellectual baggage, being, how shall we say, topped from the bottom? Indeed, what the anus does, especially when privileged, is call into question a number of overarching ideas about power and domination, particularly as related to the phallus. The anus, in a sense, speaks back to its own erasure and subsequently requires that critical theorists reorient themselves and their ideas about sexuality—for instance the predominance of the phallus—that have now become common.

Although it is easy to accept the supposition that sexuality is necessarily a dynamics of power, and that the phallus is endowed with that power, there is, I suggest, another reading. One cannot help but note that many of the phallic signifiers in this painting are obscured, put aside, or simply broken. The gun, as Francis notes, is "set aside," but the cowboy is also bent over a broken tree, which seemingly mimics the penis with its bright trunk contrasted with its bark. Moreover, the Indigenous man's penis is entirely obscured. The one erect image in the painting is that of the broken tree. At the centre of the painting, however, is the butt of the cowboy. Thus, we might ask, is it possible to read this painting not in terms of its phallic imagery, the images that most suggest the penis, but in terms of his butt? In other words, can we continue the work of reading from behind? Indeed, when we recall *Cree Master 1*, we cannot help but notice the prominence of the ass.

Its prominence highlights an interesting tension, however anecdotal, in the ass. I might be guilty here of teasing Francis's parenthetical comment about "his (attractive) butt," which I cannot help but note seems to share the shape of a butt, but there is something to this. The paintings contrast the settler butt to the Indigenous butt. In her chapter "Red Hot to the Touch: wRi(gh)ting Indigenous Erotica," Kateri Akiwenzie-Damm writes that

> [l]ike many other Anishnaabe people I have often heard people complain and make jokes about our "flat Indian asses." As I thought about it I realized how beautiful we are and how the characteristics that make us Anishnaabeck are part of that beauty—even with a "flat ass." . . . Although we joke about them, our "flat asses" are a part of what makes

us distinctly beautiful, and it seemed to me that they ought to be celebrated and admired. At that moment I decided to be the first to stand up and say it proud: flat asses are sexy! And so, through a simple spoken word piece, the humble Anishnaabe poet strives to elevate the lowly "flat ass" to its rightful place as "a muse, an inspiration, an object of beauty, a miracle."[38]

Although I am not interested in being reductive, I am interested in the idea of "flat Indian asses," which seem to hold true in *Ceci n'est pas une pipe*, at least compared with the bubble butt of the cowboy, whose ass seems to have something in common with George Quaintance's "bare chests and asses" and those "asses . . . more perfectly rounded." Likewise, Tom of Finland "would later do the same thing in his drawings, but in Tom's work, asses and chests and the gigantic muscles and pricks and cocks were exaggerated so much so that they were totally unrealistic—but *very* sexy."[39] (Incidentally, though Tom of Finland is known for the exaggerated phallus, he is quoted as having said "I'm an assman myself."[40]) So the Indigenous ass, we are told, is flat, but the attractive butt of the cowboy is anything but flat. There is a key distinction between the two: if the flat ass is not sexy, or needs to be reclaimed as sexy, then surely the cowboy's ass must be not only attractive but also sexy.

Let us return to the analysis of the image. We should not hear, for instance, how Francis speaks of the cowboy "swivel[ling] around to look at the brave." The position is about looking back at the Indigenous body and away from the action on the plain; we note the animal running to the side of the painting. Even the Indigenous man is not looking forward but looking down, below, at the behind. The ass is the focus of this image, and the ass, well, "n'est pas une pipe." What I think we should postulate here, perhaps, is not a shift in power dynamics but a genuine complication of how we think about sexuality—the penis is not the only active agent in this scene. Indeed, as far as I can tell in *Ceci n'est pas une pipe*, none of the focus is on the phallic signifier. We might even suggest—paradoxically enough—that it is an empty signifier. Indeed, the genuine phallic image in this painting, as in *Cree Master 1*, appears to be the ass.

The ass in each of these images is pleasurable, pleasure seeking, and pleasure giving. As critical theorists, we do a disservice when we position the penetrated body as the body lacking in power, the body lacking pleasure of its own. Although I recognize that feminist theory has long critiqued the phallus/penis—and rightly so—I must reluctantly admit that we have yet to free ourselves from its dominance. The idea, for instance, that Monkman's paintings provide an inversion of power highlights the phallic reality. We see a top, we see a bottom, we have a power dynamic—so goes the erotic calculus. But as I have suggested above, is it possible that this painting is about topping from the bottom?

Such a question runs the risk of invalidating the anti-colonialist or decolonizing readings, present throughout the work of Monkman. That is, we would once more affirm the power of the settler-colonialist, because he becomes the source of attention, the site of focus, the erotic body to be pleased. We need to hold on to these anti-colonial impulses that resonate throughout the work, but at the same time we cannot deny that "the early North American west was an arena of intensive contact between men of all races," and thus, as Francis notes, "the question of how white men would react to the more diverse sexual practices common among many Indigenous peoples was not preordained." Francis further observes that "Indeed, many commentators in the nineteenth and twentieth centuries openly questioned whether white settlers would prove a great and hardy race, capable of 'civilizing' themselves and these new lands, or whether they would degenerate into the morass of corrupt behaviour that was thought to characterize more 'savage' races."[41] This recognition of the duality of these visions is important precisely because it seems that the former has dominated much of the national consciousness on colonization of the west, even though the historical narrative would demonstrate, as Francis has, an overall concern about colonization and its impact on masculinity. The history of colonialism, therefore, is always rife with potential duplicity, and colonialism is slippery because it can always go "backward."

The riskiness of this reading is thus one that erases the very colonial critique that it seeks to call into question. But we should read this not as an erasure of that colonial process but as a recognition that this process always flirted with its own homoeroticism and its own potential for "degeneration."[42] But to focus squarely on the Indigenous person and settler-colonialist is also to erase a larger critique found in the work. "Monkman is playing," Francis argues, "with and against the norms of landscape painting," which *necessarily* include "the ideological uses of this genre, where representations of a fecund and light-filled country were usually seen to reflect European settlers' divine entitlement to the land."[43] That is, just as this chapter has called into question the ideological underpinning of the pastoral, we would be remiss if we failed to recognize that the content, which includes but is not limited to characters in the painting, already critiques colonialism.

Returning to the task at hand, these two images work together in this pursuit of pleasure because, as Sedgwick notes, "the sexual politics of the ass are not identical to the sexual politics of the asshole. But they are not totally separate either."[44] We might well argue that this is what these two images highlight—they are both ostensibly about the ass, but how the ass functions in both is similar but different. That is, the ass is a site of pleasure in both (or perhaps a site of non-pleasure if we accept a more violent reading, though as Francis has noted, and as I hope I have also demonstrated, this reading seems to be less convincing), and in its becoming a site of pleasure we need to rethink what David Halperin has called (with reference to sadomasochism) "a re-mapping of the body's erotic sites"; such a remapping encourages a "breakup of the erotic monopoly traditionally held by the genitals."[45] I would argue that Monkman's work explicitly urges us, as viewers, to critique, break up, and dismount that "erotic monopoly," which, we might insist, is an imposition of colonialism, and if not colonialism then surely Victorian and colonial morality.

Anal eroticism is not new, and more importantly for our purposes here it has a pre-Columbian history that still needs to be written. I am not about to extend a genealogical argument through the history of the anus in Indigenous art, but it is worth noting that "anal intercourse is the most popular sexual practice depicted in pre-Columbian art."[46] Moreover, writings of the conquest of the Americas are replete with discussions of "the sexual politics" of both the ass and the asshole. It is difficult to separate the ass from homosexuality (and, even if we know this, the larger community might continue to find doing so difficult, and we just need to pay attention to homophobic jokes that flood the media and often revolve around the queerness of the ass), particularly male homosexuality.

The anus, the ass, the rear, the rectum, and so on—all parts of a whole—have held a precarious position in the history of colonialism, particularly of the Americas. Hernán Cortés, for instance, famously declared that everyone is a sodomite in the New World,[47] a sentiment later echoed by Bernal Díaz del Castillo.[48] Sodomy, of course, referred to a large number of sexual acts that did not advance "the aim of married procreative sex" and included anal sex, fellatio, masturbation, bestiality, and so on.[49] As much as colonialism accounts and condemns these instances of sodomy, there is always the "good" Indian in these historical documents who must be saved from or who has renounced, repressed, and/or abandoned sodomy.[50]

I provide this brief discussion because the sexual morality that shocks and humiliates us as viewers of Monkman's paintings is not, at least not essentially so, a part of the Indigenous ethos. That is, renunciation of the anus as a site of pleasure might well be more intimately connected with colonialism than with any primitive culture. The erotic imaginary of a text such as *Song of the Loon* is precisely that, by leaving behind "civilization," one can return to one's own primal sexuality. This is absolutely not to suggest that a novel such as *Song of the Loon* is not without ethical and moral problems, but it is to suggest that perhaps we have focused too much on the phallocentric images that clutter the archive of colonialism. Also, it is to suggest that Monkman's paintings, in which the ass figures so prominently, might well teach us something about the ass, which apparently can be accessed only by returning to the wilderness (a theme seen in the previous chapter on *Brokeback Mountain*).

I do not want to be an apologist for problematic and offensive texts such as *Song of the Loon* or the numerous—too many to count— examples of a virginal heroine and an aggressive, suave, seductive Indigenous man in the tradition of popular romance novels (which are not inherently problematic but have a complicated history that weaves together colonialism and readerly pleasures). I am suggesting instead that we can read these texts from a different perspective, one that forces us to reconsider our own orientation and placement when viewing an image such as *Cree Master 1*. As comfortable as we have become with phallic imagery and the phallus as active, it turns out, at least by way of Monkman's paintings, that the ass can do quite a bit as well.

Indeed, the anus is filled with erotic and symbolic meaning, and the critical assumption that it can only be penetrated reduces the body in these images to meaninglessness. This can hardly be the political goal of Monkman's work. Instead, we are reminded that one can top from the bottom, that the bottom can be in control, and that in the sexual arena things are never as simple as a binary that reduces each actor to one role. Sexuality, we learn, and as I hope is becoming clear throughout *Reading from Behind*, needs to be theorized in new ways that evade the binary. In this regard, we would do well to embrace a more global theory of sexuality that recognizes the tensions between poles and that, as much as we might like to believe in a horizontal plane on which sexuality is oriented, there is always another axis.

CHAPTER 6
Unlocking Delmira Agustini's "El Intruso"

IN THIS CHAPTER, I TURN TO POETRY, MORE EXPLICITLY to one of the most canonical examples of Latin American modernist poetry, Delmira Agustini's "El Intruso" (The Intruder). Agustini is largely recognized as one of the most important modernist poets from Latin America, and her work has been of significant interest to a range of scholars, especially feminist literary critics. What has yet to be completed is a queer study—of any kind—of Agustini. This chapter, to a certain extent, aims to open the door to this kind of reading of her work, but it attempts to do so only by reading "her most famous and most anthologized" poem, as J. Andrew Brown has called "El Intruso."[1]

Madeleine Simonet, in an early scholarly article on Agustini, begins by declaring that she was "one of the greatest women poets of Latin America," and her "life and work were brief, but filled with intensity in that constant, mystical search for some higher form of love that could satisfy both her carnal and her spiritual yearnings."[2] Certainly, one of the largest concerns in scholarship on her poetry has been the slipperiness of this binary between an erotic love and a spiritual love or a kind of pursuit of transcendence. However, various critics have also sought to displace the eroticism of Agustini's verse, a task that I argue misreads—wilfully—an essential part of her oeuvre, which really is, bluntly put, erotic. To deny the eroticism is to deny a search for an "authentic feminine" voice that recognizes the complexity of femininity and female authorship.[3] In working to displace the erotic, we also run the risk of missing out on the queerer aspects of Agustini's oeuvre, which celebrates an eroticism not inherently heteronormative, not essentially heterosexist in orientation. Instead, we find a range of sexual themes that includes sexuality as pleasure (i.e., not concerned with procreation), sadism, and masochism. Her final book of poetry, Simonet observes, "scandalized the people of Montevideo, who, it is said, thought her poetry was no longer kept within the realms of decency."[4] It is imperative that we recognize the explicit and implicit eroticism in her verse and that we think about the erotic in queer terms. Sarah T. Moody has argued that, "while other *modernistas* ['modernists'] offered images of women as emblems of beauty and of formal or poetic perfection, Agustini's images directly are markedly variable and diverse, emphasizing grotesque and violent figurations that directly rebut imagery of female passivity."[5] Her poetry thus responds directly to governing ideas and ideals about "female passivity" and instead offers a radical redescription of those ideas and ideals.

In "El Intruso," readers are provided with a common enough treatment of eroticism, love, and desire. Brown explains that Agustini "describes the nocturnal encounter that marks the beginning of her relationship with the lover/intruder" and that the poem "evokes the master/slave relationship," a theme that appears often enough in erotic poetry.[6] Likewise, Ignacio Ruiz-Pérez argues that Agustini "subvierte y distorsiona el lugar común del otro" (subverts and distorts the commonplace of the other) and that "En la obra de la poeta uruguaya el hecho de mirar al otro implica tomar conciencia del abismo que separa al yo del tú" (In the work of the Uruguayan poet, the act of looking at the other implies recognizing the abysm that separates the "I" from the "you").[7] Although I recognize and embrace the validity and soundness of Brown's and Ruiz-Pérez's readings of Agustini, I am interested in pursuing queerer readings of the poem. In particular, in this chapter, I wish to displace the heteronormativity that informs so many readings of the poem and to resituate the logic of eroticism in the poem. Hence, this chapter provides queerer ways of reading "El Intruso" in the hope of showing that the poem is more complex and ambiguous than earlier critics have allowed.

Before moving further, I must attend to what I mean by heteronormativity, at least within the context of this chapter, though in many ways this project as a whole seeks to dismantle the heteronormative understandings of anality. What I mean, at bottom, is a movement away from what Michel Foucault has eloquently described as the "utilitarian and fertile" place of the parents' bedroom.[8] So I am less interested in the productive value of heteronormativity, the value so often marked by reproduction. Thus, in terms of sexuality, an approach that does not embrace heteronormativity recognizes that not all sexuality needs to be productive. Lauren Berlant and Michael Warner, for instance, in their article "Sex in Public," recognize the complexity of so-called normativity; they write about a young straight couple for whom "reproductivity governs their lives, their aspirations, and their relations to money and entailment, mediating their relations to everyone and everything else."[9] This reproductive demand is what I align with heteronormativity; deviations from it are necessarily in opposition to the impulse of productivity. Thus, when this straight couple think about "nonreproductive eroticism," they find that they can talk only with Berlant and Warner: "[Y]ou're the only people we can talk to about this; to all of our straight friends this [a vibrator] would make us perverts."[10] Heteronormativity becomes a tightly bound form of sexuality that has as its primary, if not unique, goal reproduction.

Questioning heteronormativity and heterosexual texts becomes an imperative mode of reading queerly. One can find, I argue, queer potential in texts that have been read largely through a heteronormative lens (and vice versa). David M. Halperin in *How to Be Gay* asks, "Why would we [gay men] want Edmund White, when we still have *The Golden Girls*?"[11] This question is important for a number of reasons: first, it displaces the assumption that queer studies is interested only in queer texts (i.e., those written by a gay man such as White or those that treat homosexuality) in favour of heteronormative texts (e.g., *The Golden Girls*, a sitcom almost always heterosexual in its treatment of sexuality[12]); second, Halperin's question points out that heterosexual texts (those ostensibly about heterosexual relations) have queer and, more particularly for Halperin, gay potential; and third, queer theory must recognize that its concerns can branch outward to locations that do not represent queer experience but are nevertheless consumed by queer culture. His greater critique is simple: texts about queers are not terribly enticing to queers, and often enough queer pleasure, which looks beyond the normative or embraces the normative to queer ends (i.e., *The Golden Girls*), is found in heterosexual texts. Paradoxically, of course, there is much to be said about the ways in which heterosexual culture produces and consumes so-called queer texts.

Halperin's critique is important because it dismantles and challenges notions of "gay identity," but perhaps more significant is his innovative engagement with what we might call straight texts. Halperin notes that critics and what Virginia Woolf might call "common readers" can find (and often do find) "the queer charm of certain non-gay representations" such as *The Golden Girls*.[13] For Halperin, "the queer charm" of cultural texts resides not in their treatment of "gay" themes but in the queer charms already contained within them.[14] Queer charms are the pleasures that queerly positioned audiences find in heteronormative texts. Indeed, I argue in this chapter that "El Intruso" is rich with queer charm that can be and should be exposed.

Following Halperin's recognition of queer charms, I want to expose how we might begin to read queerly or, in the words of François Cusset, how we might "invert the gaze." Cusset suggests that "every text is ambiguous" and that it is our role, as critics, "to learn to *take* the text, *turn* it over, *penetrate* it, play with its sex, slip ours into it, follow it to the end of its ambivalence, and force it along the way to assume a position."[15] Although this chapter, like the book as a whole, goes to great pains to critique the primacy of the phallus, I think that Cusset's invocation of inversion (though seemingly quite phallic) is important. The queer charms that Halperin speaks of reside in the ambiguity that Cusset wants to uncover.

"We are," he argues, "looking for details that have been ignored," and these ignored details, more often than not, are those queer elements from which homophobic culture might wish to distance itself.[16] The "ignored" quality of Agustini's poem is precisely, I shall argue, its queer charm.

My analysis of "El Intruso," therefore, provides a queer reading of the poem while also engaging with and affording a critique of earlier readings of the poem that have relied on heteronormative logic. Brown's reading of the poem, for instance, suggests that it evokes "the master/slave relationship," which sustains a sadomasochistic reading of the poem, particularly evident when one considers the power dynamics at play: "Y hoy río si tú ríes, y canto si tú cantas, / y si tú duermes, duermo como un perro a tus plantas" (And today I laugh if you laugh, sing if you sing / and if you sleep, I sleep like a dog at your feet).[17] The poem provides a logic in which there seems to be a master/slave relationship. All of this, as I have suggested above, is fair and to the point. Although I do not wish to imply that sadomasochism exists outside heterosexual culture, I do intend to demonstrate how queer theory and sadomasochism can and do inform one another.

Chiefly, my argument is that sadomasochism—like queer theory—recalculates and recalibrates notions of sexuality away from the productive, utilitarian, and fertile aspects of the parents' bedroom.[18] For Foucault, sadomasochism is about "the real creation of new possibilities of pleasure."[19] Its goal is not reproduction but pleasure. Foucault, as Halperin explains, thought that sadomasochism represents "a re-mapping of the body's erotic sites" and encourages a "breakup of the erotic monopoly traditionally held by the genitals."[20] If, as Brown argues, the poem evokes the master/slave relationship, then we must necessarily consider the ways in which this relationship works and how it undercuts and critiques heteronormativity.

The poem and so many readings of it rely on its opening line: "Amor, la noche estaba trágica y sollozante / cuando tu llave de oro cantó en mi cerradura" (Love, the night was tragic and painful / when your golden key sang in my lock).[21] The negotiation of pain, common to the master/slave relationship, is present, and the singing golden key seemingly reinforces heterosexuality (additionally, one cannot help but note how the lock and key once more reinforce the master/slave aspect of the poem). Ana Peluffo concurs that "el cuerpo femenino queda convertido en la 'cerradura' y 'la llave del oro' del amante" (the female body is converted in the "lock" and "the golden key" of the lover).[22] But why must the cerradura be—necessarily so—feminine or female? The golden key (llave de oro) and the lock (cerradura), of course, are rather common metaphors—nearly dead metaphors—for sexual expression. Is there anything in particular that requires that the heteronormative reading be the only possible reading of Agustini's poem?

This question, of course, is further complicated by the realization that Agustini avoids gendering the poetic voice. There is no instance when the poet uses, for example, an adjective that would indicate the gender of that voice, yet critics insist on the poem's heterosexuality. There is, however, one possible slip: "y si tú duermes, duermo como un perro a tus plantas." The perro (dog) here is distinctly masculine, and it is the only instance in which a reader could infer the gender of the poetic voice. If we read the poem closely, there is no particular reason, I argue, that the desire, lust, love described cannot be between men, for instance. The intruder in the scene, we know, is masculine, but the yo is never clearly defined, save, perhaps, when the yo says "duermo como un perro," which renders the voice that of a (male) dog. I argue, thus, that this gendering question becomes a "key" to rereading the poem, reading it anew, reading it, as we shall see, from behind.

No one thing, no one sign, no one symbol in the poem demands and allows for *only* vaginal penetration; after all, a key could surely sing in any orifice that resembles a lock. It seems to be fair enough to recognize that there is an anally erotic reading of this poem that maintains its poetic logic and eroticism. In other words, this reading does not disrupt or displace the erotic symbolic order of the poem; by shifting attention to the cerradura, the poem does not surrender its eroticism. Moreover, it can break up "the erotic monopoly traditionally held by the genitals," especially when we shift our attention away from the phallogocentric contexts of the poem and toward the cerradura. And ultimately it allows for a queer(er) reading of the poem that recognizes and builds upon the subversive quality of Agustini's poems that Ruiz-Pérez has noted in his study. "El Intruso" can be—and perhaps should be—read in light of the advances of queerly informed reader practices.

I begin here with an exploration of the question of pleasure, particularly what we might call *jouissance* or "bliss." What seems to be evident, indeed what is likely a generic requirement of erotic poetry, is its insistence on pleasure. Roland Barthes has defined *jouissance* as the moment when "everything is lost."[23] In many regards, reading from behind requires, in part, that "everything [be] lost" in terms of the standard hermeneutics and poetic readings of Agustini's poem. A reader who reads from behind allows for a new reading of the poem, one that leads to "a point on the horizon, an ideal point, a point that's off the map, but one whose meaning reveals its structural analysis. It is revealed perfectly by the fact of jouissance."[24] Indeed, though Jacques Lacan is not speaking about anality, it is worth noting the importance of *jouissance* to the "structural analysis" and how meaning is revealed by and through *jouissance*: "This is where the work begins. It is with knowledge as a means of jouissance that work that has a meaning, an obscure meaning, is produced. This obscure meaning is the meaning of truth."[25] I might be guilty here of misreading Lacan, but I note a similarity in how we read the poem as heteronormative. Of course, the normative reading makes sense, but what happens if we consider a more "obscure meaning"? If psychoanalysis has taught us anything, it is that *only sometimes* is a cigar really just a cigar.

The failure of readings that rely on heteroeroticism is that they reduce the orgasm to a genital-only orgasm; moreover, these readings rely on a phallogocentric understanding of orgasm. Although the Lacanian position insists on the phallus—"analytic experience attests precisely to the fact that everything revolves around phallic jouissance"[26]—my reading troubles the primacy of the phallus. Anne Koedt, for instance, has provided an important critique of the psychoanalytic understanding of the female orgasm. Although Freud insisted that the clitoral orgasm (which would have little to do with a lock) is immature and that vaginal orgasm is the ideal, Koedt has drawn attention to "the myth of the vaginal orgasm."[27]

In her famous, indeed defining, article, Koedt distinguishes between "the vaginal and clitoral orgasm," noting that "the vagina is not a highly sensitive area and is not constructed to achieve orgasm."[28] Readings of "El Intruso" that insist on the lock and key as metaphor for sexual excitation are ultimately negligent insofar as they maintain the idea that the vagina is the locus of pleasure, which runs contrary to Koedt's argument that "there is only one area for sexual climax; that area is the clitoris."[29] My intention here is not to dismiss earlier critics of Agustini's poem but to polemicize the key and lock metaphor. Indeed, historically, as Koedt notes, "men knew that the clitoris was and is the essential organ for masturbation,"[30] central, of course, to the treatment of "hysteria" in the nineteenth century. So what do we make of the erotic logic that informs so many readings of the poem? If orgasm is to be found not in the lock but around it, then what are we to do with the continued importance of the lock in critical engagements with the poem?

At this point in my argument, it should be adequately clear that the lock need not function as a gynophallic; instead, I argue, the lock defies heteronormative logic precisely because it disrupts the dominance of the phallus. That is, the lock can and does function symbolically as the anus. In such a reading, I locate the queer charms of non-gay forms and consider the possibility of anal eroticism throughout "El Intruso." The poem already contains queer charms, and we do not need to engage in extraneous biographical criticism, as is common in lesbian and gay criticism. A great deal of criticism of Agustini makes extensive use of her biography, which acts, often enough, as a guide through her poetry. For the purposes of this chapter, it is best to accept the Barthesian claim that "the birth of the reader must be at the cost of the death of the Author."[31] This is not a matter of "outing" Agustini—indeed, nothing could be less interesting for the purposes of this chapter. Instead, the goal is to engage with the queer charms of "El Intruso" by attending to another erotic and poetic logic.

Guy Hocquenghem has astutely noted that "Ours is a phallic society, and the quality of pleasure is determined in relation to the phallus."[32] His point, worth considering in relation to "El Intruso," challenges the phallus as the governing symbol. The phallus has been central to many readings of the poem precisely because it is through the lock that the phallus is able to sing—rather than the lock. Indeed, such a reading depends on a phallogocentric positioning that reifies the phallus as the singular site of pleasure and that only the phallus can allow for the lock to find pleasure, a position that Koedt has rightly called "the myth of the vaginal orgasm." As Hocquenghem has suggested, "To centre on the penis eliminates or subdues other desiring machines."[33] To focus our readings on the phallogocentric logic of the poem does a disservice to other possible readings and other possible sites of pleasure. Moreover, to focus on the phallus negates the sadomasochistic potential of the poem, especially when we accept the Foucauldian argument that sadomasochism breaks up "the erotic monopoly traditionally held by the genitals."[34] Likewise, Jeffrey R. Guss observes that "As a phallic society we are obliged to organize around recognition of the phallus; without this there is nothing."[35] Michael Moon, in accounting for Hocquenghem's position, explains that "the constitutive overvaluation of the phallus and the phallic in capitalist culture depends on a corresponding devaluation of the anus and anal desire and pleasure."[36] To focus specifically on the phallus is to foreclose any other possible readings of eroticism and pleasure intrinsic to the poem. Is it not possible to enter into the hermeneutics of the poem through the exit? That is, could the cerradura not actually be the symbolic llave de oro to deciphering Agustini's poem?

Reading the poem with a focus on anal eroticism deflates the primacy and dominance of the phallus and allows for a queerer interpretation. To these ends, I draw on the pioneering work of Eve Kosofsky Sedgwick because it has often and carefully considered the possibility of anal eroticism in literary texts. In "Is the Rectum Straight?"—a paper on Henry James's *The Wings of the Dove*—Sedgwick displaces the phallus as the primary signifier of eroticism: "As it happens in James's own, extremely dense, and highly charged associations concerning the anus did not cluster around images of the phallus. They clustered around the hand."[37] To speak about the anus as symbolic is to rewrite the primacy of the phallus, and indeed, in thinking about the anus, it is not the phallus but the hand that serves as its binary. When we look at Agustini's poem, we find initially that the presumed phallic reference is the key, but later the phallic reference is displaced altogether and replaced by the hand: "[T]iemblo si tu mano toca la cerradura" (I tremble if your hand touches my lock).[38] Between the two lines utilizing the cerradura, we find another line that references this queer possibility: "Bebieron en mi copa tus labios de frescura" (Your fresh lips drank from my cup).[39] Once more it highlights, I contend, a movement away from phallic sexuality. Although we cannot deny that Agustini initially relies on the phallic logic of penetration in the opening lines, in the latter lines the phallus is dismissed, and the mere touch of the lock by the intruder's hand causes shivering. The locus of pleasure in this line is thus found not in the phallus but in the hand.

But there is more to this than the phallic logic at play in the first line—there is much more to the poem than the opening couplet that informs so much of the criticism of the poem—and we should read it in light of what Sedgwick calls "fisting-as-écriture."[40] If the hand must touch the anus for there to be arousal, as seems to be the case, then surely this relates to the sexual practice of fisting. But within Sedgwick's notion of fisting-as-écriture "what is so productive about the fisting image as a sexual phantasmatic is that it can offer a switchpoint not only between homo- and heteroeroticism, but also between allo- and autoeroticism . . . and between the polarities that a phallic economy defines as passive and active."[41] Fisting subverts the phallic economy and allows, once again, for a queerer reading of "El Intruso." Moreover, we should recognize that this reading correlates with Brown's argument about the sadomasochistic thematics of the poem, but this vision is chiefly Foucauldian because it challenges the "erotic monopoly of the genitals."

But further still, when one recognizes that the word *cerradura* is one of the few repeated throughout the sonnet, and that the word itself buttresses the poem, one can begin to think about the larger project of reading from behind. The word and the pleasure attached to it are found at the opening and toward the closing of the poem. The focus is not on phallic *jouissance* but on the pleasures of the cerradura. Indeed, if we were to read the poem from the bottom to the top, its meaning becomes more ambiguous, or more credibly the poem resides outside the logic of the erotic monopoly of the phallus.

Although critics as diverse as Foucault, Hocquenghem, Halperin, and Sedgwick have all called for, or at least negotiated with, a recalculation of the erotic monopoly, one question that likely remains revolves around the possibility of pleasure. For many theorists, the pleasure principle is self-evident. But the question here becomes one that must attend to the logic of erotic poetry, eroticism, and *jouissance*. Agustini's poem can provide another theory of pleasure or at least require its readers to reconsider the primacy of "the myth of the vaginal orgasm" and more generally the primacy of genital orgasm. The sadomasochistic elements of the poem already highlight the need to rethink the question of pleasure, but so does a reading that focuses specifically on the primacy of the cerradura rather than the llave de oro. It is important to remember, on the one hand, that the key can sing only when positioned in the lock, but, on the other hand, there is still plenty of affect to be found in and around the lock.

If we accept the Foucauldian position that sadomasochism recalculates the erotic economy of genitalia, then we must recalculate our understanding of the orgasm. In their article "Non-Genital Orgasms," Barry R. Komisaruk and Beverly Whipple review scholarship on anal orgasms, which ranges from "anecdotal reports" to the historical reality that, as noted in the previous chapter, "anal intercourse is the most popular sexual practice depicted in pre-Columbian art."[42] Although my interest here is not in outlining a genealogy of anal eroticism, it is important to recognize that such eroticism has never been exclusively the domain of subcultural communities; instead, the imagery, at the least, is the most common thematic in pre-Columbian art. Moreover, they observe that in one study 26 percent of men "claimed that they have prostate or anal orgasms."[43]

The importance of rewriting the erotic monopoly is central, in many ways, to anal eroticism. Guss, for instance, observes that "Anal sexuality is repeatedly evoked as a location of virulent danger that threatens this process of gender creation. Multiple tasks of gender instantiation for men are embedded in the erotic arc between the penis and the anus and the cultural processes that define and structure their erotic protection."[44] I want to be careful here, for the queerer reading is not about reducing the poem to a locus of pleasure between men, as a theorist such as Guss would do—though undoubtedly this reading functions perfectly well, especially since Agustini avoids gendering the one intruded upon. Sedgwick, for instance, cautions against Guss's overdetermined reading; she rightly asks, and it is a question that we should ask often when thinking about male anal eroticism, "What about male desire for a woman's anus—is that anal desire?"[45] Although anal eroticism undoubtedly provokes questions of male desire for another man's anus, I stress that it need not be this way. Reading from behind affords another reading of "El Intruso" precisely because it undercuts and displaces the primacy of the phallus as totalizing signifier. Displacing the phallus results in a rewriting of the symbolic chain of signifiers so central to many readings of the poem.

Another reason for considering anal eroticism in Agustini's poem is that it opens up more hermeneutic possibilities. As Sedgwick notes, "one misses a lot of the action and possibility—including lesbian action and possibility—in [Henry] James's anal poetics if one is too facile in translating every image of penetration into an image of phallic penetration."[46] We are reductive if we insist on the phallus as the defining quality of any negotiation of erotic power, and we are likely to miss, as many critics before me have, the possibility of anal eroticism in Agustini's poetry. What her poem can do—and this possibility is essential to the poem—is disrupt the logic of the phallus. This gesture is important not only for queer studies but also for feminist literary criticism, which often must contend with a tradition of phallogocentrism. Like Sedgwick, "I'm not going to get started on the phallus. Personally, I can take it or leave it."[47] I insist that the continued and persistent presence of the phallus in interpretations of this poem has done a repeated disservice to its complexity.

Ultimately, we must admit that, when we position the anus as the locus of pleasure and as the hermeneutic key to this poem, we can reconsider the erotic potential of the episode, and this reading does not make the poem any simpler; rather, it makes it a great deal richer. It is worth noting that

The ass is soft and sensitive, and associated with pollution and shame, like the vagina. It is non-specific with regard to genital difference in that everybody has one. It allows access into the body, when after all only women are supposed to have a vulnerable interior space. All this makes anal eroticism a suasive point for the displacement or erasure of purely phallic boundaries.[48]

This argument is important not only because it reinforces my argument about the need to displace the primacy of the phallus, but also because it encourages another vision of the poem, perhaps a rather utopian vision. In displacing the phallus, and repositioning the anus, we are left with a new eroticism not foreclosed by orientation precisely because the anus is not restricted to one sex. Such an understanding of eroticism seems to be in line with Foucauldian thought. As Leo Bersani explains, "Foucault more or less openly praises sado-masochistic practices for helping homosexual men (many of whom share heterosexual men's fear of losing their authority by 'being under another man in the act of love') to 'alleviate' the 'problem' of feeling 'that the passive role is in some way demeaning.'"[49] With this in mind, we come full circle and return to Brown's recognition of the sadomasochistic aspects of the poem, but unlike Brown we have been more involved in rewriting the erotic monopoly of the genitals. And we have reunderstood the sadomasochistic relationship and its negotiation of power precisely because—at least in the Foucauldian understanding—some power can be found in the submissive position. In this regard, though the poem is about the "intruso," there are two actors in this scenario, and both receive pleasure, a pleasure that fundamentally resides in and is made possible through the cerradura.

By shifting critical focus away from the phallus and toward the anus, we actively rewrite the erotic monopoly of so many other readings of the poem. Moreover, and this is perhaps what is precisely at stake in this chapter, we move away from the phallogocentric impulses and demands of patriarchy. And, if our focus shifts, then we can also reread the opening couplet, which can return us to Sedgwick's notion of fisting-as-écriture. That is, the eroticism considered in Agustini's poem is not phallic but fundamentally concerned with the anus as a site of pleasure. In this rendering, we can find an intrinsically queer poem because it allows for allo- and autoeroticism insofar as no one's sexuality is excluded, and the poem becomes much more subversive and transgressive than earlier critics allowed. The poem, in the words of Cristina Santos and Adriana Spahr, is defiantly deviant[50] insofar as it rebels wildly against normative culture and the rigid straightness of heteronormative culture.

The poem can thus be read without losing any poetic logic in light of the cerradura and particularly away from the now fully displaced phallus. In what follows, I argue that this reading, in line with the Foucauldian understanding of sadomasochism, is also in line with the Barthesian "pleasure of the text" and particularly Barthes's own theory of sexuality. Throughout this chapter, I have oscillated between reading the poem as homosexual, by which I mean that there is a way to read the poem as "gay" wherein both actors are men, and contraheteronormative, because the sex described is ultimately not about the reproductive parents' bedroom. I have been intentionally ambiguous because I am not partial to either reading, for both readings are inherently in opposition to earlier readings, and both actively engage in a rewriting of the phallic economy of the poem.

Barthes provides an interesting and productive intervention in theories of sexuality precisely because his writings are so intimately linked with the practice of writing. In his course, *The Preparation of the Novel*, he links the novel fantasy with sexuality, particularly the first time. For Barthes, the novel fantasy—the fantasy of writing a novel—"starts out from *a few* novels and to that extent rests on (takes as its starting point) something like the First Pleasure (of reading)."[51] To write a novel requires an awareness of a few novels that will motivate the writing of our own novel, "and, from our knowledge of erotic pleasure, we recognize the force of that First Pleasure, which traverses a lifetime."[52] The intimacy between writing and sexuality cannot be ignored, and there is a correlation between the first novel and the first (erotic) time—it will affect the life of the author-lover. Nowhere, of course, is this correlation more clearly elucidated than in Barthes's seminal *The Pleasure of the Text*.

Jane Gallop, always an extraordinary reader, admits to having "fantasized teaching [*The Pleasure of the Text*] not as literary theory but as a theory of sexuality," and one can certainly imagine how this course might unfold, especially "since the advent of queer theory."[53] Likewise, Carol Mavor acknowledges that it was not until "recently" that she became "more literate in the nuances of his queer sensibility."[54] Not as a scholar writing "since the advent" but as someone for whom queer theory was always present, she has always sensed something queer about Barthes. This queerness was not just because of his queer affairs with his mother,[55] or the fact that "Barthes was at times mockingly referred to by the students of the Collège de France as *tante* (which in French is not only 'aunt' but also slang for nancy-boy),"[56] but also because he celebrates hedonism in *The Pleasure of the Text*, writes "boyishly" (to borrow Mavor's term) about love in *A Lover's Discourse*, and at one moment pronounces the death of the author only to publish later *Roland Barthes by Roland Barthes*.[57]

For Barthes, *jouissance*, distinct from pleasure, can be understood as orgasm, but "Barthes also regularly connects jouissance with perversion."[58] Indeed, if we are to find pleasure in Agustini's text, it cannot be just about *plaisir*—"comfortable, ego-assuring, recognized, and legitimated by culture"—but must also be about *jouissance*: "shocking, ego-disruptive, and in conflict with the canons of culture."[59] To read "El Intruso" from a queer perspective is to recognize the *plaisir* of the text and, more importantly, to recover its many layers of pleasure and ultimately *jouissance*.

This *jouissance* of the text, we must recognize, "does not come in its own good time."[60] I contend that this is precisely what unfolds in the poem. The meaning of the poem does not come in the opening couplet but must be uncovered only in the closing verses—the exit—when we return to the cerradura. Gallop, in her brilliant reading of *The Pleasure of the Text*, observes that "The next sentence in the translation is 'Everything is wrought to a transport at one and the same moment,'" which she would rather translate as "Everything goes off (or everything explodes) at once (or at one go)."[61] Once more, I would argue, this is precisely what happens at the second instance of cerradura, at the moment when "everything goes off" or, erotically, when everything becomes known, much like the first pleasure of reading. The *plaisir* of the text might well be found in the singing key, but the *jouissance* is found in the now opened lock.

Ultimately, as I move toward a conclusion, I offer one last observation that must be included in any "fantasy" of a Barthesian theory of sexuality. Barthes "wished to create the Neuter, a new value that would 'un-realize' the antinomies and binarisms that restrain sexual experience."[62] This "new value" corresponds, as I shall show, to my reluctance to privilege one reading of Agustini's poem over another. It is clear that "Barthesian eroticism is plural, expansive in the very sense in which it avoids any constraining and privileged localization."[63] Admittedly, I have focused on the anus as the "key" to understanding the poem, but there is more than one way to read it. For Barthes, eroticism and sexuality should not be dependent, at least following Pierre Saint-Amand, and reduced to genitality, and Barthes is particularly interested in "unsettling the *meaning* of erotic gestures."[64] If we are careful, and if we follow the Barthesian lesson, when we read "El Intruso" we can negotiate how it unsettles many of the meanings of "erotic gestures." It is imperative that as critics we pay attention to "the surface in its multiplicity and its infinity."[65]

"El Intruso" provides no grammatical key to the genders of its actors. This reading, once more, is in line with the Barthesian "neutral," which "suffers the weight (the shadow) of grammar" because it is interested in "what is neither masculine nor feminine."[66] This notion of "the weight . . . of grammar" is important because the neuter is as much a desired construct as it is "truly impossible in our language."[67] In considering Balzac's *Sarrasine* and the figure of the castrato, Barthes tells us that

> were [the neuter] possible, it would be no less dangerous discursively, for it would either reveal the castrato too early (neither man nor woman: we have seen that in our mythology the neuter is perceived as a desexualisation and not as "disanimation"), or it would mark the will of not choosing between the two sexes, which would already be saying too much.[68]

As I have suggested above, the only possible instance of grammatical identification is the use of the word *perro*, grammatically masculine. But, like Balzac's *Sarrasine* and Barthes's reading of it, the ambiguity of the gender is what sustains the reading. The pleasure of the text is neither too early (indeed, as we have seen above, the meaning of the poem comes perhaps too late for most readers) nor too much. The poem, therefore, is neutral and shimmers, as Barthes might suggest: "[T]he Neutral is the shimmer: that whose aspect, perhaps whose meaning, is subtly modified according to the angle of the subject's gaze."[69] This is what I have done in this reading of "El Intruso": I have resituated not only the reader's gaze but also the reader's position in reading, literally, from behind. "[W]e don't need to take sides against this image"; instead, we can embrace the ways in which the neutral, like Agustini's poem, "plays on the razor's edge."[70]

Reading from behind encourages another reading of "El Intruso," one that indeed engages with the sadomasochism that Brown has considered, one that more elaborately considers the subversive quality that Ruiz-Pérez has advocated, and ultimately one that fully works to understand the phallic economy that has so often informed earlier criticisms. In this reading of the poem, we have actively engaged with Foucauldian paradigms of pleasure, repositioned the erotic monopoly of genitalia, and luxuriated in the richly complex Barthesian *jouissance* and eroticism. This reading does not, I believe, harm the poem, nor does it need to make the poem gay; instead, it demonstrates the very reasons why "El Intruso" remains Agustini's most well-known and most collected poem, and it has to do with much more than the simplicity of "tu llave de oro cantó en mi cerradura." Indeed, as I hope I have shown, the key is able to sing only because of the lock, and we are able to read this poem anew only if we focus on how the lock gives meaning not only to the singing key but also to the poem as a whole.

Shameful Matrophilia
in *Doña Herlinda y su hijo*

IN THE PREVIOUS CHAPTER, WE EXPLORED ANAL eroticism in Delmira Agustini's canonical poem "El Intruso," in particular a reading of the poem that reimagines the erotic calculus that unfolds on that "tragic and painful night." In this chapter, we will once more consider poetry; in this case, a poem becomes a key to understanding a film. Our attention will focus on the Mexican film *Doña Herlinda y su hijo* (1985; Doña Herlinda and Her Son), in which we are introduced to a queer family: Rodolfo, Doña Herlinda's son, lives with his lover, Ramón, in Rodolfo's mother's home. Meanwhile, his mother has arranged a marriage for Rodolfo to Olga. The film is rich in queer potential. In this chapter, we will explore how the film participates in and informs an effeminophobic project by way of the mother-loving Rodolfo. In a sense, he embodies the Barthesian claim "I want maternity and genitality."[1] Throughout the film, we watch Rodolfo struggle to memorize a poem, which he hopes to recite publicly for his mother. The poem, which Ramón has no difficulty memorizing, also explains, as I argue, Rodolfo's many conflicted loves and in many ways becomes a source of shame. This shame oscillates, as we shall see, around anal eroticism. Hence, this chapter works to understand how effeminophobia and matrophilia—both of which are represented as shameful—inform one another and participate in the construction of Rodolfo's anal eroticism.

Jaime Humberto Hermosillo's *Doña Herlinda y su hijo* is a queer film not just because it deals with gay men. The film feels queer. It never feels quite right (or its queerness feels just right). Rodolfo, a pediatrician, falls in love with Ramón, a student at the music conservatory. Meanwhile, Doña Herlinda has arranged a marriage between Olga, a worker at Amnesty International, and Rodolfo. Ultimately, and somewhat miraculously, they all end up living together (happily ever after) in Doña Herlinda's home, expanded and renovated to accommodate this very queer family. Indeed, in summarizing the film, the pioneering film historian and critic Vito Russo explains that "Mama is smart enough to see if she breaks them [Rodolfo and Ramón] up, her son will hate her, so she engineers a plot that will make everyone happy."[2] Russo rightly notes the importance of Doña Herlinda, particularly the ways in which she can sustain a notion of "happiness" while allowing for the queer (re)definition of the family.

Critics of the film have largely focused on its non-heteronormativity or what we might more commonly call its queerness, but discussions have not extended queerness beyond the sexuality of the protagonist. Daniel Balderston, for example, asks about the "excluded middle," or bisexuality, in the film.[3] Meanwhile, David William Foster focuses not on bisexuality but on how the film queers patriarchy.[4] Russo's argument attends to the way that the film explores masculinity, machismo, and the macho male. All of these readings are done well and raise important questions about what is arguably one of Mexico's most interesting and provocative films exploring queer relations and subjectivity.[5] Indeed, the film, viewed today (nearly thirty years later), seems to address "the new normal" *avant la lettre*.

Critical recognition of the importance of Doña Herlinda allows for our return to *Doña Herlinda y su hijo*. Russo, of course, is not alone in his commentary. Foster, for example, calls her "the crucial axis"[6] and "pivotal figure"[7] of the film. The Cuban director Néstor Almendros suggested that Doña Herlinda is "un nuevo arquetipo de las artes narrativas: Doña Herlinda es como Don Juan, Don Quijote, Hamlet, La Celestina, etc.; un personaje que quedará siempre como un modelo. Ella . . . es la madre de todos los homosexuales, con sus ambigüedades, su saber y no saber, su querer y no querer reconocer, con su amor y comprensión" (a new archetype of the narrative arts: Doña Herlinda is like Don Juan, Don Quijote, Hamlet, La Celestina, etc.; a character that always remains a model. She . . . is the mother of all homosexuals, with their ambiguities, her knowing and not knowing and not wanting to recognize, with her love and comprehension).[8] In this chapter, I suggest that the mother, as earlier critics have noted, is a crucial figure, but I extend their arguments to suggest that the film and its queerness—its feeling queer—depend on the mother. One might go as far as to suggest that the mother functions as a fabulous shibboleth of the film's queerness.

David M. Halperin speaks of "the obsession with the mother figure" as one of the "great value[s] of traditional gay male culture" yet, of course, one of "its most despised and repudiated features."[9] It is hard not to return to the archetypal image of the overbearing but loving mother, particularly in the context of gay male culture. *Doña Herlinda y su hijo*, as the title suggests, is very much about this relationship, however true or false the archetype. Instead of seeing this as the site for clinical work, a paranoid search for symptoms so as to confirm homosexuality, I want to attend to the complex and loving relationship between a mother and her son, a son and his mother. I am not interested in the diagnostic work of "outing" or ascribing sexuality; rather, my approach recognizes, as Eve Kosofsky Sedgwick would remind us, that "People are different from each other."[10] What might appear to be gay for one need not be gay for another; however, to be clear, the question of orientation is not what is being called into question. We are concerned with the relationship between mother and son, and how it is queer.

Doña Herlinda y su hijo "shakes things about, like mothers and sons and boys and men," as Carol Mavor writes of her own (maternal) *Reading Boyishly*.[11] Like Mavor, I am interested in reading *boyishly*, which is "to covet the mother's body as a home both lost and never lost, to desire her as only a son can, as only a body that longs for her, but will never become Mother, can."[12] The film is indebted, no doubt, to notions of the family romance, particularly the Oedipal complex, which, like the gay boy and his mother, has nearly become a tired, but nevertheless exciting, cliché. Unlike the Oedipal scenario, however, in *Doña Herlinda y su hijo*, there is no father to kill. Doña Herlinda is always—in the film at least—a widow; the father is always already absent. Rodolfo, in a sense, has thus fulfilled the Oedipal complex and can "covet [his] mother's body as a home both lost and never lost."

The British psychoanalyst D. W. Winnicott rightly noted that "the full Oedipal situation is but seldom enacted in real life": that is, though "some boys do express in so many words and quite openly their *in-love* feeling for their mother and their wish to marry her, and even to give her children, . . . many do not."[13] Rodolfo, as we shall see, is one of those boys who does express such feelings for his mother. This feeling of love is further complicated by the queerness of the Oedipal situation explored in *Doña Herlinda y su hijo*, for one could read this narrative as an inversion of the Oedipal complex. For example, one could suggest that it is the mother who loves to the extreme, that it is she who killed her husband to be able to love her son fully and without the burden of her spouse. However, such a reading requires too much liberty of the critic: that is, the text, while certainly flirting with this possibility, never provides enough signs to confirm it. My argument therefore pays particular attention to how Rodolfo explores the feeling of which Winnicott speaks and how he covets his mother's body.

In the closing sequence of the film, Rodolfo publicly recites poetry. "Nocturno" is a love poem written by Mexican poet Manuel Acuña and dedicated to Rosario de la Peña y Llerena. Balderston explains that the poem "is famous for its association with the poet's suicide in 1873, and the dedication of it to Rosario de la Peña has spawned the persistent theory that Acuña committed suicide after being rejected by Rosario."[14] For Balderston, "what is most jarring about the poem is the poet's yearning for a world where he could share his life with his beloved Rosario and also with his beloved and saintly mother."[15] Although it is easy to imagine the discomfort that Balderston feels about the amorous relationship with the mother, French theorist Roland Barthes wrote that "the writer plays with the mother's body . . . in order to glorify it, to embellish it."[16] I argue throughout this chapter that this is precisely what happens not only in the poem but also (and perhaps most importantly) in the closing sequence of the film—Rodolfo achieves Acuña's goal of sharing his life with both his lover and his mother. Or Rodolfo, like Barthes, fulfills "the stereotype of being too passionately close to his mother."[17]

Whereas earlier critics have focused on the gay or bisexual aspects of the film, I suggest that this amorous maternal relationship is indeed worthy of further consideration. There is no doubt about the sexuality of Rodolfo, but where we locate instances of queerness can extend beyond the bedroom. The queerness of the film's closing scene is multiple: the discomfort noted by Balderston with regard to the poem, the very queerness of Acuña's poem, the closing sequence in which Rodolfo recites the poem with his mother beside him, and the queer implications of the film for Acuña's poem. Moreover, I suggest here that his poem structures the total narrative of *Doña Herlinda y su hijo*, and consequently, I argue, the film calls into question his own sexuality. I am thus suggesting that Acuña's poem functions like the Barthesian punctum, the "sting, speck, cut, little hole,"[18] that emerges from the image. Acuña's poem, to which I will devote attention, is the "detail" of *Doña Herlinda y su hijo* that "overwhelms the entirety of my reading."[19]

Acuña's poem is straightforward enough insofar as it is a love song for Rosario, yet jarringly, suddenly, and queerly the poet's mother appears. The poem opens with

yo necesito	(I need
decirte que te adoro	to tell you that I adore you
decirte que te quiero	to tell you that I love you
con todo el corazón.[20]	with all my heart.)

On the surface, there is nothing particularly exceptional about the poem. It is repetitive and juvenile in its simplicity and sweetness.

Indeed, one might even suggest that it is overly sentimental and clichéd. One is reminded of how Barthes speaks of love: "To try to write love is to confront the *muck* of language: that region where language is both *too much* and *too little*, excessive (by the limitless expansion of the *ego*, by emotive submersion) and impoverished (by the codes on which love diminishes and levels it)."[21] Likewise, Adam Phillips writes that falling in love is "traditionally overwhelming, [an] excessive experience."[22] As much as literary critics are cautious about the excesses of love, it is important to note, I believe, as Barthes does, that trying to put love into words often results in this strange tension between being "both *too much* and *too little*." The film repeatedly calls our attention to the "excessive experience" of love, particularly via the mother. One is reminded here of Julia Kristeva, who writes that, "contrasted with the love that binds a mother to a son, all other 'human relationships' burst like blatant shams."[23]

However, by the third stanza of Acuña's poem, readers can begin to confront what is undoubtedly "the *muck* of language" and its inherent and discomforting complexity:

De noche, cuando pongo	(At night, when on the pillow
mis sienes en la almohada	I lay my weary head,
y hacia otro mundo quiero	and bid my spirit follow
mi espíritu volver,	back to another world
camino mucho, mucho,	on and on I walk
y al fin de la jornada	and at the journey's end
las formas de mi madre	the forms of my mother vanish
se pierden en la nada	leaving nothingness in her stead
y tú de nuevo vuelves	and once again in my soul
en mi alma a aparecer.	you, my love, are unfurled.)

The position of the mother is ambiguous, for she is present during the day yet slips quickly into the "nada" that equally completes the "jornada." She falls into the darkness in which her body is juxtaposed with the nocturnal dreams of Rosario. In the evening, the mother disappears, and like the Barthesian mother she celebrates "with relief: the night is over."[24]

This juxtaposition of mother and lover is less about creating distance between two bodies and more about folding together the bodies, a duplicitous love. I am reminded here again of Barthes: "I am then two subjects at once: I want maternity *and* genitality."[25] This declaration of love for the mother, "as much as his homosexuality," as Wayne Koestenbaum explains, "separates Barthes from customary behavior."[26] For Koestenbaum, there is an intimate connection between Barthes's homosexuality and his love for his mother: his matrophilia. I agree with Koestenbaum that this "separates Barthes from customary behavior," but what does such a separation mean for Acuña and his poem and subsequently *Doña Herlinda y su hijo*?

On the one hand, I do not want to suggest that Acuña was homosexual; on the other, it is important to flirt with a certain amount of queerness, especially since this is what Hermosillo's film does. Flirting "creates the uncertainty it is also trying to control," as Phillips has written,[27] and Hermosillo's film disturbs and calls into question the sexuality of Acuña without ever having to suggest it explicitly. We are flirting with that possibility. We will find no "smoking gun" in Acuña's poem, but there is certainly something queer unfolding in it. Something that speaks as much to maternity as it does, seemingly, to genitality. I imagine that what is "most jarring" is likely this duplicitous subjectivity that desires the maternal and the genital. Love for the mother is a flirtation with the incest taboo and with one of the "most despised and repudiated features"[28] of gay male subjectivity, the devoted son and his beloved and adored mother.

With this flirtation in mind, I focus on the poem's queerer moments and consider how we might read the poem queerly. In the fourth stanza of Acuña's poem, we are presented with what might be understood as the shameful aspects of his love. The complexity of love is considered once more, particularly in terms of recognition and reciprocity. The poet, moreover, is almost too recognized by his amorous other, and he is a lover who recognizes too much.

comprendo que en tus ojos	(I know that never again
no me he de ver jamás,	can I see my face in your eyes
y te amo y en mis locos	yet in my delirious pain

y ardientes desvaríos	my love for you still burns.
bendigo tus desdenes,	I give thanks for your disdain,
adoro tus desvíos,	adore your evasive turns
y en vez de amarte menos	and instead of loving you less,
te quiero mucho más.	my passion soars to new skies.)

This stanza, at least initially, relies on recognition. It calls on the eyes of the beloved, who sees the poet in all of his "locos y ardientes desvaríos." But what is this madness for which he begs "tus desdenes" and for which he adores "tus desvíos"? What we confront here, of course, is one of queer theory's most persistent and written about affects: shame. Although a theorist such as Michael Snediker[29] has cautioned readers and fellow queer theorists about privileging what Silvan Tomkins calls "negative affect," this stanza, I believe, requires recognition and discussion of shame, particularly queer shame. Douglas Crimp writes in his essay "Mario Montez, for Shame" that "shame is both productive and corrosive of queer identity, the switching point between a stage fright and a stage presence, between being a wallflower and a diva, so too is it simultaneously productive and corrosive of queer reevaluations of dignity and worth."[30] One can read the fourth stanza as being caught in this tension "between introversion and extroversion," as Sedgwick suggests.[31] The poet recognizes his "locos y ardientes desvaríos" and acknowledges the displeasure of his amorous other: he has been shamed, yet in this shame he continues to love. This doubling tension directs the amorous—yet shameful—attention toward the mother as much as his amorous other. From whom is the poet begging "tus desdenes"? This shamefulness is all the more present in the closing scene, in which Rodolfo recites this poem with his mother seated beside him.

Before moving analysis of the film and poem further, I want to attend to the question of shame, particularly in the context of Hispanic and Latin studies. One essential problem, at least for some scholars, with Crimp's argument about shame is its negation of race. Lawrence La Fountain-Stokes, for example, argues in his remarkably astute article "Gay Shame, Latina- and Latino-Style: A Critique of White Queer Performativity" that "Crimp doesn't make much out of Móntez's Puerto Ricanness or of her ethnoracial difference or colonial status; in fact it is almost as if her Puerto Ricanness were irrelevant, except to mark her Catholic religiosity and origins in the culture of machismo."[32] I want to be cautious here in my treatment of shame, particularly given the controversy surrounding not only Crimp's essay but also the entire collection of essays, *Gay Shame*, from which I take his essay.[33] My contention here is that what is shameful about Acuña's poem is what makes a reader such as Balderston uncomfortable. The shame is about a boy in love with his mother. Mavor, for instance, in summarizing one of Winnicott's case studies, observes how Winnicott "turns the sweet, maternal play of the boy into a place of shame and anxiety."[34] My contention about shame here is less about the "ethnoracial difference or colonial status" of Acuña and more about the shame and anxiety surrounding the "sweet, maternal play of the boy." Indeed, this shame is intimately connected to effeminophobia, "a pervasive fear of effeminate boys."[35] As Mavor further writes, "such shame is familiar to all boys and 'boyish men' who love their mothers in a culture of what Eve Kosofsky Sedgwick calls 'effeminophobia.'"[36] Thus, the shame that I am negotiating here is one that a boy who loves his mother feels or that we are made to feel on his behalf.

Doña Herlinda y su hijo contains only the fifth, sixth, and seventh stanzas, or the centre, of Acuña's poem. As viewers of the film, we are privileged to hear only these stanzas, undoubtedly the queerest stanzas in which the idealization of mother and lover are most clearly elaborated. More importantly, the film does not deny the queerness of these stanzas; indeed, I would argue, it *insists* on it. Balderston writes of the scene that "this melodramatic lyric is worthy of being transformed into a bolero,"[37] which, for knowing critics, is a genre that José Quiroga has understood in queer terms. Quiroga argues that "boleros allow gay men to deploy and suspend the borders implicit in the genre, and to motivate them according to their own wishes and desires."[38] Acuña's poem, thus, if "worthy of being transformed into a bolero," must also be part of a queer genre in which gay men can appropriate these songs for "their own wishes and desires." This is precisely what Hermosillo does in *Doña Herlinda y su hijo*.

The stanzas at the film's close have proven to be difficult for Rodolfo to memorize. Viewers have heard parts of the poem when he "memorized it in the sauna with the help of Ramón, who seems to have a better memory for poetry than he does."[39] The closing sequence of the film returns us to the earlier sauna scene, and we are reminded, as viewers, that the poem has been recited between just Rodolfo and Ramón before its public recitation by Rodolfo. The poem has thus been heard by Ramón in both a remarkably private space and subsequently a public space. In the sauna scene, we hear the following verse:

A veces pienso en darte	(Sometimes I think I should give you
mi eterna despedida,	a final, eternal farewell,
borrarte de mis recuerdos	erase you from all recollection,
y hundirte en mi pasión	submerge you beneath passion's waves,
mas si es en vano todo	but if all of this is in vain,
y el alma no te olvida,	if your presence, my soul can't dispel,
¿Qué quieres tú que yo haga,	what do you want me to do,
pedazo de mi vida?	O love of my life, pray tell?
¿Qué quieres tú que yo haga,	What do you want me to do
con este corazón?	with this heart that still yearns, still craves?)

The poem's questions are important particularly in the sauna scene, in which Rodolfo negotiates many loves: Olga, Doña Herlinda, and of course Ramón. Why is Ramón able to memorize the poem, or why does he already know the poem? One can certainly imagine that the poem is all too prescient for him. In this moment, it is no longer a monologue but a dialogue between Rodolfo and Ramón. The film could lose its promise of "happily ever after," as is so common in our love stories. Indeed, this part of the film seems to flirt with the tragic possibility of the failure of Rodolfo's amorous relations, particularly since viewers have learned that Ramón is thinking of finding a place of his own. Rodolfo knows that he is flirting with failure and asks Ramón what he wants him to do. Ramón, as Rodolfo knows, is but a "pedazo" of his life.

Failure to memorize the poem is perhaps troubled by realization that, in reciting it, Rodolfo negotiates several loves while necessarily also admitting, as Kristeva would suggest, that, "contrasted with the love that binds a mother to a son, all other 'human relationships' burst like blatant shams." The sham and the shame of eros are brought to the forefront in the poem, and Rodolfo must account for his many failures in this moment: his confusion about his relationships with his mother, Olga, and Ramón and his inability to put into words each of these loves, even when the words are provided for him through the poem. One is reminded here that stuttering is often a "hostile anal-sadistic manifestation" and that analysts look "to an earlier stage of development where the infant struggles between states of fusion and the aggression associated with the healthy urge to separate from a mother whose need is for the child to remain merged."[40] If we read the inability to utter the poem without the stutter, then perhaps we can see this failed memory as symptomatic, once more, of the incomplete Oedipal cycle. Likewise, Ernest Jones notes that Freud asked Ferenczi if stammering might be "caused by a displacement upwards of conflicts over excremental functions."[41] Clearly, the inability to remember the poem has profound psychoanalytic implications that revolve around the mother and the anus. More particularly and clinically, we might go so far as to suggest that Rodolfo is plagued by alexithymia, a dysfunctional emotional awareness of himself and those around him; however, I would contend that much of this alexithymia is necessarily attached to the earlier psychoanalytic challenges that remain unresolved.

The poem is used in a variety of ways and for a variety of audiences. Its seventh stanza, which we hear for the first time in the closing sequence, is perhaps the most discomforting—or our discomfort has been growing throughout—because it brings together all of the amorous and erotic tensions in the film:

¡Qué hermoso hubiera sido	(How lovely it would have been
vivir bajo aquel techo,	to live beneath one crest,
los dos unidos siempre	united and bound forever,
y amándonos los dos;	same home, same roof, same sod;
tú siempre enamorada,	you, enamoured always,
yo siempre satisfecho,	me, contented, at rest,
los dos una sola alma,	the two of us, one soul,

los dos un solo pecho,   the two of us, one breast,
y en medio de nosotros   and, held in an embrace between us,
mi madre como un Dios!   my mother, like a God!)

In this stanza, the poet, like Rodolfo, recognizes that he is conflicted by his desire for both maternity and genitality. The stanza tells the love story of Rodolfo; more particularly, it shows that he has accomplished what Acuña never could. Balderston explains that "What was impossible in the Mexico of 1873, the coexistence of passionate love with the bourgeois family, and is posed as a utopian dream of a home with the beloved Rosario and the loved mother is made real in the film."[42] Balderston is correct, but the film goes further. Rodolfo accomplishes quite a bit more than Acuña's poem, for he has managed to live "bajo aquel techo" with Olga, his "madre como un Dios," and the unspoken (though already spoken to) Ramón. All of this culminates in the question from the previous stanza: "¿Qué quieres tú que yo haga / pedazo de mi vida?" If Rodolfo recites the poem to his beloved, then it is important to ask which "pedazo de [su] vida" is the beloved. There are, as viewers of the film know, many elements in Rodolfo's amorous life.

As complex as all of this surely is, there is still more happening. Mavor has suggested that to read boyishly "is to covet the mother's body as a home both lost and never lost."[43] *Doña Herlinda y su hijo* is perhaps one of the clearest examples of the architecture of matrophilia. Rodolfo, of course, will never again inhabit his mother's body; however, the home becomes a part of—metonymous with—the mother's own body, a body that the mother is always willing to expand in a form of metaphorical pregnancy. "When Rodolfo and Olga return from their honeymoon," Balderston explains, Doña Herlinda "proposes the ultimate wedding gift . . . architectural drawings showing various new rooms added to the house, including a tower room where Ramón can practice his French horn."[44] The house, like the pregnant mother's body, the body with a growing child, can always expand to accommodate the family. Unlike the pregnant body, however, in Doña Herlinda's world there is no particular need to deliver Rodolfo from the body. Rodolfo can literally always be a part of and stay perpetually in his mother's home. In psychoanalytic terms, we have a problem. Christina Wieland notes that "separation from the mother is part of the working through of the Oedipus complex,"[45] and in the case of *Doña Herlinda y su hijo* this "working through" can never take place since Doña Herlinda's body is always expanding, always accommodating, and never failing Rodolfo.

Rodolfo, in many ways, is always a boy in his mother's home. Throughout the film, one finds toys scattered around the home. A toy car, for example, explores the contours of the male body. His "boyish ways keep him tied to his mother's apron strings. To be 'tied to the apron strings (of a mother . . .),' so says the *Oxford English Dictionary*, is to be wholly under her influence."[46] Rodolfo is almost literally tied to his mother's body—the corporal body and the architectural body of the home—bodies always willing to change, to grow, to expand, all in the hope of continually accommodating his "boyish ways." Moreover, Acuña's poem reinforces Mavor's notion of a boy who is wholly under the influence of his mother. In the poem, the mother is understood as if she were "como un Dios." Rodolfo, the boyish man, surrounded by children in his profession as a pediatrician, luxuriates in the presence of his mother. He demands her presence.

Mavor writes that "In the beginning of an infant's life he understands himself to be one with his mother. He is not separate from his mother. The attentive mother understands this and gives into it, with pleasure."[47] Although Mavor is concerned with the Winnicottian mother, one cannot help but note how Doña Herlinda, in a sense, is the mother at the "beginning of an infant's life," yet, of course, Rodolfo is hardly an infant. Indeed, by the end of the film, this boyish man is the father of an infant.

What is arguably discomforting to critics and viewers of the film, I would argue, is this effeminate boy who has undoubtedly fallen in love with his mother. Although I am reluctant to suggest that critics are effeminophobic, I do contend that there is a general reluctance to accept the effeminate boy/man. I agree with Sedgwick that even "the gay movement has never been quick to attend to the issues concerning effeminate boys."[48] The challenge that a film such as *Doña Herlinda y su hijo* and a poem such as Acuña's present is not just the discomfort associated with the Oedipal complex but—perhaps especially—the fear of effeminate boys.

This effeminophobic question is made all the more clear when we begin to consider the sexuality of Rodolfo. His boyishness extends far beyond just his relationship with his mother. Throughout the film, we come to see him as a typical "macho" male. Indeed, Olga suggests to Ramón at one point that Rodolfo is a macho. However, in the private spaces, slowly but surely, we are less and less certain of this claim. This question reaches its climax in the tower room. In their analyses, Foster, Balderston, and Russo all seem to agree that this scene is particularly important because of how it subverts—indeed calls into question—our expectations of gender and sexuality. "Although Ramón is generally portrayed in the feminized role of the insertee, in this scene . . . it is Rodolfo," Foster explains, "who is leisurely serviced by Ramón."[49] Like Foster, I want to dwell on this scene because it is through this scene, delicately buttressed between the two readings of Acuña's poem, that we can further explore the shameful aspects of *Doña Herlinda y su hijo*.

A lot of "meaning" happens in this scene but likely goes unnoticed. I do not think that it is an accident that Foster, for example, has discussed this scene; nor do I think that it is merely critical excitement about the bottoming macho. Instead, this scene brings together the many loves—many shameful loves—that Rodolfo tries to negotiate. Indeed, in what follows, I suggest that what is most noticeable about sexuality in *Doña Herlinda y su hijo* is the missing phallus.

Annie Potts has observed that "there exists a synecdochal relationship between the man and his penis" and that "the penis stands in and up for the man."[50] Although I am not interested in contesting the veracity of this claim—for indeed it seems to be (is?) axiomatic—I suggest that the queerness of the film resides not in the fact that it is about a gay man but in the fact that it deflates this "synecdochal relationship." Likewise, though Peter Lehman argues that "the phallus most easily retains its awe and mystique when the penis is hidden,"[51] Hermosillo makes no effort to hide the penis in *Doña Herlinda y su hijo*. Particularly, the film does not seem to be interested in the phallus at all; rather, it is fundamentally inter-

7.1 *Film still from Doña Herlinda*

ested in, intrigued by, and fascinated with the anus. Rodolfo's anus becomes the site where meaning can be found, the site where the various shameful threads can be tied together. Ultimately, I argue, his sexual positioning is intimately related to his matrophilia and the attending effeminophobia, which renders the film so discomforting and provides its queer feeling.

On the one hand, Balderston's invocation of the French horn is important because it seemingly revolves around the oral-phallic; on the other, Balderston speaks of the French horn in relation to Ramón's private space.[52] In both instances, but especially the first, when viewers see Ramón playing the French horn, his fist is lodged in its mouth.

Although this is customary for the instrument, so as to manipulate pitch, it is also our first clue that perhaps Ramón is not quite the effeminate man that he might seem to be. The visual focus throughout this scene is not on the oral-phallic component of the instrument but on the fist lodged in it. Hermosillo clearly directs our attention to the positioning of the hand; indeed, once we are made aware of this image, it is nearly impossible to ignore. As in

Acuña's poem, which "overwhelms the entirety of my reading," I am struck by this fisting image in the opening sequence of the film.

Barthes speaks in *Camera Lucida* of punctum as the "sting, speck, cut, little hole" of the image. It is hard not to misread the Barthesian "little hole" in light of the image of Ramón's fist tightly lodged in the French horn. The anus, and especially sexuality attached to it, have become "the essence of homosexuality, the very ground zero of gayness,"[53] and this must be acknowledged in the context of *Doña Herlinda y su hijo*. The piercing image that opens the film is indicative of something, which becomes clear only as viewers watch the film.

What should be clear when viewing *Doña Herlinda y su hijo* is that the film, like anal eroticism, "subverts categories and complicates notions of gender and power that long for stability."[54] Scholars of Latin American sexuality, particularly male homosexuality, have long noted the canonical and popular presence of Octavio Paz's *El laberinto de la soledad* (The Labyrinth of Solitude), and I contend that Hermosillo actively engages with and critiques Paz's theory of sexuality. For Paz, the verb *chingar* "es un verbo masculino, activo, cruel: pica, hierre, desgarra, mancha. Y provoca una amarga resentida satisfacción en el que lo ejecuta" ("The verb is masculine, active, cruel: it stings, wounds, gashes, stains. And it provokes a bitter, resentful satisfaction").[55] Moreover, Paz explains that "El chingón es el macho, el que abre," and thus, in contrast, "[l]o chingado es lo pasivo, lo inerte y abierto" ("The chingón is the macho, the male; he rips open the chingada, the female, who is pure passivity, defenseless, [and opened]").[56] It is not a stretch of the imagination to associate this discourse with male homosexuality, particularly in Latin contexts. Tomás Almaguer, for instance, argues through Paz that "Aggressive, active, and penetrating sexual activity, therefore, becomes the true marker of the Mexican man's tenuous masculinity."[57] This "tenuous masculinity" continues in more recent scholarship on male homosexuality: "While the *pasivo* role is associated with femininity and a man who is penetrated is seen as less of a man, the *activo* role in anal sex carries less stigma and at times may even enhance the social standing of the performer."[58] For this reason, *Doña Herlinda y su hijo* is so surprising (and discomforting). Viewers have been led to believe that Rodolfo is "el que abre" (he who opens), and in the end they realize that it is Ramón who is "el macho."[59]

However, a close reading of the film shows that we have been provided with cues and clues that Rodolfo might not be as big a macho as we are led to believe. The opening sequence of the film is important because it "pica, hiere, desgarra, mancha" ("stings, wounds, gashes, stains"),[60] just as the Barthesian punctum is a "sting, speck, cut, little hole." Moreover, we should not forget that the punctum "should be revealed only after the fact."[61] Indeed, this is precisely what happens in our reading of the film. The first viewing of *Doña Herlinda y su hijo* likely does not reveal the opening punctum; instead, viewers become aware of it only as the film progresses, and likely they miss the punctum in the same way, as Vito Russo notes, that they miss "the jar of lubricant [given] for his birthday."[62] *Doña Herlinda y su hijo* reveals its complexity only in the closing sequence, in which Rodolfo recites Acuña's poem, the moment when viewers are most discomforted by his matrophilia, intimately linked, as I shall argue, to effeminophobia and his effeminate position.

But, before getting ahead of myself, let us pay attention to the tower scene, in which Rodolfo and Ramón retire to a room in a tower that Doña Herlinda has had constructed for Ramón as a wedding gift for Rodolfo and Olga. This scene, considered by Foster and Balderston, absolutely challenges gender norms and expectations because Rodolfo is the recipient of the action. He is the passive partner. However, considering the opening image of Ramón playing his French horn, we might well reconsider this scene. What kind of action is Rodolfo receiving? Foster and Balderston are likely correct in their assertion that this is a sexual episode, but again what kind of sex is it? I suggest—even if only in the realm of flirting with the possibility—that the scene can be (and perhaps should be) read as an example of fisting. It is telling, for example, that throughout the scene we can only see one of Ramón's hands (or one of his arms). Where then, we might ask, is the other hand, and what is it doing?

James Miller describes fisting as "[a] long and elaborate ritual" that involves "the slow, gradual introduction of first fingers, then the hand, and eventually the arm, lubricated with vast quantities of Crisco."[63] It is telling that before we see Rodolfo and Ramón we see clothing

7.2 Film still from Doña Herlinda

strewn over the floor of the tower room and an open Nivea tin, missing a fistful of cream. We can only speculate on what precisely happens in this scene, but clearly Rodolfo, in the words of Paz, is "lo pasivo, lo inerte y abierto." Our earliest introduction to Ramón is with his hand in the bell of his French horn, and that image penetrates our visual awareness of his identity. It is fascinating that the oral-phallic quality of the musical instrument is almost entirely negated in the film in favour of the anal dimensions of the instrument.

In *Three Essays on Sexuality*, Freud observes that "Certain regions of the body, such as the mucuous membrane of the mouth and anus, . . . seem, as it were, to be claiming that they should themselves be regarded and treated as genitals."[64] Although there is undoubtedly an oral-phallic component to the French horn (indeed to many instruments), telling is that the French horn also requires manipulation of the bell, which symbolizes the anus, by the hand. Most interesting, for our purposes, is the way in which Hermosillo focuses not on the oral dimensions but on the anal dimensions of the instrument. As I have argued throughout *Reading from Behind*, we can recognize the role of the phallus, but we do not aim to reify it.

The challenge, therefore, is to move away from the phallus. We are too accustomed to the idea that "if sex means penetration, and penetration means penis, then there's no sex in the absence of a penis."[65] However, in the context of the scene in question, sex undoubtedly occurs in it. My contention, however, is that the sex need not be read as phallically dependent, and if we pay attention to the cues throughout the film we most often see images of Ramón with his fist tightly lodged in an aperture. Moreover, as Lehman has suggested, if "the phallus most easily retains its awe and mystique when the penis is hidden," then Hermosillo does the phallus no favours by showing it. The anus, on the other hand, is nearly always hidden, nearly always private. The "awe and mystique" in *Doña Herlinda y su hijo* are the shame of anal eroticism, especially since Rodolfo is the receptive partner.

The complex relationship between the receptive partner and anal pleasure has long been theorized in sexuality studies, particularly in Latin American studies. The receptive partner is "lo pasivo, lo inerte y abierto," as Paz has suggested. It is telling that he uses "neuter" forms of language or has neutered the noun. Likewise, Halperin writes that

> Any gay man who forsakes the ranks of the privileged gender and the designed gender style, who lowers himself to the undignified, abject status of the effeminate, the fairy, the poof, the bitch, the sissy, the flaming queen, incurs the easy ridicule and cheap contempt of both the straight world and the gay world—and even, for all he knows (or fears), the disdain of his own lover.[66]

My argument, as I have been stressing throughout, is that this shameful forsaking of "gender style" is discomforting for critics of *Doña Herlinda y su hijo*. The challenge is undoubtedly twofold: Rodolfo is a mama's boy, and he has lowered himself "to the undignified, abject status" noted by Halperin.

We will recall that "to be penetrated is to abdicate power,"[67] at least following the Foucauldian paradigm established in *The History of Sexuality* but also as we have seen in various writings on Latin sexuality. But this abdication of power does quite a bit more in *Doña Herlinda y su hijo*. Bersani argues that "Nothing is more threatening to culturally enforced boundaries between men and women than a man participating in the jouissance of real or fantasmatic female sexuality."[68] In the psychoanalytic reading of jouissance, it is telling that for Rodolfo we never witness any sort of phallic jouissance, unless we anticipate and endorse a notion of the phallic anus, as Guss has attempted to do in his work. He explains that "The anus becomes active as it becomes a source of pleasure, an organ of desire, an urgent, engorged organ that demands to be recognized."[69] But this does not seem to be the narrative in *Doña Herlinda y su hijo*, for the anus has largely been repressed or hidden. Clearer is the abdication of phallic power and the "jouissance of real or fantasmatic female sexuality." Bersani has suggested that "the rectum is the grave in which the masculine ideal . . . of proud subjectivity is buried."[70] My intention here is not to misread Bersani's comment or to impose a particular remark about the AIDS crisis on Rodolfo's body (though, at this point in our history, it is hard not to see the foreshadowing) but to contend that his rectum is ultimately the place where any notion of the masculine ideal or macho is necessarily buried. We might go so far as to suggest that his dream of a masculine ideal and macho identity for himself can only ever be buried in the rectum precisely because Rodolfo can never achieve the masculine ideal since he is always, and forever will be (as Acuña's poem makes clear), the son of Doña Herlinda.

It is imperative, I believe, that we carefully and critically read male femininity, effeminophobia, precisely because of its correlation with the renunciation of phallic power, which discomforts viewers of the film. I am thus suggesting that we are discomforted not by the matrophilia per se, but by the correlation between matrophilia and male femininity. This discomfort is effeminophobic, even though we might have no known or declared hatred of the effeminate male. We must remember, as Sedgwick has noted, that "the gay movement has never been quick to attend to issues concerning effeminate boys."[71] Halperin goes further: "To participate openly and avowedly in cultural practices that seem to express transgendered subjectivity, or that are marked as feminine . . . is socially, and erotically, risky for gay men."[72] The discomfort that *Doña Herlinda y su hijo* provokes is negotiated by effeminophobia, the abdication of phallic and male power, and above all because Rodolfo *should not be* the receptive partner. Indeed, even when we are provided with cues and clues, we largely choose—consciously or otherwise—to ignore them.

Doña Herlinda y su hijo, as I have suggested above, is a queer film, but its queerness occurs not only because it deals with gay men but also because it leads to discomfort among viewers, which brings together Rodolfo's matrophilia and effeminophobia. The problem is that seemingly, at least within the context of the film, one cannot have one without the other. The film ensures the possibility of—indeed the need for—effeminophobia through its repeated renunciation of phallic power in favour of anal jouissance or what Lacan and others might call "feminine jouissance." The queerest moments of the film are ostensibly found in the ways that it continues to disrupt and subvert the viewer's experience of it.

CHAPTER 8

Vengeful Vidal

Both heterosexuality and homosexuality are the
precarious outcome of a desire which knows no name.
—GUY HOCQUENGHEM

IN THIS LAST CHAPTER, WE RETURN TO AMERICAN
literature: Gore Vidal's *Myra Breckinridge* (1968), an
over-the-top novel that includes one of the most famous
rape scenes in twentieth-century literature. But this
scene, I argue, is worthy of consideration and should be studied
in a slow and methodical fashion because of the ways in which it
challenges our ideas about anal desire, anal sexuality, and anal orientations. Above all, this book brings together elements from each
of the earlier chapters, so we see anal desire, anal sexuality (fingers,
dildos, penetration), and the impossibility of orientation.

In summarizing *Myra Breckinridge*, John Carlevale explains that,
"Until her sex-change operation in Copenhagen, Myra Breckinridge
was one Myron Breckinridge, a struggling New York intellectual
and film critic, whose frustrated efforts to dominate other men by
submitting to them sexually led him to seek fulfilment as a woman."[1]
Myra Breckinridge is Myra's story of her life as Myra. The novel
functions like a diary or narrative therapy, wherein she writes her

daily routine, her desires and dreams, and we become aware that her analyst, Randolph Montag, is the intended reader. Myra is a complex character "whom no man will ever possess."[2] We are told that she "is a creature of fantasy, a daydream revealing the feminine principle's need to regain once more the primacy that she lost at the time of the Bronze Age when the cock-worshipping Dorians enslaved the West."[3] In a sense, Vidal's novel, as we shall see, is a lengthy critique of phallocentrism and thus becomes an ideal text for a project such as *Reading from Behind*.

As a novel, *Myra Breckinridge* is an "iconoclastic, gender-bending novel that simultaneously exploited and exploded traditional genres,"[4] which makes it, for some critics, complex and confused. Purvis E. Boyette, for instance, suggests that it "is not a novel at all, in the same sense that *Tristram Shandy* is not a novel."[5] Once more, it seems, we must attend to generic orientation when we deal with questions of sexual orientation. Boyette's solution is to think in terms of satire, particularly what Northrop Frye calls Menippean satire, which features "an attack on a philosophy, grotesque exaggeration, caricature, the diminution of human beings into animals or machines, and a radical dislocation of conventional perspectives."[6] Frye argues that "characters are stylized, stereotyped, presented as incarnations of theory,"[7] different from Fiedler's "innocent homosexuality," not a stereotype but an archetype found in literary fiction. The stereotype itself is stylized, presented as if it were a theory. Frye further suggests that "the type of fantasy peculiar to the Menippean form is not allegorical, nor romantic, nor humorously grotesque, but a deliberate attempt to get away from customary association, to reduce sense experience to one of many possible categories, to bring out the tentative, *als ob* basis of our thinking."[8] I return to Frye not to advocate a Frygian reading of *Myra Breckinridge* (though it might be a useful pursuit for another critic) but to urge us to avoid the temptation to read Vidal's text as merely allegorical, as I think critics are often prone to do. Even Boyette, who positions the text as a Menippean satire, ultimately succumbs to temptation and positions it as an allegory about the demise of American culture (long before Allan Bloom and others would during yet another game of the culture wars).

Meanwhile, a more recent critic, Carlevale, has read the fiction of the 1960s by attending to the "Dionysian Revival." He argues that *Myra Breckinridge* "is the era's most complete prophet of the Dionysian."[9] Dionysus, of course, is "the god of intoxication, madness, ecstasy, and metamorphosis."[10] The Dionysian thus has much in common with how Boyette understands the Menippean satire: a poetic form of excess in which we always flirt with and ultimately go beyond imposed limits and boundaries. Or, at the least, the poetic form has called into question the imposition of those very limits and boundaries that govern our society.

Initial response to the novel was governed chiefly by moralistic tyranny. Boyette establishes this tyranny in the opening paragraph of his article:

> I had first thought to entitle this essay "*Myra Breckinridge* Is Queer; or the Omission of an Article," so that my title would make two points: that the novel is not about *a* homosexual and that we have to watch carefully Gore Vidal's facetious use of language. In other words, I intend to take *Myra Breckinridge* seriously as a work of fiction and, in its kind, as a serious work of art. In academic circles, one is inclined to regard "coast-to-coast bestsellers" with scarcely disguised contempt, and my first impulse is to applaud newspaper critics like Josh Greenfield who dismiss popular novels with "serious criticism need not apply." But if *Myra Breckinridge* is to be salvaged from the pornographer's bin, we shall have to look at the work rather more seriously than the thousands who have read the book for prurient reasons alone.[11]

Boyette's invocation of queer, as we shall see, is important; however, for the time being, we should note how Boyette speaks of "scarcely disguised contempt" being the modus operandi for "serious critics" when considering a "coast-to-coast bestseller." I suppose, then, that the difference between serious critics and other critics is that, unlike the former, the latter are honest and need not scarcely disguise their contempt. *Time* magazine, for instance, includes a review that begins thus: "Has literary decency fallen so low—or has fashionable camp risen that high?"[12] *Myra Breckinridge*, its reception, and its adaptation have all been caught up in questions of literary value, which, I must admit, are some of the most boring questions that literary scholars and critics can take up, especially when a work is not intended to be read alongside those of our so-called geniuses.

Nevertheless, Harold Bloom writes, "after many readings, *Myra Breckinridge* continues to give wicked pleasure, and still seems to have fixed the limit beyond which the most advanced aesthetic neopornography ever can go."[13] His sentiment was unchanged by the time he wrote *The Western Canon: The Books and School of the Ages* (1994), in which he declares that *Myra Breckinridge* is "sublimely outrageous."[14] Even while he laments the rise of the "School of Resentment," which seeks to destroy the canon in the name of "multiculturalism," he cannot let go of his appreciation of Vidal's novel. I would go so far as to argue that, for all of Bloom's cantankerous comments deriding multiculturalism, there is something of a queer streak, particularly a gay one, that runs through his canons. But his continued appreciation of *Myra Breckinridge* is interesting, to say the least, especially since it seemingly represents everything that he laments, yet, as he himself admits, the novel is a work to be read and reread.

Nevertheless, the novel has remained largely unstudied, especially if we compare it with Vidal's earlier *The City and the Pillar* (1948), now recognized as one of his most important contributions to literature. However, scholars have worked to attend to *Myra Breckinridge* and offer a range of critiques of it. In an early article, "*Myra Breckinridge*: A Study in Identity," John F. Wilhelm and Mary Ann Wilhelm position the novel alongside Nathaniel West's *The Day of the Locust* and F. Scott Fitzgerald's *The Last Tycoon*, both of which use "Hollywood as a microcosm of society."[15] Unfortunately, they ultimately speak of how the novel and its author demonstrate "a pathological and destructive way of life."[16] What I want to highlight here is that Vidal's novel is complex and complicated; so too is its reception.

Charles Berryman imagined, as early as 1980, that "no doubt a few graduate students are now at work on dissertations comparing the *Wife of Bath* with *Myra Breckinridge*."[17] Neville Hoad explains that in *Fear of a Queer Planet* Michael Warner positions "Myra Breckinridge as a messiah for global queerness."[18] Likewise, in an obituary for Vidal, Dennis Altman argues that *Myra Breckinridge* "should be read as the founding text of queer theory, even if it is far too frivolous to appear on graduate school reading lists."[19] Declarations of its place in queer theory are not without their own problems. Joanne Meyerowitz, for instance, observes that "Vidal appropriated the [male-to-female or MTF] confessional autobiography and reworked it as a social satire and a saga of sexual conquest," and she faults him for "not relat[ing] an arduous transition in which an uncomfortable man embarked on a new life as a woman; rather, he began with a self-made woman who reverts happily to male at the novel's end."[20] I am not entirely convinced that Myra's return to being a man is indeed a "happily ever after," as Meyerowitz would figure it, but I do recognize why some transsexual historians, theorists, and activists might be offended by the novel. Indeed, Meyerowitz explains that "Many transsexuals . . . found it wholly offensive. One MTF called it 'the worst possible publicity for the transsexual cause,' and another wrote, 'I burn every copy I can get.'"[21] The authenticity is questioned: "He [Vidal] may or may not have read the transsexual autobiographies available,"[22] and Christine Jorgenson says that he "had no scientific knowledge of his subject."[23] All of this, however, presumes that Vidal intended to provide an objective study of transsexuality in *Myra Breckinridge*, which, by all accounts, he failed to do. I am not trying to excuse Vidal or apologize for him, but trying to admit that his novel was never anything more than a literary work of prose fiction (and, of course, nothing is ever just a literary work of prose fiction, for readers will engage a text and respond to it in a variety of modes).

Unfortunately, even with the many opinions and controversies, studies of the novel, as I have noted, remain few and far between. To a certain extent, it is surprising that so few studies have been written, particularly in an age such as ours, which has benefited enormously from queer readings of literary fiction. In this spirit, I return to *Myra Breckinridge* and read it from behind, especially because of its treatment of orientation and sexuality. My argument, once more, is that anal desire and sexual orientation, though often aligned, are not inherently attached to one another. What does it mean to desire an anus, and how does this desire inform and affect our theories of sexuality, theories so often indebted to an idea of the "normal." If we accept that *Myra Breckinridge* is just a satire, then perhaps we can enter into it without fear that it is a realist text, and I am content to accept this logic if it enables study of the text. However, I do think that there is something else at stake in reading *Myra Breckinridge* from behind: a serious consideration of anal poetics, precisely at the heart of this book. What does the anus mean and do in fiction, and how do we think about it in complicated, complex, confusing, and cluttered scenarios? As with so many of the texts studied in *Reading from Behind*, Vidal's novel is difficult. What makes *Myra Breckinridge* difficult is twofold: first, as Eve Kosofsky Sedgwick wrote of Marcel Proust's *In Search of Lost Time*, it is "dizzyingly impossible";[24] second, there is, I believe, a metacritical and self-reflexive reading practice required when dealing with a text such as *Myra Breckinridge*, precisely because it unsettles and discomforts its reader.

A central challenge of *Reading from Behind* has been dealing with discomfort, and *Myra Breckinridge* thrives on it. It is important to stress the value of discomfort and its affective resonances because through discomfort we confront our deepest fears, anxieties, paranoias, and perhaps even wishes. Boyette, for instance, seems to be remarkably uncomfortable when considering the novel (one wonders why he would write an article about it given his sentiments):

> Although Vidal has written elsewhere (and quite rightly) that we can live full lives without procreating, he makes Myra's transexuality an assault on the fundamental basis of life. No pop psychology in the world can persuade us that allowing one's penis to be cut off is anything but desperate hysterical insanity, however articulate. The transexual Myra is thus the radical figure of our cultural impotence and spiritual sterility, and as the archetype pervert she is the image of a debased and debauched society.[25]

Boyette perhaps misses the point here. Admittedly, he was writing in 1971, but today it is easily fathomable that one would allow his "penis to be cut off." Nevertheless, I highlight this passage to note the "hysterical insanity" at play in responding to *Myra Breckinridge*. Boyette almost seems to protest too much. For him, the novel is an allegory of what Oswald Spengler might have called "the decline of the west" and what Allan Bloom would call "the closing of the American mind."[26]

The *irony*, a favourite word for critics of Vidal's novel (the other favourite word being *failure*), occurs when Boyette explains that "Any man who has read a substantial number of good novels suspects that Vidal has launched what amounts to a *frontal* attack on literary form as it is traditionally understood."[27] Boyette is too phallic a reader for Vidal, and we must remember that the novel is deeply skeptical of the "splendid penis,"[28] though at no point does *Myra Breckinridge* advocate what would be tantamount to a "frontal attack," which is to say castration. Vidal has had enough "cock-worshipping." Sexuality, as he shows, is far more complex, as were many other American writers during the sexual revolution; one thinks here, of course, of *Portnoy's Complaint* (1969) by Philip Roth and *Couples* (1968) by John Updike. Vidal is not providing a frontal attack but attacking literary form, so-called good novels, and sexuality from behind. In other words, a critic such as Boyette becomes all too much like Rusty Godowsky, who "allow[s] himself to be raped by a woman [Myra] wearing a dildo."[29]

Myra Breckinridge is perhaps most famous for that scene, the longest chapter in the book. Every critic writing about the novel has mentioned, at least in passing, this aspect of the narrative. In one of the first scholarly essays on the novel, Wilhelm and Wilhelm write that "The huge irony of Rusty's sham physical check-up by Myra shows him up as a terror stricken adolescent before Myra's aggressive sexual assault."[30] Catharine R. Stimpson, who devotes more attention to this scene, notes that "Myra's rape of Rusty is still ugly [today], but Myra's sadistic shouts of ecstasy as she rides her 'sweating stallion into forbidden country' revolt us, not her dildo."[31] Douglas Eisner also returns to this scene:

> To call Rusty's rape camp is to attest to both the violence
> of queer representation and the violence of gender confor-

mity. To unman Rusty requires a violent act because his own masculinity is so embattled: "the last bastion." More important, however, this violence is conjoined with humor to undercut the violence. Are we supposed to be offended or amused, repulsed or turned on?[32]

These questions are important precisely because the scene, like so much of the novel, oscillates between polarities. There is surely something repulsive about the rape, just as there is something rather titillating about it. Incidentally, one is reminded here of the use of rape in the films of Pedro Almodóvar, which provoke a range of affective responses.[33] Likewise, in considering the film's adaptation of this scene, David Scott Diffrient speaks of its being "admittedly disturbing yet hilarious."[34] One film critic for the popular press, upon the release of *Myra Breckinridge* on DVD, writes that "fucking straight guys is the best revenge."[35] This is a complicated and complex scene to consider, not least because of the violence of the event; however, it seems to be a scene that once more richly illustrates our equally complicated and complex relation to the anus.

Although much has been made of the phallus and penis as symbols, Vidal's novel carefully deflates this myth and urges us to think about other potential symbols, and in raping Rusty's "never-used entrance"[36] Myra shows just how symbolic the anus is in American culture. Critical theorists such as Catherine Waldby and Brian Pronger "posit anal receptivity, rather than castration anxiety, as the more destabilizing spectre of the hyperbolically phallic subject," and "Both view psychic resistance to anal reception as part of the motivating force behind misogynist and homophobic projective violence, and, correspondingly, both see feminist and queer political potential in attempts to dephallicize the straight male body by openly celebrating, or celebratively opening, the heterosexual male anus."[37] I want to be careful here because there is a difference, of course, between rape and "openly celebrating . . . the heterosexual male anus"; however, the correlation between phobic cultures and the anus is to the point. Indeed, the point of *Myra Breckinridge* is about the relationship between the homophobic nature of male culture and the "never-used entrance," which paradoxically is used a great deal in the construction of homophobic cultures. Pronger, for instance, explains that the "asshole . . . is the tightly closed orifice of the phallic conqueror, as well as the (perhaps) reluctantly opened orifice of the phallically conquered," and "Masculine desire protects its own phallic production by closing openings."[38] In this spirit, to allow for the opening of one of these closings is fundamentally in opposition to the definition of masculinity. To be penetrated is to be conquered, whereas to penetrate is to conquer. Leo Bersani, as noted previously, famously speaks of the rectum as the "grave in which the masculine ideal . . . of proud subjectivity is buried."[39] *Myra Breckinridge*, in many respects, foreshadows so much of the theoretical discussion that would unfold in the age of HIV/AIDS. However, we cannot help but note the ways in which, through unfolding of the buttocks in *Myra Breckinridge*, we witness "proud subjectivity" revealed in all of its shame and humiliation.

All of this admitted, there is a great deal of curiosity surrounding the anus and its pleasures, which is why various critics have begun to think about the potential of "openly celebrating, or celebratively opening, the heterosexual male anus." *Reading from Behind* as an intellectual project is perhaps overly invested in this argument, but the anus is a fully loaded symbol that we need to think about in a careful and critical fashion. Although Waldby might argue that "what theoretical feminism needs now is a strap-on,"[40] I am reluctant to insist on the literal penetration of the anus as necessary for the deconstruction of male hegemony, homophobia, and so on, for it seems that many critics of *Myra Breckinridge* were thoroughly shocked and terrorized by the anal rape scene. My argument is less about the literal need for this and more about what it means in literary and cultural texts. It is possible to think and speak about the ass and its eroticism without getting "on your knees," as Pronger might suggest (incidentally, the euphemism is remarkably ambiguous).[41] *Myra Breckinridge* imagines so much of this discussion about the anus, masculinity, and homophobia long before critical theorists began to undertake this intellectual work.

In what follows, I analyze the anus in *Myra Breckinridge* slowly and carefully by closely reading the text and highlighting how Vidal encourages us to think about the ass, and particularly how a theory of reading from behind is already contained in his novel. My devotion to slowness here is informed by Wayne Koestenbaum, who notes, in his reading of *Myra Breckinridge*, that "acts of literary production . . . may be slow."[42] What remains obvious to me is that our literary texts are sites where our theories can come into being rather than being imposed on literary texts. Theory and textual analysis work together in a delicate game of illuminating one another.

Throughout the novel, Rusty's posture is called into question; we learn that this is because of his days as a football player when Rusty broke several ribs. Thus, he tilts slightly to the left. He is, of course, in Myra's posture class. After one class, he is summoned to her office. We are told that "Rusty came to my office and sat on the straight chair beside the desk, listing to one side, legs wide apart. He was not in the least nervous. In fact, he was downright defiant, even contemptuous of me, so secure did he think himself in his masculine superiority."[43] The tension between Myra and Rusty is palpable. In a psychoanalytic sense, the scene is rich with transference, of which surely Dr. Montag is aware as he reads these notes. Myra theorizes that "Today there is nothing left for the old-fashioned male to do, no ritual testing of his manhood through initiation or personal contest, no physical struggle to survive or mate."[44] There is a ritual, of course, that tests Rusty's manhood that Myra does not acknowledge: that is, homophobia. The boy soon to become a man must prove his masculinity and his claim to manhood by renouncing what he is not: a queer, a fag, an invert, and so on. Yet, of course, his claim to masculinity is persistently called into question by Myra. Indeed, *Myra Breckinridge* as a novel might well be a significant meditation on masculinity, not least because of her own relation to masculinity and repudiation of it in both a physical and a psychic sense.

During Rusty's first private encounter with Myra, she inspects his back, with the promise of a chiropractic intervention. Myra, however, can barely contain herself when Rusty dances for her, and "the effect [was] almost unbearably erotic."[45] She speaks of "waves of lust [that] made me dizzy as those strong deep buttocks slowly moved."[46] The emphasis in this scene, as in much of the novel, is resolutely not on the phallus but on the possibility of "those strong deep buttocks" to arouse, to be gazed upon. Rusty takes off his shirt so that Myra can inspect his back: "[T]he shirt rose higher. About two inches above the navel, more hairs began."[47] His body becomes the object of her gaze, and Rusty knows this. "Aware of my interested gaze, he blushed. . . . Like so many male narcissists, he is . . . paradoxically modest: he enjoys revealing himself but only on his terms."[48] So much of this scene is caught up in the tension between eroticism and humiliation. Rusty is repeatedly humiliated by Myra: "[I]t was a moment to cherish, to exult in, to give a life for. His embarrassment was palpable" as he stands, hands against the wall, while Myra inspects his back.[49] Throughout much of this scene, his penis is hidden. Myra "pulled [his] shorts down to his knees. He gave a strangled cry, looked back over his shoulder at me, face scarlet, mouth open, but no words came," and she explains that Rusty "started to pull away from me, then stopped, recalling that he was for all practical purposes nude."[50]

The nudity further humiliates Rusty, and we need to think carefully about what Myra is doing in this scene. She highlights the "paradoxically modest" nature of the young man but does not fully reveal his body. In a sense, we might agree here with Giorgio Agamben, who suggests that "nudity is not actually a state but rather an event" and that "We can . . . only experience nudity as a denudation and a baring, never as a form and a stable possession."[51] Agamben is correct in thinking of nudity as an event rather than an essence or a state of being: that is, as readers we wait for revelation, the moment when the body will finally be revealed. And Myra does a rather spectacular job of mapping Rusty's body:

> I touched the end of the spine, a rather protuberant bony tip set between the high curve of buttocks now revealed to me in all their splendor . . . and splendor is the only word to describe them! Smooth, white, hairless except just beneath the spinal tip where a number of dark coppery hairs began only to disappear into the deep crack of the buttocks so tightly clenched that not even a crowbar could have pried them apart.[52]

His tightly clenched buttocks speak to his anxiety, fear, and humiliation in this scene. We, as readers, are located in the event of nudity, the moment of "a denudation and a baring" of Rusty's body. But only "half of the mystery" is revealed in this scene, and "the rest must wait for a more propitious time."[53] Everything about this scene aligns, I believe, with Agamben's nudity. We are witnessing a textual striptease, "an event that never reaches its completed form."[54] We know, in reality, that nakedness itself is not much of an ideological problem when contained in a private space, but it becomes problematic, erotic, enticing when it becomes an event, precisely what happens in this first scene between Myra and Rusty. In a sense, when a second scene occurs, as readers we want this striptease to be less of a tease; we want, as it were, the Full Monty.

Before the rape, Myra continues to fantasize about Rusty's eventual deflowering, as it were. She says that Rusty will soon "be shattered by me into a million fragments, that I may then rearrange him along other and more meaningful lines."[55] This moment in the novel is itself a kind of shattering because it seems to call on Bersani's notion of shattering, so central to his theories of sexuality; however, these theories would not be developed for nearly two decades. The language of Myra mimics the language of Bersani—what becomes more startling, perhaps, is that few (if any) critics have negotiated his use of shattering alongside Myra's use of shattering. (One might even be tempted to ask whether *Myra Breckinridge* influenced Bersani.)

"Self-shattering," for Bersani, "disrupts the ego's coherence and dissolves its boundaries,"[56] which makes sense when we think about the difficulty that a critic faces when trying to negotiate the various orientations at play in this scene. To wit (to queer), W. B. Yeats's "The Second Coming":

Things fall apart; the centre cannot hold;
Mere anarchy is loosed upon the world,
The blood-dimmed tide is loosed, and everywhere
The ceremony of innocence is drowned;
The best lack all conviction, while the worst
Are full of passionate intensity.[57]

Self-shattering is about the moment when "Things fall apart; the centre cannot hold," when all is lost, when one experiences "the joy of self-dissolution."[58] Although earlier critics have commented on the name Rusty, they miss the point. The point is not that his name is not Polish or not Catholic[59] but that it contains his subjectivity. As a sexual subject, he is rusty, and like rust he falls apart. His name already includes the dissolution of his subjectivity. Sexuality is "a defeat of power, a giving up, on the part of an otherwise hyperbolically self-affirming and phallocentrically constituted ego."[60] The point that we must take as essential is that "The body liberated from what Foucault scornfully called the machismo of proud male ejaculation is also the male body liberated from what may be its first experience, at once sobering and thrilling, of the limits of power."[61] Self-shattering shifts attention away from "the erotic monopoly traditionally held by the genitals"[62] and, I argue in the case of Rusty, toward his "defenceless bottom, quivering at [Myra's] touch."[63]

The ruse at play in the second scene between Myra and Rusty is that he requires a physical examination, which, for one reason or another, she is in a position to perform (or at least he is gullible enough to believe that this is the case). Although much of the attention has been focused on the strap-on dildo, which appears toward the close of this scene, I want to stress that there are two anal penetrations that should be accounted for by the literary critic. Rusty has a hole in his sock, "through which the big toe protruded," and as he begins to undress he says, "Guess I'm full of holes."[64] This is a curious quip, especially since it is not Rusty who is "full of holes" but his sock. But what it demonstrates is a discomfort with holes being used in ways that they ought not to be used or holes making themselves known that should not be known. Another set of holes, for instance, appears "beneath the elastic [of frayed Jockey shorts], two round holes, like eyes," and Myra explains, "Teasingly, I put my finger in one of those holes."[65] The various holes that appear throughout this scene are explored, poked, probed, and prodded.

Throughout this scene, Myra humiliates Rusty's masculinity, noting, for instance, that his ticklishness "is a sign of sexual fear."[66] This humiliation reaches a climax—and there are many—when she notes that Rusty feels hot and says, "we'd better take your temperature."[67] She has just commented on "The total unveiling of the buttocks . . . accomplished in an absolute, almost religious silence. They were glorious," but he has "craftily contrived to hold [his Jockey shorts] up in front, and so his honor, he believed, was only half lost."[68] Myra is telling us, without telling us, that this humiliation will only grow in severity. And, of course, it does when she takes his temperature:

> As I went over to the surgical table and prepared the ther-mometer, he watched me dully, like a trapped animal. Then I returned to my quarry and, putting one hand on each cheek at the exact point where the buttock joins thigh, I said, "Relax now."
>
> He raised up on his arms and looked around at me, eyes suddenly bright with alarm. "What?"
>
> "I've got to take your temperature, Rusty."
>
> "But . . . there?" His voice broke like a teenage boy's.[69]

The scene is entirely infantilizing. Myra continually notes his youth-fulness. And she "pushed the cheeks apart until everything—secret sphincter and all—was revealed."[70] His ass has been spread apart, and she is about to insert a thermometer into it. But is it true that his ass has never been used? After all, surely his temperature has been taken there once before, and undoubtedly this is a moment when we are called to think about anal erotics.

> Then I grew bolder. I inserted my finger into the tight hot place as far as it would go. I must have touched the prostate for he suddenly groaned, but said nothing. Then, either deliberately or through uncontrollable reflex, he brought the full force of his youthful muscularity to bear on the sphincter muscle and for a moment it felt as though my finger might be nipped off.
>
> With my free hand, I slapped his tight buttock smartly. "Relax!" I commanded. He mumbled something I could not hear and the sphincter again loosened. I then removed

my finger and inserted the thermometer, after teasing the
virginal orifice with delicate probes that made him squirm.[71]

There is no denying that this scene is rich with anal eroticism, and
like so much eroticism it is not necessarily one of mere pleasure.
We are reminded of the important negotiation of pain and pleasure
intrinsic to the erotic. Moreover, his anus becomes, in a sense, masculine, powerful, phallic, for at one moment his sphincter muscle
becomes the active agent that destabilizes the previously phallic
finger. As much as we might agree that "any social use of the anus
. . . creates the risk of a loss of identity,"[72] when "the full force of his
youthful muscularity" is called on, Rusty is "taking responsibility,"[73]
not in terms of being responsible for the situation, but in terms of
being responsible for protecting himself from identity loss, a kind
of self-shattering.

In this moment, his tightening sphincter seems to have something in common with the radical female power inscribed in the
myth of the vagina dentata, "a gruesomely direct transcription of
female power and male fear": "Metaphorically, every vagina has
secret teeth, for the male exits as less than when he entered."[74]
More to the point, and worth noting here, is that "Physical and
spiritual castration is the danger every man runs in intercourse with
a woman."[75] But Vidal rewrites this myth to include the anus. One
mode of theorizing male sexuality is that the man is likely to lose
his identity, self-shatter, or be castrated. Indeed, one might go so
far as to argue that any castration would necessarily always already
involve a loss of identity culminating in self-shattering. The point is
that, though we are horrified by what happens to Rusty, the reality
is that every man fears, in one sense or another, that he will end as
less of a man than when he began. "Sex is a struggle for identity,"
argues Camille Paglia,[76] and this certainly seems to be the case
throughout *Myra Breckinridge*. When Rusty's sphincter grabs hold
of Myra's finger, both identities are necessarily called into question,
particularly because both have renegotiated their relations to power.
Rusty has attempted to reclaim his power.

This shift in power, however, is momentary. Myra reasserts her
power throughout the remainder of the scene. As she explains,

"Carefully I was reducing his status from man to boy to child to—ah, the triumph!" For her, "The sense of power was overwhelming."[77] She explains that she needs to check Rusty for a hernia, which puts an end to the erotic striptease that has been central to the narrative. He refuses to remove his underwear, to which Myra offers "a statesmanlike compromise": "I shall have to insert my hand inside the shorts and press each testicle as required by the chart."[78] Of course, the scene is hardly over, and readers are presented with "the slow unveiling" of "Rusty's manhood in its entirety."[79] But, as Myra explains in her notes, in yet another moment of shaming, "The penis . . . was not a success, and I could see now why he was so reluctant to let me see just how short it is."[80] All of this is as much about revealing the body as it is about shaming Rusty. Throughout this scene, he becomes confused and asks Myra, "Do you want me to . . . well, to ball you?" Myra responds, "Rusty! Do you know who you are talking to?"[81] The scene reaches yet another climax when she says, "However, as a lesson, I shall ball you."[82] The roles have been fully reversed, and Myra balls him.

Throughout the chapter, readers have been teased by an ever-increasing scene of humiliation and shame, and now Myra will fully humiliate, once and for all, Rusty. She says, "Now you will find out what it is the girl feels when you play the man with her," and she reveals her strap-on dildo, which causes Rusty to exclaim, "Jesus, you'll split me!"[83] Although we would be mistaken to assume that the anus becomes a substitute or pseudo-vagina (though such a logic does exist), important here is the feminizing role at play. For Myra, penetrating Rusty will give him a sense of what it feels like for a woman. Bersani would echo these sentiments: "Women and gay men spread their legs with an unquenchable appetite for destruction. This is an image with extraordinary power . . . the infinitely more seductive and intolerable image of a grown man, legs high in the air, unable to refuse the suicidal ecstasy of being a woman."[84] In exclaiming "you'll split me," Rusty confronts the "suicidal ecstasy of being a woman" or at least something *like* a woman.

> As I approached him, dildo in front of me like the god
> Priapus personified, he tried to wrench free of his bonds,

but failed. Then he did the next best thing, and brought his knees together in an attempt to deny me entrance. But it was no use. I spread him wide and put my battering ram to the gate.

For a moment I wondered if he might not be right about the splitting: the opening was the size of a dime while the dildo was over two inches wide and nearly a foot long.[85]

Invocation of Priapus is important because, though resolutely associated with the phallic, it is through the overly endowed phallus that Myra will gain access to "the eternal feminine."[86] For the time being, however, rewriting the vagina dentata is possible through what is apparently an excessively large penis—at least from Rusty's perspective. Even Myra, however, imagines that perhaps "he might . . . be right about the splitting." In this scenario, then, it is not the vagina dentata that destroys but the phallus that is ultimately able to ruin the cavity that it penetrates. Indeed, so much of the narrative mimics and alludes to the seemingly interchangeable nature of the vagina and anus: "The pink lips opened."[87] Myra ultimately claims success: "I savored my triumph. . . . Now, in the person of Rusty, I was able, as Woman Triumphant, to destroy the adored destroyer."[88] In the language of Bersani, the shattering has been wholly completed. Rusty has been made into, as it were, a woman; his homophobia has been fully explained to him with the large dildo that penetrates "the mystery that even Mary-Ann had never seen, much less violated."[89] For Myra, this scene becomes "one of the great victories for her sex" and provides her with access to "know[ledge of] what it is like to be a goddess enthroned, and all-powerful."[90]

Penetration of the anus is the ultimate taboo for the male body, yet, as Myra points out, it has been done before. The thermometer that reads a temperature necessarily enmeshes itself between the folds. But more problematic here is what this means for the orienting of desire and sexuality. Rusty, we learn, abandons Mary-Ann for Leticia, with whom he has orgasmic sex, but he never seems to be as content as Leticia. By the close of the novel, he is "a complete homosexual," for which Myra "feel[s] a certain degree of responsibility and guilt."[91] In teaching Rusty "what it is the girl feels when you play the man with her," Myra has seemingly converted him into a gay man, so she believes. Of course, none of this is true. But in penetrating his virgin ass, she has turned him into a "complete homosexual" now thriving in the pleasure of the ass.

Before closing this chapter, I want to offer a brief commentary on rape culture and Vidal's novel. In a rape culture such as ours, this scene is horrifying, but equally it seems to expose a number of hidden fantasies. The myth of the "rape fantasy" for women—that is, that women desire to be raped—has been rightly critiqued by a range of feminist theorists (and exposed as a myth), but there is something to be said, one imagines, for the rape of the rapist, the rape of the misogynist, the rape of the homophobe. And this is what is at stake in Vidal's narrative. I want to be careful here: his narrative is *not an apology for rape*, nor is it a confirmation of rape fantasies. Even if such fantasies were true, this cannot ever be a defence for rape. It is a challenging of these very myths that informs a rape culture.

Vidal's narrative is successful precisely because it accepts the principle that perhaps these myths are true, and then in a parodic and carnivalesque fashion it fully rewrites them and turns the tables on the male body and consciousness. There is something of a reparative gesture here: rape fantasy is not about the fantasy of being raped, just as penis envy is not about a desire among women for a penis but a desire among men for a bigger penis. This scene brings together a number of supposed fantasies that women contend with on a daily basis and rewrites them in such a way that they are enacted upon the male body. There is a radical potential, in a certain regard, in this narrative, especially for queer and feminist theorists who have worked to destabilize the phallocentric nature of critical thought.

This radical potential is found in Koestenbaum's remarkable essay "The Rape of Rusty," which carefully articulates and thinks about his own readings of *Myra Breckinridge*. Although Koestenbaum has not been afforded a starring role in *Reading from Behind*, he remains a rather interesting anal theorist. As such, in what remains, I attend to his reading of this novel because it is one of the queerest readings to date and brings to the forefront what I think could be the radical potential of *Myra Breckinridge*.

Koestenbaum speaks of "butt-centeredness" as a critical posture that he "once occupied"; he proposes "that we might escape repressive structures if we focus on the ass rather than the potentially procreative genitals," but he admits that "I no longer live in that conceptual universe, but I admit affinity with the punished, and with the bodily site where punishment occurs: the rear."[92] I am not sure that he is not still "butt-centered," especially since so much of his work revolves around the butt, teasing its folds and pushing us to imagine not a world without the phallus but a world in which the butt becomes a centre, if not the centre, of attention.

Ultimately, even though Vidal's narrative makes use of a rather significant phallus, at least in terms of its size, the greater symbolic power is found in the anus. What is so shocking is that the anus is endowed with so much meaning. Through it, shattering occurs—the phallus can penetrate any hole, as it were, and retain its power. But when Rusty's ass is penetrated, the possibility of symbolic unity is called into question. Myra Breckinridge the character and *Myra Breckinridge* the novel demonstrate just how important the anus is, how its symbolism works and allows for the subject to be constitutionally whole. Again I want to be careful because Rusty is raped by Myra, but what this scene illuminates, as *Reading from Behind* as a whole has tried to do, is that the anus is remarkably significant. It has the power to restructure our identities in a way that the phallus cannot, unless, of course, through castration, at the heart of the fear that motivates male sexuality.

Notes

INTRODUCTION—No Wrong Doors: An Entryway

1   Christina Garibaldi, "Jennifer Lopez on the Year of the Booty: 'It's about Time,'" MTV *News*, October 1, 2014, http://www.mtv.com/news/1949743/jennifer-lopez-year-of-booty/.

2   Drishya Nair, "Pippa Middleton Catches Attention of Plastic Surgery Lovers," *International Business Times*, July 30, 2011, http://www.ibtimes.com/pippa-middleton-catches-attention-plastic-surgery-lovers-photos-820119.

3   "The Parking Spot Escalation," episode 9, season 6, of *The Big Bang Theory*.

4   Jack Morin, *Anal Pleasure and Health: A Guide for Men, Women, and Couples* (San Francisco: Down There Press, 2010), 11.

5   The Clinton administration instituted the "Don't ask, don't tell" policy in 1994. It enabled LGBT citizens to serve in the armed forces. However, the principle privileged silence, thus not allowing LGBT citizens to participate "openly" in service. Nor could questions be asked about sexual orientations of service people. This policy was repealed during the Obama administration in 2010.

6   Morin, *Anal Pleasure and Health*, 11.

7   Ibid.

8   Ibid., 12–13.

9   Jeffrey R. Guss, "Men, Anal Sex, and Desire: Who Wants What?," *Psychoanalysis, Culture, and Society* 12 (2007): 39.

10   Jonathan Branfman and Susan Ekberg Stiritz, "Teaching Men's Anal Pleasure: Challenging Gender Norms with 'Prostage' Education," *American Journal of Sexuality Education* 7, 4 (2012): 405.

11   Adam Phillips, *On Flirtation: Psychoanalytic Essays on the Uncommitted Life* (Cambridge, MA: Harvard University Press, 1994), 41.

12   Dan Savage, "Savage Love: No Homo," October 1, 2009, http://www.thestranger.com/seattle/SavageLove?oid=2358429.

13   Sergio Merino-Salas, Miguel Angel Arrabal-Polo, and Miguel Arrabal-Martin, "Vaginal Vibrator in the Rectum of a Young Man," *Archive of Sexual Behaviour* 38 (2009): 457.

14   Donald Meltzer, "The Relation of Anal Masturbation to Projective Identification," *International Journal of Psychoanalysis* 47 (1966): 335.

15   Bruce Fink, *A Clinical Introduction to Lacanian Psychological Theory and Technique* (Cambridge, MA: Harvard University Press, 1997), 122.

16   Branfman and Stiritz, "Teaching Men's Anal Pleasure," 417.

17   Ibid., 415.

18   Robyn Wiegman, "The Times We're In: Queer Feminist Criticism and the Reparative 'Turn,'" *Feminist Theory* 15, 1 (2014): 8.

19   Eve Kosofsky Sedgwick, *Tendencies* (Durham: Duke University Press, 1993), 23.

20   Wiegman, "The Times We're In," 7.

21   Eve Kosofsky Sedgwick, *Touching Feeling: Affect, Pedagogy, Performativity* (Durham: Duke University Press, 2003), 146.

22   Ibid., 144.

23   Ibid., 146.

24   Ibid.

25   Ibid., 125.

26   Wiegman, "The Times We're In," 7.

27   Ibid., 9.

28   Jonathan Goldberg, "Introduction," in *The Weather in Proust,* by Eve Kosofsky Sedgwick (Durham: Duke University Press, 2011), xiv.

29   Wiegman, "The Times We're In," 9.

30   The earliest version of this paper appeared in the opening issue of *GLQ: A Journal of Lesbian and Gay Studies* 1, 1 (1993): 1–16 and was revised as late as 2009 in *Gay Shame*, ed. David M. Halperin and Valerie Traub (Chicago: University of Chicago Press, 2009), 49–62. When I cite from this paper, like my citations of "Paranoid Reading and Reparative Reading," I rely on the latest version.

31   Jackie Stacey, "Wishing Away Ambivalence," *Feminist Theory* 15, 1 (2014): 40.

32   Sedgwick, *Touching Feeling,* 145.

33 Following Wiegman's lead in "The Times We're In" in thinking about the various versions of Sedgwick's paper, I will provide citations from earlier versions when there are substantive changes. In one of the earliest iterations of this paper, "Queerer than Fiction," *Studies in the Novel* 28, 3 (1996): 277–80, Sedgwick writes that it "has come to seem naïve and complaisant" (277).

34 Sedgwick, *Touching Feeling*, 126.

35 Ibid.

36 Ibid., 136.

37 Silvan Tomkins, *Shame and Its Sisters: A Silvan Tomkins Reader*, ed. Eve Kosofsky Sedgwick and Adam Frank (Durham: Duke University Press, 1995), 74.

38 Michael D. Snediker, *Queer Optimism: Lyric Personhood and Other Felicitous Persuasions* (Minneapolis: University of Minnesota Press, 2009).

39 David M. Halperin and Valerie Traub, "Beyond Gay Pride," in *Gay Shame*, ed. David M. Halperin and Valerie Traub (Chicago: University of Chicago Press, 2009), 3–40.

40 Wayne Koestenbaum, *Humiliation* (New York: Picador, 2011).

41 Sianne Ngai, *Ugly Feelings* (Cambridge, MA: Harvard University Press, 2005).

42 Ann Cvetkovich, *Depression: A Public Feeling* (Durham: Duke University Press, 2012).

43 Carol Mavor, *Black and Blue: The Bruising Passion of* Camera Lucida, La Jetée, Sans soleil, *and* Hiroshima mon amour (Durham: Duke University Press, 2012).

44 José Esteban Muñoz, "Feeling Brown, Feeling Down: Latina Affect, the Performativity of Race, and the Depressive Position," *Signs* 31, 3 (2006): 675–88.

45 Lauren Berlant, *Cruel Optimism* (Durham: Duke University Press, 2011).

46 Judith Halberstam, *The Queer Art of Failure* (Durham: Duke University Press, 2012).

47 Lauren Berlant and Lee Edelman, *Sex, or the Unbearable* (Durham: Duke University Press, 2014).

48 José Esteban Muñoz, "Thinking beyond Antirelationality and Antiutopianism in Queer Critique," PMLA 121, 3 (2006): 826.

49 Sedgwick, *Touching Feeling*, 64–65.

50 Christian Lassen, *Camp Comforts: Reparative Gay Literature in Times of* AIDS (Bielefeld: Transcript Verlag, 2011), 13n1.

51 Sedgwick, *Touching Feeling*, 134.

52 Ann Cvetkovich, "Public Feelings," *South Atlantic Quarterly* 106, 3 (2007): 462–63.

53 Sedgwick, *Touching Feeling*, 146.

54 Northrop Frye, *Collected Works of Northrop Frye*, gen. ed. Alvin A. Lee, 30 vols. (Toronto: University of Toronto Press, 1996–2012), 22: 65–66. All citations from Frye are from *Collected Works of Northrop Frye*, with volume and pagination given.

55 Lassen, *Camp Comforts*, 13n1.

56 Mavor, *Reading Boyishly: Roland Barthes, J. M. Barrie, Jacques Henri Lartigue, Marcel Proust, and D. W. Winnicott* (Durham: Duke University Press, 2007), 73.

57 José Esteban Muñoz, *Cruising Utopia: The Then and There of Queer Futurity* (New York: New York University Press, 2009), 12.

58 Wiegman, "The Times We're In," 7.

59 Sedgwick, *Touching Feeling*, 137.

60 Roland Barthes, *The Pleasure of the Text*, trans. Richard Miller (New York: Hill and Wang, 1975), 3.

61 Erin Murphy and J. Keith Vincent, "Introduction," *Criticism* 52, 2 (2010): 168.

62 Cvetkovich, "Public Feelings," 463.

63 Nishant Shahani, *Queer Retrosexualities: The Politics of Reparative Return* (Bethlehem: Lehigh University Press, 2012), 10.

64 Roland Barthes, *A Lover's Discourse: Fragments*, trans. Richard Howard (New York: Hill and Wang, 1978), 73.

65 Sedgwick, *Touching Feeling*, 123; Shahani, *Queer Retrosexualities*, 10.

66 Valerie Rohy, "In the Queer Archive: Fun Home," *GLQ: A Journal of Lesbian and Gay Studies* 16, 3 (2010): 343.

67 Ann Cvetkovich, *An Archive of Feelings: Trauma, Sexuality, and Lesbian Public Cultures* (Durham: Duke University Press, 2003), 254.

CHAPTER 1—Anal Theory, or Reading from Behind

1 Annie Potts, "'The Essence of the Hard On': Hegemonic Masculinity and the Cultural Construction of 'Erectile Dysfunction,'" *Men and Masculinities* 3 (2000): 85.

2 David M. Friedman, *A Mind of Its Own: A Cultural History of the Penis* (New York: Penguin Books, 2001), 6.

3 Mels van Driel, *Manhood: The Rise and Fall of the Penis* (London: Reaktion Books, 2009), 272.

4 Micha Ramakers, *Dirty Pictures: Tom of Finland, Masculinity, and Homosexuality* (New York: St. Martin's Press, 2000), 100.

5 Ilan Stavans, "The Latin Phallus," in *Muy Macho: Latino Men Confront Their Manhood*, ed. Ray González (New York: Random House, 1996), 145.

6 Sandra M. Gilbert and Susan Gubar, *The Madwoman in the Attic: The Woman Writer and the Nineteenth-Century Literary Imagination* (New Haven: Yale University Press, 2000), 3–4.

7   Sandra M. Gilbert and Susan Gubar, *No Man's Land: The Place of the Woman Writer in the Twentieth Century* (New Haven: Yale University Press, 1988), 3.

8   Elaine Showalter, "Feminist Criticism in the Wilderness," in *The New Feminist Criticism: Essays on Women, Literature, and Theory*, ed. Elaine Showalter (New York: Pantheon, 1985), 250.

9   Judith Butler, *Gender Trouble: Feminism and the Subversion of Identity* (New York: Routledge, 2000), 6.

10   Cited in Ann Rosalind Jones, "Writing the Body: Toward an Understanding of l'Écriture féminine," in *The New Feminist Criticism: Essays on Women, Literature, and Theory*, ed. Elaine Showalter (New York: Pantheon, 1985), 365.

11   Cited in ibid., 364.

12   Hayden White, *Tropics of Discourse: Essays in Cultural Criticism* (Baltimore: Johns Hopkins University Press, 1978), 254.

13   Jeffrey R. Guss, "Men, Anal Sex, and Desire: Who Wants What?," *Psychoanalysis, Culture, and Society* 12 (2007): 39.

14   Leo Bersani, *Homos* (Cambridge, MA: Harvard University Press, 1995), 5.

15   Eve Kosofsky Sedgwick, *Epistemology of the Closet* (Berkeley: University of California Press, 1990), 25.

16   Eric Anderson, "Adolescent Masculinity in an Age of Decreased Homohysteria," *Thymos: Journal of Boyhood Studies* 7, 1 (2013): 79.

17   R. W. Connell, *Masculinities*, 2nd ed. (Berkeley: University of California Press, 2005), 77–78.

18   Eric Anderson, *Inclusive Masculinity: The Changing Nature of Masculinities* (New York: Routledge, 2009).

19   Anderson, "Adolescent Masculinity," 82.

20   Ibid., 83, 85.

21   Ibid., 82.

22   David William Foster, "Of Gay Caballeros and Other Noble Heroes," *Bilingual Review* 29, 2–3 (2008): 26.

23   Bruce Fink, *A Clinical Introduction to Lacanian Psychological Theory and Technique* (Cambridge, MA: Harvard University Press, 1997), 122.

24   Mark McCormack, *The Declining Significance of Homophobia: How Teenage Boys Are Redefining Masculinity and Heterosexuality* (Oxford: Oxford University Press, 2012), 44.

25   Guy Hocquenghem, *Homosexual Desire*, trans. Daniella Dangoor (Durham: Duke University Press, 1993), 100.

26   Jeffrey Weeks, introduction to *Homosexual Desire,* by Guy Hocquenghem (Durham: Duke University Press, 1993), 38; emphasis added.

27   Leonard Shengold, *Halo in the Sky: Observations on Anality and Defense* (New Haven: Yale University Press, 1988), 3.

28 Hilda C. Abraham and Ernst L. Freud, eds., *A Psycho-Analytic Dialogue: The Letters of Sigmund Freud and Karl Abraham, 1907–1926*, trans. Bernard Marsh and Hilda C. Abraham (New York: Basic Books, 1965), 27.

29 Peter Gay, *Freud: A Life for Our Time* (New York: W. W. Norton and Company, 1988), 336.

30 Ibid.

31 Sigmund Freud, *The Standard Edition of the Complete Psychological Works of Sigmund Freud*, ed. and trans. James Strachey (London: Hogarth Press, 1953–74), 9: 169. All quotations from Freud are taken from this edition of his works, documented by volume and page number.

32 Cited in Eve Kosofsky Sedgwick, *Touching Feeling: Affect, Pedagogy, Performativity* (Durham: Duke University Press, 2003), 123.

33 Freud, *The Standard Edition*, 9: 170.

34 Ibid.

35 Ibid.

36 Sedgwick, *Touching Feeling*, 130.

37 Freud, *The Standard Edition*, 7: 186.

38 Lee Edelman, *No Future: Queer Theory and the Death Drive* (Durham: Duke University Press, 2004), 75.

39 Adam Phillips, *The Beast in the Nursery: On Curiosity and Other Appetites* (New York: Vintage Books, 1998).

40 Freud, *The Standard Edition*, 9: 171n2.

41 Ibid., 9: 169.

42 Foster, "Gay Caballeros."

43 Owen Berkeley-Hill, "The Psychology of the Anus," *Indian Medical Gazette* 48 (1913): 302.

44 A. A. Brill, "Anal Eroticism and Character," *Journal of Abnormal Psychology* 7, 3 (1912): 199.

45 Ernest Jones, "Anal-Erotic Character Traits," in *Papers on Psycho-Analysis* (London: Maresfield Reprints, 1977), 413.

46 Ibid.

47 Freud, *The Standard Edition*, 9: 169.

48 Jones, "Anal-Erotic Character Traits," 418.

49 Adam Phillips, *On Balance* (New York: Farrar, Straus and Giroux, 2010), 1.

50 Ibid., 4.

51 Ibid., 5.

52 Jones, "Anal-Erotic Character Traits," 423.

53 Ibid., 427.

54 Michel Foucault, *History of Sexuality*, trans. Robert Hurley, 3 vols. (New York: Vintage Books, 1978–86), 3: 29.

55 Ibid., 2: 46.

56   Leo Bersani, *Is the Rectum a Grave? And Other Essays* (Chicago: University of Chicago Press, 2010), 19.

57   Kathryn Bond Stockton, *Beautiful Bottom, Beautiful Shame: Where "Black" Meets "Queer"* (Durham: Duke University Press, 2006), 2.

58   Ibid., 5.

59   Ibid., 7.

60   Hocquenghem, *Homosexual Desire*, 95.

61   Ibid.

62   Ibid.

63   Ibid., 96.

64   Ibid., 100.

65   Judith Halberstam, *The Queer Art of Failure* (Durham: Duke University Press, 2011), 150.

66   Tim Dean, *Unlimited Intimacy: Reflections on the Subculture of Barebacking* (Chicago: University of Chicago Press, 2009), xi.

67   Michael Warner, *The Trouble with Normal: Sex, Politics, and the Ethics of Queer Life* (Cambridge, MA: Harvard University Press, 1999), 214; emphasis added.

68   Stockton, *Beautiful Bottom, Beautiful Shame*, 68.

69   Dean, *Unlimited Intimacy*, 40–41; emphasis added.

70   See Trevor Hoppe, "Loaded Meaning," *Journal of Sex Research* 48, 5 (2011): 506–08; and Octavio R. Gonzalez, review of *Unlimited Intimacy: Reflections on the Subculture of Barebacking*, by Tim Dean, *Cultural Critique* 81 (2012): 125–32.

71   Halberstam, *The Queer Art of Failure*, 150.

72   David M. Halperin, *What Do Gay Men Want? An Essay on Sex, Risk, and Subjectivity* (Ann Arbor: University of Michigan Press, 2007), 23.

73   Tim Dean, "Bareback Time," in *Queer Times, Queer Becomings*, ed. E. L. McCallum and Mikko Tuhkanen (Albany: SUNY Press, 2011), 77; emphasis added.

74   Ibid., 77–78.

75   Dean, *Unlimited Intimacy*, 50–51.

76   Lisa Duggan, *The Twilight of Equality? Neoliberalism, Cultural Politics, and the Attack on Democracy* (Boston: Beacon Press, 2003), 50.

77   Bersani, *Is the Rectum a Grave?*, 10.

78   Dean, *Unlimited Intimacy*, 51.

79   Cited in Stephen M. Whitehead, *Men and Masculinities* (London: Polity, 2002), 93.

80   Joon Oluchi Lee, "The Joy of the Castrated Boy," *Social Text* 23, 3–4 (2005): 35–56.

81   David M. Halperin, *How to Be Gay* (Cambridge, MA: Harvard University Press, 2012).

82 Eve Kosofsky Sedgwick, "How to Bring Your Kids Up Gay: The War on Effeminate Boys," in *Tendencies* (Durham: Duke University Press, 1993), 154–64.

83 Carol Mavor, *Reading Boyishly: Roland Barthes, J. M. Barrie, Jacques Henri Lartigue, Marcel Proust, and D. W. Winnicott* (Durham: Duke University Press, 2007).

84 Dean, *Unlimited Intimacy*, 66.

85 Ibid., 51.

86 Ibid., 52.

87 Ibid., 55.

88 Ibid., 56.

89 Jack Halberstam, "Queer Betrayals," in *Queer Futures: Reconsidering Ethics, Activism, and the Political*, ed. Elahe Haschemi Yekani, Eveline Kilian, and Beatrice Michaelis (Burlington: Ashgate, 2013), 184.

90 Richard Fung, "Looking for My Penis: The Eroticized Asian in Gay Video Porn," in *Men's Lives*, 6th ed., ed. Michael Kimmel and Michael A. Messner (Boston: Pearson, 2004), 546.

91 Nguyen Tan Hoang, *A View from the Bottom: Asian American Masculinity and Sexual Representation* (Durham: Duke University Press, 2014), 3–4.

92 Ibid., 6.

93 Hocquenghem, *Homosexual Desire*, 103.

94 Tan Hoang, *A View from the Bottom*, 7.

95 Gabriel García Márquez, *Autumn of the Patriarch*, trans. Gregory Rabassa (New York: Harper Perennial, 1999), 159.

CHAPTER 2—Orienting Virginity

1 Hanne Blank, *Virgin: The Untouched History* (New York: Bloomsbury, 2007); Anke Bernau, *Virgins: A Cultural History* (London: Granta Books, 2007).

2 In a forthcoming collection of essays, *Virgin Envy: Beyond the Hymen*, edited by Jonathan A. Allan, Cristina Santos, and Adriana Spahr (Regina: University of Regina Press, forthcoming), we see significant discussions of virginity that move beyond the "standard" heteronormative treatment. This collection includes essays on queer and male virginities that explicitly ask about the erasure of these virginities in scholarship.

3 Michael Amico, "Gay Youths as 'Whorified Virgins,'" *Gay and Lesbian Review* 12, 4 (2005): 34.

4 Steven G. Underwood, *Gay Men and Anal Eroticism: Tops, Bottoms, and Versatiles* (Binghamton: Harrington Park Press, 2003), 47.

5 Ibid., 145.

6 Ibid., 197.

7   Michael Hattersley, "Men in Exciting Positions," review of *Gay Men and Anal Eroticism: Tops, Bottoms, and Versatiles,* by Steven G. Underwood, *Gay and Lesbian Review* 10, 4 (2003): 44.

8   Kate Monro, *The First Time: True Tales of Virginity Lost and Found (Including My Own)* (London: Icon Books, 2011), also offers narratives of virginity loss from a range of perspectives and experiences. Likewise, the film project *How to Lose Your Virginity* includes, on its webpage, a series of first-person narratives on virginity loss; see http://www.virginitymovie.com/. For a socio-cultural study of these kinds of heterosexual narratives, see Jodi McAlister, "True Tales of the First Time: An Introduction to the Virginity Loss Confessional Genre," *Colloquy* (forthcoming).

9   Mario J. Valdés, *World-Making: The Literary Truth-Claim and the Interpretation of Texts* (Toronto: University of Toronto Press, 1992), 3.

10 Melina M. Bersamin et al., "Defining Virginity and Abstinence: Adolescents' Interpretations of Sexual Behaviors," *Journal of Adolescent Health* 41 (2007): 182–88; Laura M. Carpenter, *Virginity Lost: An Intimate Portrait of First Sexual Experiences* (New York: New York University Press, 2005); Hayley DiMarco, *Technical Virgin: How Far Is Too Far?* (Grand Rapids: Revell, Baker Publishing Group, 2006); Stephanie R. Medley-Rath, "'Am I Still a Virgin?' What Counts as Sex in 20 Years of *Seventeen,*" *Sexuality and Culture* 11, 2 (2007): 24–38; Jamie Mullaney, "Like a Virgin: Temptation, Resistance, and the Construction of Identities Based on 'Not Doings,'" *Qualitative Sociology* 24, 1 (2001): 3–24; Mark Regnerus and Jeremy Uecker, *Premarital Sex in America: How Young Americans Meet, Mate, and Think about Marrying* (Oxford: Oxford University Press, 2011); Jeremy E. Uecker, Nicole Angotti, and Mark D. Regnerus, "Going Most of the Way: 'Technical Virginity' among American Adolescents," *Social Science Review* 37 (2008): 1200–15; Jessica Valenti, *The Purity Myth: How America's Obsession with Virginity Is Hurting Young Women* (Berkeley: Seal Press, 2010).

11 Edward Sagarin, "Typologies of Sexual Behavior," *Journal of Sex Research* 7, 4 (1971): 282–88.

12 Marie C. Stopes, "The Technique of Contraception: The Principles and Practices of Anti-Conceptional Methods," *Eugenics Review* 21, 2 (1929): 136–38.

13 Ulrich Clement, "Surveys of Heterosexual Behaviour," *Annual Review of Sex Research* 1, 1 (1990): 45–74.

14 Carol A. Darling and J. Kenneth Davidson, "The Relationship of Sexual Satisfaction to Coital Involvement: The Concept of Technical Virginity Revisited," *Deviant Behavior* 8, 1 (1987): 27–46. Biblical scholarship also made use of the term "technical virgin" as early as 1967; see George Allan and Merle Allshouse, "Current Issues in Process Theology: Some Reflections," *Christian Scholar* 50, 3 (1967): 167–76. However, today the term has

been adopted by mainstream/secular and religious cultures. Evangelical books on virginity, purity, chastity, and technical virginity (especially when coupled with reclaiming purity) are too many to list; however, they are targeted at both men and women.

15 David G. Berger and Morton G. Wenger, "The Ideology of Virginity," *Journal of Marriage and Family* 35, 4 (1973): 668.

16 Jonathan A. Allan, "Theorising Male Virginity in Popular Romance," *Journal of Popular Romance Studies* 2, 1 (2011): n. pag., http//jprstudies.org/2011/10/theorising-male-virginity/.

17 Sandra L. Caron and Sarah P. Hinman, "'I Took His V-Card': An Exploratory Analysis of College Student Stories Involving Male Virginity Loss," *Sexuality and Culture* 17, 4 (2012): 538.

18 Irving B. Tebor, "Male Virgins: Conflicts and Group Support in American Culture," *Family Life Coordinator* 9, 3–4 (1961): 42.

19 Laura M. Carpenter, "Virginity Loss in Reel/Real Life: Using Popular Movies to Navigate Sexual Initiation," *Sociological Forum* 24, 2 (2009): 821.

20 Ibid., 805.

21 There are some exceptions to this rule, as I have argued, for "virginity in popular romance fiction is never simple, even—or perhaps especially— . . . when the virgin is the romance hero"; "romance novels have been criticised and even discarded by many in the academy for the ways in which they apparently reinforce patriarchal norms, but when we read these novels with a particular focus on male virginity, we find that romance novelists are quite conscious of these norms, and they sometimes break new ground in both gender and genre. Male virginity may receive its most honest and most complete fictional treatment in the genre pervasively written 'by women, for women': the popular romance novel." Allan, "Theorising Male Virginity."

22 Eve Kosofsky Sedgwick, *Epistemology of the Closet* (Berkeley: University of California Press, 1990), 3.

23 Ibid.

24 Ibid.

25 Ibid., 4.

26 Eve Kosofsky Sedgwick, *Tendencies* (Durham: Duke University Press, 1993).

27 Underwood, *Gay Men and Anal Eroticism*, 5.

28 Leo Bersani, *Is the Rectum a Grave? And Other Essays* (Chicago: University of Chicago Press, 2010), 19.

29 Underwood, *Gay Men and Anal Eroticism*, 9.

30 Sarah S. G. Frantz, "'How We Love Is Our Soul': Joey W. Hill's BDSM Romance Holding the Cards," in *New Approaches to Popular Romance Fiction*, ed. Sarah S. G. Frantz and Eric Murphy Selinger (Jefferson:

McFarland Press, 2012), 48. For recent studies on BDSM and orientation, see Elizabeth Freeman, *Time Binds: Queer Temporalities, Queer Histories* (Durham: Duke University Press, 2010); Niklas Nordling et al., "Differences and Similarities between Gay and Straight Individuals Involved in Sadomasochistic Subculture," *Journal of Homosexuality* 50, 2–3 (2006): 41–57; and Margot Weiss, *Techniques of Pleasure:* BDSM *and the Circuits of Sexuality* (Durham: Duke University Press, 2011).

31 Sedgwick, *Epistemology of the Closet*, 67–68.

32 McAlister, "True Tales of the First Time," TS4.

33 Ibid.

34 Björn Krondorfer, *Male Confessions: Intimate Revelations and the Religious Imagination* (Stanford: Stanford University Press, 2010), 4.

35 Ibid., 15.

36 Sedgwick, *Epistemology of the Closet*, 79.

37 Underwood, *Gay Men and Anal Eroticism*, 3.

38 Eve Kosofsky Sedgwick, "Anality: News from the Front," in *The Weather in Proust*, ed. Jonathan Goldberg (Durham: Duke University Press, 2011), 172.

39 Susan Kippax and Gary Smith, "Anal Intercourse and Power in Sex between Men," *Sexualities* 4, 4 (2001): 413–34; Jeffrey R. Guss, "The Danger of Desire: Anal Sex and the Homo/Masculine Subject," *Studies in Gender and Sexuality* 11, 3 (2010): 124–40; Sedgwick, "Anality."

40 One thinks here, for instance, of how anal sexuality and sexual orientation become complicated in Hispanic, Latino, and Chicano communities, wherein penetration is highly regulated (see Chapter 7). See also Tomás Almaguer, "Chicano Men: A Cartography of Homosexual Identity and Behavior," in *The Lesbian and Gay Studies Reader*, ed. Henry Abelove, Michèle Aina Barale, and David M. Halperin (New York: Routledge, 1993), 255–73; Peter M. Beattie, "Measures of Manhood: Honor, Enlisted Army Service, and Slavery's Decline in Brazil, 1850–90," in *Changing Men and Masculinities in Latin America*, ed. Matthew C. Guttman (Durham: Duke University Press, 2003), 233–55; Alex Carballo-Diéguez et al., "Looking for a Tall, Dark, Macho Man . . . Sexual-Role Behavior Variations in Latino Gay and Bisexual Men," *Culture, Health, and Society* 6, 2 (2004): 159–71; and David William Foster, *Sexual Textualities: Essays on Queer/ing Latin American Writing* (Austin: University of Texas Press, 1997).

41 Cited in Merle Miller, *On Being Different: What It Means to Be a Homosexual* (London: Penguin, 2012), 6.

42 Underwood, *Gay Men and Anal Eroticism*, 21.

43 David M. Halperin, *How to Be Gay* (Cambridge, MA: Harvard University Press, 2012), 456.

44 Underwood, *Gay Men and Anal Eroticism*, 22.

45 Ibid.

46 Ibid., 25.

47 Monro, *The First Time*, 86–87.

48 Underwood, *Gay Men and Anal Eroticism*, 27.

49 Ibid.

50 Ibid., 26.

51 Ibid., 56.

52 Ibid., 57, 60.

53 Ibid., 56.

54 Ibid., 57.

55 Ibid., 60.

56 Ibid., 61.

57 Ibid., 71.

58 Ibid., 81–82.

59 Ibid., 60.

CHAPTER 3—Topping from the Bottom:
Anne Tenino's *Frat Boy and Toppy*

1 Steven G. Underwood, *Gay Men and Anal Eroticism: Tops, Bottoms, and Versatiles* (Binghamton: Harrington Park Press, 2003).

2 Lisa Fletcher, *Historical Romance Fiction: Heterosexuality and Performativity* (Hampshire: Ashgate, 2008), 73n1.

3 Amanda Firestone, "'I Was with Edward in My Happy Place': The Romance of the *Twilight* Saga as an Aca-Fan," *Monsters and the Monstrous* 2, 2 (2012): 71–72.

4 Ibid.

5 Kate Thomas, "Post Sex: On Being Too Slow, Too Stupid, Too Soon," in *After Sex: On Writing since Queer Theory*, ed. Janet Halley and Andrew Parker (Durham: Duke University Press, 2011), 66.

6 Sarah S. G. Frantz and Eric Murphy Selinger, eds., New Approaches to Popular Romance Fiction (Jefferson, nc: McFarland Press, 2012).

7 Thomas, "Post Sex," 67–68.

8 Ibid., 66.

9 Hans-Jürgen Döpp, *In Praise of the Backside* (New York: Parkstone Press, 2011), 88.

10 Guy Hocquenghem, *Homosexual Desire*, trans. Daniella Dangoor (Durham: Duke University Press, 1993), 100.

11 Jayne Ann Krentz, "Introduction," in *Dangerous Men and Adventurous Women: Romance Writers on the Appeal of Romance*, ed. Jayne Ann Krentz (Philadelphia: University of Pennsylvania Press, 1992), 1.

12 Pamela Regis, "What Do Critics Owe the Romance?," *Journal of Popular Romance Studies* 2, 1 (2011): n. pag., http://jprstudies.org/2011/10/"what-do-critics-owe-the-romance-keynote-address-at-the-second-annual-conference-

of-the-international-association-for-the-study-of-popular-romance"-by-pamela-regis/.

13   Northrop Frye, *Collected Works of Northrop Frye,* gen. ed. Alvin A. Lee, 30 vols. (Toronto: University of Toronto Press, 1996–2012), 27: 260.

14   However, this has been a contested point in Frye scholarship; see A. C. Hamilton, *Northrop Frye: Anatomy of His Criticism* (Toronto: University of Toronto Press, 1990), 21–25; and, more recently, Jean O'Grady, "Re-Valuing Value," in *Northrop Frye: New Directions from Old,* ed. David Rampton (Ottawa: University of Ottawa Press, 2009), 226–46.

15   Elio Iannacci, "What Women Want: Gay Male Romance Novels," *Globe and Mail,* February 11, 2011, http://www.theglobeandmail.com/life/relationships/what-women-want-gay-male-romance-novels/article565992.

16   Cited in Mala Bhattarcharjee, "It's Raining Men: Tackling the Torrents of Male/Male Romantic Fiction Flooding the Market," RT *Book Reviews,* September 2012, 22–26.

17   Dan Brown, *Angels and Demons* (New York: Washington Square Press, 2000), 19.

18   Anne Tenino, *Frat Boy and Toppy* (Hillsborough: Riptide Publishing, 2012), 1: 68. Citations are organized by chapter and then line number.

19   Ibid., 1: 70, 73.

20   Jeffrey R. Guss, "Men, Anal Sex, and Desire: Who Wants What?," *Psychoanalysis, Culture, and Society* 12 (2007): 39.

21   David M. Halperin, *Saint Foucault: Towards a Gay Hagiography* (New York: Oxford University Press, 1995), 88.

22   Jason Edwards, *Eve Kosofsky Sedgwick* (London: Routledge, 2009), 75.

23   Heidi Cullinan, *Dirty Laundry* (Hillsborough, NJ: Riptide Publishing, 2013).

24   Cited in Sarah Wendell and Candy Tan, *Beyond Heaving Bosoms: The Smart Bitches' Guide to Romance Novels* (New York: Simon and Schuster, 2009), 161.

25   Toni Carrington, *Private Sessions* (Don Mills, ON: Harlequin, 2010).

26   Jack Morin, *Anal Pleasure and Health: A Guide for Men, Women, and Couples* (San Francisco: Down There Press, 2010), 30.

27   Ibid., 29.

28   Ibid., 30.

29   Tenino, *Frat Boy and Toppy,* 27: 1940.

30   Ibid., 2: 187.

31   Ibid., 2: 189.

32   Ibid., 7: 497.

33   Ibid., 7: 559.

34   Ibid., 7: 562.

35   Ibid., 5: 299.

36 Robin Harders, "Borderlands of Desire: Captivity, Romance, and the Revolutionary Power of Love," in *New Approaches to Popular Romance Fiction*, ed. Sarah S. G. Frantz and Eric Murphy Selinger (Jefferson, NC: McFarland, 2012), 133.

37 For a larger discussion of race, particularly the "whiteness" of popular romance fiction, see Jayashree Kamblé, "White Protestantism: Race and Religious Ethos in Romance Novels," in *Making Meaning in Popular Romance Fiction: An Epistemology* (New York: Palgrave Macmillan, 2014), 131–56.

38 Janice Radway, *Reading the Romance: Women, Patriarchy, and Popular Literature* (Chapel Hill: University of North Carolina Press, 1991), 128.

39 Michel Foucault, *History of Sexuality*, trans. R. Hurley, 3 vols. (New York: Vintage Books, 1978–86), 2: 194.

40 Tenino, *Frat Boy and Toppy*, 16: 1099.

41 Leo Bersani, *Is the Rectum a Grave? And Other Essays* (Chicago: University of Chicago Press, 2010), 29.

42 Sarah Frantz, review of *Frat Boy and Toppy*, by Anne Tenino, *Dear Author: A Romance Review Blog for Readers by Readers*, March 28, 2012, http://dearauthor.com/book-reviews/overall-b-reviews/b-plus-reviews/review-frat-boy-and-toppy-by-anne-tenino.

43 Tenino, *Frat Boy and Toppy*, 4: 256.

44 Ibid., 4: 257.

45 Ibid., 4: 266.

46 Ibid., 4: 269.

47 Ibid., 4: 272.

48 Ibid., 4: 274.

49 Leo Bersani, *Homos* (Cambridge, MA: Harvard University Press, 1995), 101, 97.

50 Tenino, *Frat Boy and Toppy*, 4: 284.

51 Ibid., 27: 1940.

52 Ibid., 4: 292.

53 Ann Snitow, "Mass Market Romance: Pornography for Women Is Different," in *Women and Romance: A Reader*, ed. Susan Ostrov Weisser (New York: New York University Press, 2001), 309.

54 It is worth noting here that Jodi McAlister has written the history of the virgin heroine in romance in her PhD dissertation, "The Origins, Historical Evolution, and Representations of the Virgin Heroine in English Literature" (Macquarie University, Australia).

55 Ritch C. Savin-Williams, *The New Gay Teenager* (Cambridge, MA: Harvard University Press, 2005), 137.

56 Tenino, *Frat Boy and Toppy*, 3: 208, 24: 1620.

57 Aaron James, *Assholes: A Theory* (New York: Doubleday, 2012), 11–12.

58 There is much to be said about the relationship between an asshole as a repugnant person and an asshole as a body part. In *Assholes*, James writes that "Something is deeply bothersome about them, something beyond mere material costs: something bad enough to drive an otherwise coolheaded person into a fit of rage; something that lingers in one's memory like a foul stench; something that warrants a name we use for a part of the body we hide in public, a part of the body that many people feel alienated from and perhaps wish wasn't there" (ibid.). In future work, I will tease this out further. For instance, how does the asshole as a repugnant person shift when we are interested in the asshole as a part of the body that we seek to expose, embrace, and accept? Incidentally, this task will be complicated by considering similar words, for example *lameass* and *dumbass*, both of which also appear in *Frat Boy and Toppy*.

59 Savin-Williams, *The New Gay Teenager*, 34.

60 David M. Halperin, *How to Be Gay* (Cambridge, MA: Harvard University Press, 2012).

61 Tenino, *Frat Boy and Toppy*, 11: 801.

62 Halperin, *How to Be Gay*, 6–7.

63 Ibid., 8.

64 Tenino, *Frat Boy and Toppy*, 12: 815–17.

65 Morin, *Anal Pleasure and Health*, 21.

66 Ibid.

67 Tenino, *Frat Boy and Toppy*, 12: 908.

68 Ibid., 12: 909.

69 Foucault, *History of Sexuality*, 2: 199.

70 Tenino, *Frat Boy and Toppy*, 12: 918.

71 Ibid., 12: 946.

72 Ibid., 14: 1008–09.

73 Ibid., 14: 1010.

74 Ibid., 22: 1463, 22: 1466.

75 Ibid., 22: 1484.

76 Ibid., 1: 70.

77 Döpp, *In Praise of the Backside*, 88.

78 Tenino, *Frat Boy and Toppy*, 15: 1086.

79 Ibid., 38: 2380.

80 Ibid., 27: 1949.

81 Ibid., 27: 1950.

82 Underwood, *Gay Men and Anal Eroticism*, 5.

83 Ibid., 27.

84 Tenino, *Frat Boy and Toppy*, 11: 801.

CHAPTER 4—Orienting *Brokeback Mountain*

1   Michael Cobb, "God Hates Cowboys (Kind Of)," *GLQ: A Journal of Lesbian and Gay Studies* 13, 1 (2006): 103.

2   David M. Halperin, *How to Be Gay* (Cambridge, MA: Harvard University Press, 2012), 97.

3   Joshua Clover and Christopher Nealon, "Don't Ask, Don't Tell," *Film Quarterly* 60, 3 (2007): 63.

4   Sheila J. Nayar, "A Good Man Is Impossible to Find: *Brokeback Mountain* as Heteronormative Tragedy," *Sexualities* 14, 2 (2011): 237.

5   Richard N. Pitt, "Downlow Mountain? De/Stigmatizing Bisexuality through Pitying and Pejorative Discourses in Media," *Journal of Men's Studies* 14, 2 (2006): 255.

6   D. A. Miller, "On the Universality of *Brokeback*," *Film Quarterly* 60, 3 (2007): 50.

7   Clifton Snider, "Queer Persona and the Gay Gaze in *Brokeback Mountain*: Story and Film," *Psychological Perspectives: A Quarterly Journal of Jungian Thought* 51, 1 (2008): 57; emphasis added.

8   Elaine Showalter, *A Jury of Her Peers: Celebrating American Women Writers from Anne Bradstreet to Annie Proulx* (New York: Vintage, 2010), 509.

9   David Wilbern, "Like Two Skins, One inside the Other: Dual Unity in *Brokeback Mountain*," *PsyArt: An Online Journal for the Psychological Study of the Arts* (2008), http://www.psyartjournal.com/article/show/wilbern-like_two_skins_one_inside_the_other_dual; Ginger Jones, "Proulx's Pastoral: *Brokeback Mountain* as Sacred Space," in *Reading* Brokeback Mountain: *Essays on the Story and the Film,* ed. Jim Stacy (Jefferson: McFarland Press, 2007), 19–28.

10 Nayar, "A Good Man Is Impossible to Find," 238.

11 Erika Spohrer, "Not a Gay Cowboy Movie? *Brokeback Mountain* and the Importance of Genre," *Journal of Popular Film and Television* 37, 1 (2009): 26.

12 Harry Brod, "They're Bi Shepherds, Not Gay Cowboys: The Misframing of *Brokeback Mountain*," *Journal of Men's Studies* 14, 2 (2006): 252.

13 B. Ruby Rich, *New Queer Cinema: The Director's Cut* (Durham: Duke University Press, 2013), 186.

14 Lucy Lockwood Hazard, *The Frontier in American Literature* (New York: Thomas Y. Crowell Company, 1927), 19.

15 William Calin, *The Twentieth-Century Humanist Critics: From Spitzer to Frye* (Toronto: University of Toronto Press, 2007), 101.

16 Ibid., 118.

17 Cited in Eric Cheyfitz, "Matthiessen's *American Renaissance*: Circumscribing the Revolution," *American Quarterly* 41, 2 (1989): 341.

18 Ibid., 350.

19   It is worth noting here that Harvard has a rather complicated history when it comes to homosexuality. See, for instance, William Wright, *Harvard's Secret Court: The Savage 1920 Purge of Campus Homosexuals* (New York: St. Martin's Press, 2005); and Douglass Shand-Tucci, *The Crimson Letter: Harvard, Homosexuality, and the Shaping of American Culture* (New York: St. Martin's Press, 2003).

20   Northrop Frye, *Collected Works of Northrop Frye*, gen. ed. Alvin A. Lee, 30 vols. (Toronto: University of Toronto Press, 1996–2012), 8: 308.

21   Cheyfitz, "Matthiessen's *American Renaissance*," 350.

22   F. O. Matthiessen, *American Renaissance: Art and Expression in the Age of Emerson and Whitman* (London: Oxford University Press, 1941), 535; emphasis added.

23   Jay Grossman, "The Canon in the Closet: Matthiessen's Whitman, Whitman's Matthiessen," *American Literature* 70, 4 (1998): 799.

24   Matthiessen, *American Renaissance*, 535.

25   Arthur Redding, "Closet, Coup, and Cold War: F. O. Matthiessen's *From the Heart of Europe*," *Boundary 2* 33, 1 (2006): 172.

26   Cited in ibid., 171.

27   Robert K. Martin, "Newton Arvin: Literary Critic and Lewd Person," *American Literary History* 16, 2 (2004): 290.

28   Newton Arvin, *Whitman* (New York: Russell and Russell, 1969), 275.

29   Ibid.

30   In 2001, Barry Werth published a biography of Arvin, *The Scarlet Professor: Newton Arvin, a Literary Life Shattered by Scandal* (New York: Talese, 2001), which itself has become a site of controversy but also fostered a renewed interest in Arvin. See Martin, "Newton Arvin"; Eric Savoy, "Arvin's Melville, Martin's Arvin," *GLQ: A Journal of Lesbian and Gay Studies* 14, 4 (2008): 609–15; and Chris Castiglia, "'A Democratic and Fraternal Humanism': The Cant of Pessimism and Newton Arvin's Queer Socialism," *American Literary History* 21, 1 (2009): 159–82.

31   Arvin, *Whitman*, 276.

32   Eve Kosofsky Sedgwick, *Epistemology of the Closet* (Berkeley: University of California Press, 1990), 22.

33   Arvin, *Whitman*, 277.

34   Travis M. Foster, "Matthiessen's Public Privates: Homosexual Expression and the Aesthetics of Sexual Inversion," *American Literature* 78, 2 (2006): 235.

35   Redding, "Closet, Coup, and Cold War," 176.

36   Cited in Judith Halberstam, *The Queer Art of Failure* (Durham: Duke University Press, 2011), 87.

37   Ibid.

38   Leslie A. Fiedler, *Love and Death in the American Novel* (New York: Stein and Day, 1966), 13.

39 Anonymous, review of *Love and Death in the American Novel*, by Leslie Fiedler, *Daedalus* 92, 1 (1963): 170.

40 Leslie Fiedler, "Come Back to the Raft Ag'in, Huck Honey!," in *Leslie Fiedler and American Culture*, ed. Steven G. Kellman and Irving Malin (Cranbury, NJ: Associated University Press, 1999), 29.

41 Nishant Shahani, *Queer Retrosexualities: The Politics of Reparative Return* (Bethlehem: Lehigh University Press, 2012), 110.

42 Fiedler, *Love and Death in the American Novel*, 338.

43 Ibid.

44 Ibid.

45 Lee Edelman, *No Future: Queer Theory and the Death Drive* (Durham: Duke University Press, 2004), 29.

46 Cited in Grossman, "The Canon in the Closet," 809.

47 Fiedler, *Love and Death in the American Novel*, 338.

48 Carol Mavor, *Reading Boyishly: Roland Barthes, J. M. Barrie, Jacques Henri Lartigue, Marcel Proust, and D. W. Winnicott* (Durham: Duke University Press, 2007), 72.

49 Fiedler, *Love and Death in the American Novel*, 339.

50 Ibid., 341.

51 Fiedler, "Come Back to the Raft,," 27.

52 Eve Kosofsky Sedgwick, *Between Men: English Literature and Male Homosocial Desire* (New York: Columbia University Press, 1985).

53 Fiedler, *Love and Death in the American Novel*, 344.

54 Richard Chase, "Leslie Fiedler and American Culture," *Chicago Review* 14, 3 (1960): 15.

55 Herman Melville, *Moby-Dick, or The Whale* (New York: Penguin, 1992), 28.

56 Fiedler, *Love and Death in the American Novel*, 349.

57 Ibid., 348.

58 Ibid., 349.

59 Cited in Jerome Loving, *Walt Whitman: The Song of Himself* (Berkeley: University of California Press, 1999), 184–85.

60 Walt Whitman, *Leaves of Grass: The First (1855) Edition*, ed. Malcolm Cowley (New York: Penguin, 1959), 109.

61 Fiedler, *Love and Death in the American Novel*, 349.

62 K. C. Glover, "Males, Melville, and *Moby-Dick*: A New Male Studies Approach to Teaching Literature to College Men," *New Male Studies: An International Journal* 2 (2013): 64.

63 Newton Arvin, *Herman Melville* (New York: Sloan, 1950).

64 Leslie A. Fiedler, "On Becoming a Pop Critic: A Memoir and a Meditation," *New England Review and Bread Loaf Quarterly* 5, 1–2 (1982): 196.

65 Fiedler, *Love and Death in the American Novel*, 349–50.

66 Ibid., 350.

67   Ibid., 350–51.

68   Leslie A. Fiedler, "Reestablishing Innocence: A Conversation with Leslie A. Fiedler," with Geoffrey Green, *Interdisciplinary Humanities* 20, 1 (2003): 96.

69   Fiedler, *Love and Death in the American Novel*, 355.

70   Christopher Looby, "'Innocent Homosexuality': The Fiedler Thesis in Retrospection," in *Adventures of Huckleberry Finn: A Case Study in Critical Controversy*, ed. Gerald Graff and James Phelan (Boston: Bedford-St. Martin's Press, 1995), 535–50.

71   Marjorie Garber, "Translating F. O. Matthiessen," *Raritan* 30, 3 (2011): 104.

72   Adam Phillips, *On Flirtation: Psychoanalytic Essays on the Uncommitted Life* (Cambridge, MA: Harvard University Press, 1994), 41.

73   John Alberti, "'I Love You, Man': Bromances, the Construction of Masculinity, and the Continuing Evolution of Romantic Comedy," *Quarterly Review of Film and Video* 30, 2 (2013): 159.

74   Ibid., 165.

75   Elizabeth J. Chen, "Caught in a Bad Romance," *Texas Journal of Women and Law* 21, 2 (2012): 246.

76   Ibid., 248.

77   Gore Vidal, *The City and the Pillar* (New York: Vintage, 1995), 24.

78   Mark Twain, *Adventures of Huckleberry Finn*, ed. Emory Elliot (Oxford: Oxford University Press, 1999), 108–09.

79   Mark Twain, *The Adventures of Tom Sawyer* (New York: Modern Library, 2001), 119–20.

80   For a discussion of nakedness and clothing in Mark Twain, see Steven Petersheim, "'Naked as a Pair of Tongs': Twain's Philosophy of Clothes," *Papers on Language and Literature: A Journal for Scholars and Critics of Language and Literature* 48, 2 (2012): 172–96.

81   Vidal, *The City and the Pillar*, 24.

82   Ian Scott Todd, "Outside/In: Abjection, Space, and Landscape in Brokeback Mountain," *Scope* 13 (2009), http://www.scope.nottingham.ac.uk/article.php?issue=13&id=1098.

83   Leigh Boucher and Sarah Pinto, "'I Ain't Queer': Love, Masculinity, and History in *Brokeback Mountain*," *Journal of Men's Studies* 15, 3 (2007): 311.

84   Chase, "Leslie Fiedler and American Culture," 12.

85   Mark John Isola, "Discipling Desire: The Fluid Textuality of Annie Proulx's *Brokeback Mountain*," *Nordic Journal of English Studies* 7, 1 (2008): 33.

86   Linda Hutcheon, *A Theory of Adaptation* (New York: Routledge, 2006), 6–7.

87   Matthew Bolton, "The Ethics of Alterity: Adapting Queerness in *Brokeback Mountain*," *Adaptation* 5, 1 (2011): 44.

88   Ibid., 45.

89 Fiedler, *Love and Death in the American Novel*, 368.
90 Sedgwick, *Epistemology of the Closet*, 77.
91 Eve Kosofsky Sedgwick, *Tendencies* (Durham: Duke University Press, 1993), 31.
92 Ibid.
93 Phillips, *On Flirtation*, 41.
94 Wolfgang Iser, *The Implied Reader: Patterns of Communication in Prose Fiction from Bunyan to Beckett* (Baltimore: Johns Hopkins University Press, 1974), 282.
95 For a larger and more refined discussion of advance retrospection and generic fiction, see Tania Modleski, *Loving with a Vengeance: Mass-Produced Fantasies for Women* (New York: Routledge, 2008), 27–49, especially 32–33.
96 Melville, *Moby-Dick*, 56–57.
97 Fiedler, *Love and Death in the American Novel*, 366.
98 Melville, *Moby-Dick*, 58.
99 Harold Bloom, *The Anxiety of Influence: A Theory of Poetry* (New York: Oxford University Press, 1997), 14.
100 Jeffrey R. Guss, "Men, Anal Sex, and Desire: Who Wants What?," *Psychoanalysis, Culture, and Society* 12 (2007): 39.
101 Annie Proulx, *Brokeback Mountain* (New York: Scribner, 1997), 14.
102 Mark J. Blechner, "The Darkest Continent," *Studies in Gender and Sexuality* 11, 3 (2010): 146.
103 Proulx, *Brokeback Mountain*, 18.
104 Ibid., 19.
105 Jeffrey Q. McCune Jr., *Sexual Discretion: Black Masculinity and the Politics of Passing* (Chicago: University of Chicago Press, 2014), 4.
106 Ibid., 6.
107 José Esteban Muñoz, *Disidentifications: Queers of Color and the Performance of Politics* (New York: New York University Press, 1999), 5.
108 Eve Kosofsky Sedgwick, "Anality: News from the Front," in *The Weather in Proust*, ed. Jonathan Goldberg (Durham: Duke University Press, 2011), 172.
109 Muñoz, *Disidentification*, 5.
110 Sedgwick, *Tendencies*, 73.
111 Guy Hocquenghem, *Homosexual Desire*, trans. Daniella Dangoor (Durham: Duke University Press, 1993), 103.
112 Fiedler, *Love and Death in the American Novel*, 351.
113 Proulx, *Brokeback Mountain*, 15.
114 Fiedler, *Love and Death in the American Novel*, 349.
115 Ibid., 351.
116 Ibid.
117 Sedgwick, *Epistemology of the Closet*, 1.
118 Sedgwick, *Tendencies*, 8.

CHAPTER 5—Spanking Colonialism

1 Richard Amory, *Song of the Loon* (1966; reprinted, Vancouver: Arsenal Pulp Press, 2005).

2 Ibid., 28.

3 I am referring here to the concept of "mansplaining." Rebecca Solnit, in *Men Explain Things to Me* (Chicago: Haymarket Books, 2014), 4–5, explains that "Men explain things to me, and other women, whether or not they know what they're talking about. Some men. Every woman knows what I'm talking about. It's the presumption that makes it hard, at times, for any woman in any field; that keeps women from speaking up and from being heard when they dare; that crushes young women into silence by indicating, the way harassment on the street does, that this is not their world. It trains us in self-doubt and self-limitation just as it exercises men's unsupported confidence."

4 Ian Mozdzen, "Reflections on *Song of the Loon* at Forty," *Gay and Lesbian Review* 13, 2 (2006): 40.

5 Ken Furtado, "Between the Covers," *Echo Magazine* 16, 21 (2005): 68.

6 Mozdzen, "Reflections on *Song of the Loon* at Forty," 40.

7 Sianne Ngai, *Ugly Feelings* (Cambridge, MA: Harvard University Press, 2005).

8 Daniel Heath Justice, Bethany Schneider, and Mark Rifkin, "Heaven and Earth: From the Guest Editors," *GLQ: A Journal of Lesbian and Gay Studies* 16, 1–2 (2010): 1.

9 Margot Francis, *Creative Subversions: Whiteness, Indigeneity, and the National Imaginary* (Vancouver: UBC Press, 2011), 151–52.

10 Justice, Schneider, and Rifkin, "Heaven and Earth," 1.

11 Northrop Frye, *Collected Works of Northrop Frye*, gen. ed. Alvin A. Lee, 30 vols. (Toronto: University of Toronto Press, 1996–2012), 12: 275.

12 Kent Monkman, "Kent Monkman: The Canadian Artist Who Is Exploding the Mythology of the West—One Brushstroke at a Time," interview with David Furnish, *Interview* 36, 2 (2006): 136–37.

13 Shirley J. Madill, "Intelligent Mischief: The Paintings of Kent Monkman," in *The Triumph of Mischief*, ed. David Liss and Shirley J. Madill (Hamilton: Art Gallery of Hamilton, 2008), 28.

14 Margaret Atwood, *Survival: A Thematic Guide to Canadian Literature* (Toronto: McClelland and Stewart, 2004), 145–46.

15 Jennifer Reid, *Louis Riel and the Creation of Modern Canada: Mythic Discourse and the Postcolonial State* (Albuquerque: University of New Mexico Press, 2008), 61.

16 Frye, *Collected Works of Northrop Frye*, 12: 498.

17 Elizabeth Freeman, *Time Binds: Queer Temporalities, Queer Histories* (Durham: Duke University Press, 2010), xvi–xvii.

18   Ibid., xvii.

19   Rebecca F. Plante, "Sexual Spanking, the Self, and the Construction of Deviance," *Journal of Homosexuality* 50, 2–3 (2006): 60.

20   Sigmund Freud, *The Standard Edition of the Complete Psychological Works of Sigmund Freud*, ed. and trans. J. Strachey, 24 vols. (London: Hogarth Press, 1953–74), 17: 181.

21   Francis, *Creative Subversions*, 152.

22   Jason Edwards, *Eve Kosofsky Sedgwick* (London: Routledge, 2009), 59.

23   Eve Kosofsky Sedgwick, *Tendencies* (Durham: Duke University Press, 1993), 177.

24   Edwards, *Eve Kosofsky Sedgwick*, 74–75.

25   Sedgwick, *Tendencies*, 182.

26   Ibid., 183.

27   Wayne Koestenbaum, *Humiliation* (New York: Picador, 2011), 8.

28   Sedgwick, *Tendencies*, 183.

29   Colleen Lamos, "James Joyce and the English Vice," *Novel: A Forum on Fiction* 29, 1 (1995): 23–24.

30   Silvan Tomkins, *Shame and Its Sisters: A Silvan Tomkins Reader*, ed. Eve Kosofsky Sedgwick and Adam Frank (Durham: Duke University Press, 1995), 133.

31   Ibid., 134.

32   Koestenbaum, *Humiliation*, 7.

33   Francis, *Creative Subversions*, 152.

34   Ibid.

35   Ibid.

36   Ibid.

37   Jane Gallop, *Anecdotal Theory* (Durham: Duke University Press, 2002), 15.

38   Kateri Akiwenzie-Damm, "Red Hot to the Touch: wRi(gh)ting Indigenous Erotica," in *Me Sexy: An Exploration of Native Sex and Sexuality*, ed. Drew Hayden Taylor (Vancouver: Douglas and McIntyre, 2008), 121.

39   John Butler, *The Gay Utopia* (Herndon: Starbrooks, 2004), 47.

40   Dian Hanson, ed., *Tom of Finland: Bikers, Vol. 2* (Cologne: Taschen, 2012), 206.

41   Francis, *Creative Subversions*, 152.

42   Ibid.

43   Ibid., 153.

44   Sedgwick, *Tendencies*, 203.

45   David M. Halperin, *Saint Foucault: Towards a Gay Hagiography* (New York: Oxford University Press, 1995), 88.

46   Barry R. Komisaruk and Beverly Whipple, "Non-Genital Orgasms," *Sexual and Relationship Therapy* 26, 4 (2011): 359.

47 Jonathan Goldberg, *Sodometries: Renaissance Texts, Modern Sexualities* (Stanford: Stanford University Press, 1992), 193.

48 Michael J. Horswell, *Decolonizing the Sodomite: Queer Tropes of Sexuality in Colonial Andean Culture* (Austin: University of Texas Press, 2005), 73.

49 Goldberg, *Sodometries*, 19.

50 Ibid., 185–86.

CHAPTER 6—Unlocking Delmira Agustini's "El Intruso"

1   J. Andrew Brown, "Feminine Anxiety of Influence Revisited: Alfonsina Storni and Delmira Agustini," *Revista canadiense de estudios hispánicos* 23, 2 (1999): 197.

2   Madeleine Simonet, "Delmira Agustini," *Hispania: A Journal Devoted to the Teaching of Spanish and Portuguese* 39, 4 (1956): 397.

3   Cristina Santos, *Bending the Rules in the Quest for an Authentic Female Identity: Clarice Lispector and Carmen Boullosa* (New York: Peter Lang, 2004).

4   Simonet, "Delmira Agustini," 401.

5   Sarah T. Moody, "Radical Metrics and Feminist Modernism: Agustini Rewrites Darío's Prosas Profanas," *Chasqui* 43, 1 (2014): 59.

6   Brown, "Feminine Anxiety of Influence Revisited," 197.

7   Ignacio Ruiz-Pérez, "Contra-escrituras: Delmira Agustini, Alfonsina Storni, y la subversión del modernism," *Revista hispánica moderna* 61, 2 (2008): 194. All Spanish-English translations by the author, unless otherwise credited.

8   Michel Foucault, *History of Sexuality*, trans. R. Hurley, 3 vols. (New York: Vintage Books, 1978–86), 1: 3.

9   Lauren Berlant and Michael Warner, "Sex in Public," *Critical Inquiry* 24, 2 (1998): 564.

10 Ibid.

11 David M. Halperin, *How to Be Gay* (Cambridge, MA: Harvard University Press, 2012), 123.

12 *The Golden Girls* (1985–92) on numerous occasions flirted with and openly discussed queer concerns. The opening episode includes a gay cook, only ever seen once in the series; Rose Nylund is tested for HIV in another episode; Dorothy Zbornak's female friend falls in love with Rose; Blanche Devereaux's brother, Clayton Hollingsworth, comes out in one episode, later brings his partner to meet Blanche, and ultimately "marries" his partner; and Phil, the brother of Dorothy and the son of Sophia Petrillo, wears women's clothing.

13 Halperin, *How to Be Gay*, 110.

14 Ibid.

15 François Cusset, *The Inverted Gaze: Queering the French Literary Classics in America*, trans. David Homel (Vancouver: Arsenal Pulp Press, 2011), 27.

16 Ibid., 20.

17 Delmira Agustini, "El Intruso," in *Poesías completas* (Barcelona: Editorial Labor, 1971), 143.

18 Foucault, *History of Sexuality*, 1: 3.

19 Cited in James Miller, *The Passion of Michel Foucault* (New York: Simon and Schuster, 1993), 27.

20 David M. Halperin, *Saint Foucault: Towards a Gay Hagiography* (New York: Oxford University Press, 1995), 88.

21 Agustini, "El Intruso," 143.

22 Ana Peluffo, "'De todas las cabezas quiero tu cabeza': Figuraciones de la 'Femme Fatale' en Delmira Agustini," *Chasqui* 34, 2 (2005): 141.

23 Roland Barthes, *The Pleasure of the Text*, trans. Richard Miller (New York: Hill and Wang, 1975), 39.

24 Jacques Lacan, *The Other Side of Psychoanalysis*, trans. Russell Grigg (New York: W. W. Norton and Company, 2007), 46.

25 Ibid., 51.

26 Jacques Lacan, *Encore: On Feminine Sexuality, the Limits of Love, and Knowledge, 1972–1973*, ed. Jacques-Alain Miller, trans. Bruce Fink (New York: W. W. Norton and Company, 1988), 7.

27 Anne Koedt, "The Myth of the Vaginal Orgasm," in *Feminism and Sexuality: A Reader*, ed. Stevi Jackson and Sue Scott (New York: Columbia University Press, 1996).

28 Ibid., 111.

29 Ibid.

30 Ibid., 113.

31 Roland Barthes, "The Death of the Author," in *Image-Music-Text*, trans. Stephen Heath (New York: Hill and Wang, 1977), 148.

32 Guy Hocquenghem, *Homosexual Desire*, trans. Daniella Dangoor (Durham: Duke University Press, 1993), 95.

33 Ibid., 120.

34 Halperin, *Saint Foucault*, 88.

35 Jeffrey R. Guss, "The Danger of Desire: Anal Sex and the Homo/Masculine Subject," *Studies in Gender and Sexuality* 11, 3 (2010): 126.

36 Michael Moon, "New Introduction," in *Homosexual Desire*, by Guy Hocquenghem (Durham: Duke University Press, 1993), 18.

37 Eve Kosofsky Sedgwick, *Tendencies* (Durham: Duke University Press, 1993), 99.

38 Agustini, "El Intruso," 143.

39 Ibid.

40 Sedgwick, *Tendencies*, 99.

41 Ibid., 101.

42 Barry R. Komisaruk and Beverly Whipple, "Non-Genital Orgasms," *Sexual and Relationship Therapy* 26, 4 (2011): 359.

43 Ibid.

44 Guss, "The Danger of Desire," 124.
45 Eve Kosofsky Sedgwick, *The Weather in Proust*, ed. Jonathan Goldberg (Durham: Duke University Press, 2011), 172.
46 Sedgwick, *Tendencies*, 98–99.
47 Ibid., 98.
48 Catherine Waldby, "Destruction: Boundary Erotics and the Refiguration of the Heterosexual Male Body," in *Sexy Bodies: The Strange Carnalities of Feminism*, ed. Elizabeth Grosz and Elspeth Probyn (New York: Routledge, 1995), 272.
49 Leo Bersani, *Is the Rectum a Grave? And Other Essays* (Chicago: University of Chicago Press, 2010), 19.
50 Cristina Santos and Adriana Spahr, eds., *Defiant Deviance: The Irreality of Reality in the Cultural Imaginary* (New York: Peter Lang, 2006).
51 Roland Barthes, *The Preparation of the Novel*, trans. Kate Briggs (New York: Columbia University Press, 2011), 13.
52 Ibid.
53 Jane Gallop, "Precocious Jouissance: Roland Barthes, Amatory Maladjustment, and Emotion," *New Literary History* 43, 2 (2012): 565.
54 Carol Mavor, *Reading Boyishly: Roland Barthes, J. M. Barrie, Jacques Henri Lartigue, Marcel Proust, and D. W. Winnicott* (Durham: Duke University Press, 2007), 33.
55 Ibid., 30.
56 Carol Mavor, *Black and Blue: The Bruising Passion of* Camera Lucida, La Jetée, Sans soleil, *and* Hiroshima mon amour (Durham: Duke University Press, 2012), 48.
57 For Barthes and his mother, see Roland Barthes, *Camera Lucida: Reflections on Photography*, trans. Richard Howard (New York: Hill and Wang, 1981); Roland Barthes, *Mourning Diary*, trans. Richard Howard (New York: Hill and Wang, 2010); and Mavor, *Reading Boyishly*. For Barthes and the death of the author, see Jane Gallop, *The Deaths of the Author: Reading and Writing in Time* (Durham: Duke University Press, 2011), especially 27–84.
58 Gallop, "Precocious Jouissance," 566.
59 Ibid.
60 Barthes, *The Pleasure of the Text*, 52.
61 Gallop, "Precocious Jouissance," 568.
62 Pierre Saint-Amand, "The Secretive Body: Roland Barthes, Gay Erotics," trans. Charles A. Porter and Noah Guynn, *Yale French Studies* 90 (1996): 157–58.
63 Ibid., 158.
64 Ibid., 159.
65 Ibid.
66 Roland Barthes, *The Neutral*, trans. Rosalind E. Krass and Denis Hollier (New York: Columbia University Press, 2005), 72–73.

67 Roland Barthes, cited in Lawrence R. Schehr, *The Shock of Men: Homosexual Hermeneutics in French Writing* (Stanford: Stanford University Press, 1995), 88.
68 Ibid.
69 Barthes, *The Neutral*, 51.
70 Ibid., 73.

CHAPTER 7—Shameful Matrophilia in *Doña Herlinda y su hijo*

1   Roland Barthes, *A Lover's Discourse: Fragments*, trans. Richard Howard (New York: Hill and Wang, 1978), 104–05.
2   Vito Russo, *The Celluloid Closet: Homosexuality in the Movies* (New York: Quality Paperback Book Club, 1987), 314.
3   Daniel Balderston, "Excluded Middle? Bisexuality in *Doña Herlinda y su hijo*," in *Sex and Sexuality in Latin America*, ed. Daniel Balderston and Donna J. Guy (New York: New York University Press, 1997), 190–99.
4   David William Foster, "Queering the Patriarchy in Hermosillo's *Doña Herlinda y su hijo*," in *Sexual Textualities: Essays on Queer/ing Latin American Writing* (Austin: University of Texas Press, 1997), 64–72. The same argument appears in David William Foster, *Queer Issues in Contemporary Latin American Cinema* (Austin: University of Texas Press, 1997).
5   For a historical discussion of male homosexuality in Mexican cinema, see Michael Schuessler, "'Vestidas, Locas, Mayates,' and 'Machos': History and Homosexuality in Mexican Cinema," *Cinematic and Literary Representations of Spanish and Latin American Themes*, special issue of *Chasqui* 34, 2 (2005): 132–44.
6   Foster, "Queering the Patriarchy," 66.
7   Ibid., 67, 68.
8   Cited in Aaraón Díaz Mediburo, *Los hijos homoeróticos de Jaime Humberto Hermosillo* (Mexico: Plaza y Valdés, 2004), 102. All Spanish-English translations by the author, unless otherwise credited.
9   David M. Halperin, *How to Be Gay* (Cambridge, MA: Harvard University Press, 2012), 38.
10 Eve Kosofsky Sedgwick, *Epistemology of the Closet* (Berkeley: University of California Press, 1990), 22.
11 Carol Mavor, *Reading Boyishly: Roland Barthes, J. M. Barrie, Jacques Henri Lartigue, Marcel Proust, and D. W. Winnicott* (Durham: Duke University Press, 2007), 30.
12 Ibid., 31–32.
13 D. W. Winnicott, *The Child, the Family, and the Outside World* (Cambridge, MA: Perseus Publishing, 1987), 149.
14 Balderston, "Excluded Middle?," 194.
15 Ibid.

16 Roland Barthes, *The Pleasure of the Text*, trans. Richard Miller (New York: Hill and Wang, 1975), 37.

17 Carol Mavor, "Black and Blue: The Shadows of *Camera Lucida*," in *Photography Degree Zero: Reflections on Roland Barthes's Camera Lucida*, ed. Geoffrey Batchen (Cambridge, MA: MIT Press, 2008), 230.

18 Roland Barthes, *Camera Lucida: Reflections on Photography*, trans. Richard Howard (New York: Hill and Wang, 1981), 27.

19 Ibid., 49.

20 I graciously thank Jeannine Pitas for translating Acuña's poem for this chapter.

21 Barthes, *A Lover's Discourse*, 99.

22 Adam Phillips, *On Balance* (New York: Farrar, Straus and Giroux, 2010), 9.

23 Julia Kristeva, "Stabat Mother," in *Tales of Love*, trans. Leon S. Roudiez (New York: Columbia University Press, 1987), 247.

24 Roland Barthes, *Mourning Diary*, trans. Richard Howard (New York: Hill and Wang, 2010), 5.

25 Barthes, *A Lover's Discourse*, 104–05.

26 Wayne Koestenbaum, "Foreword: In Defence of Nuance," in *A Lover's Discourse: Fragments*, by Roland Barthes, trans. Richard Howard (1978; reprinted, with a foreword, New York: Hill and Wang, 2010), xvi.

27 Adam Phillips, *On Flirtation: Psychoanalytic Essays on the Uncommitted Life* (Cambridge, MA: Harvard University Press, 1994), xvii.

28 Halperin, *How to Be Gay*, 38.

29 Michael D. Snediker, *Queer Optimism: Lyric Personhood and Other Felicitous Persuasions* (Minneapolis: University of Minnesota Press, 2009).

30 Douglas Crimp, "Mario Montez, for Shame," in *Gay Shame*, ed. David M. Halperin and Valerie Traub (Chicago: University of Chicago Press, 2009), 71.

31 Eve Kosofsky Sedgwick, "Shame, Theatricality, and Queer Performativity: Henry James's *The Art of the Novel*," in *Gay Shame*, ed. David M. Halperin and Valerie Traub (Chicago: University of Chicago Press, 2009), 52.

32 Lawrence La Fountain-Stokes, "Gay Shame, Latina- and Latino-Style: A Critique of White Queer Performativity," in *Gay Latino Studies: A Critical Reader*, ed. Michael Hames-García and Ernesto Javier Martínez (Durham: Duke University Press, 2011), 63.

33 For critiques of *Gay Shame*, chiefly the conference, see Judith Halberstam, "Shame and White Gay Masculinity," *Social Text* 23, 3–4, 84–85 (2005): 219–33; Hiriam Pérez, "You Can Have My Brown Body and Eat It, Too!" *Social Text* 23, 3–4, 84–85 (2005): 171–91; and La Fountain-Stokes, "Gay Shame." For the response of conference organizers, see David M. Halperin and Valerie Traub, "Beyond Gay Pride," in *Gay Shame*, ed. David

M. Halperin and Valerie Traub (Chicago: University of Chicago Press, 2009), 3–40.

34 Mavor, *Reading Boyishly*, 71.

35 Ibid., 72.

36 Carol Mavor, *Black and Blue: The Bruising Passion of* Camera Lucida, La Jetée, Sans soleil, *and* Hiroshima mon amour (Durham: Duke University Press, 2012), 48.

37 Balderston, "Excluded Middle?," 195.

38 José Quiroga, *Tropics of Desire: Interventions from Queer Latino America* (New York: New York University Press, 2000), 162. Quiroga is certainly not the first, nor will he be the last, to assign a genre to gay male subjectivity. Before him, Wayne Koestenbaum explored male homosexuality and opera in *The Queen's Throat: Opera, Homosexuality, and the Mystery of Desire* (New York: Farrar, Straus and Giroux, 1993); D. A. Miller provided a reading of the Broadway musical and male homosexuality in *Place for Us: Essay on the Broadway Musical* (Cambridge, MA: Harvard University Press, 1998); and more recently Halperin explored the melodrama as an ideal space of male homosexuality in *How to Be Gay*. Although not the goal of this study, a new question arises: what, then, is *not* a gay genre? That is, is there a genre that could be excluded, or is there a genre that is "lesbian" or "straight"?

39 Balderston, "Excluded Middle?," 194.

40 Margaret Wilkinson, "His Mother-Tongue: From Stuttering to Separation, a Case History," *Journal of Analytical Psychology* 46 (2001): 266.

41 Ernest Jones, *The Life and Works of Sigmund Freud*, 3 vols. (New York: Basic Books, 1953–57), 2: 183.

42 Balderston, "Excluded Middle?," 195.

43 Mavor, *Reading Boyishly*, 30.

44 Balderston, "Excluded Middle?," 195.

45 Christina Wieland, "Human Longings and Masculine Terrors: Masculinity and Separatism from the Mother," *British Journal of Psychotherapy* 22, 1 (2005): 72.

46 Mavor, *Reading Boyishly*, 72.

47 Ibid., 62.

48 Eve Kosofsky Sedgwick, *Tendencies* (Durham: Duke University Press, 1993), 157.

49 Foster, "Queering the Patriarchy," 65.

50 Annie Potts, "'The Essence of the Hard On': Hegemonic Masculinity and the Cultural Construction of 'Erectile Dysfunction,'" *Men and Masculinities* 3 (2000): 85.

51 Peter Lehman, "Crying over the Melodramatic Penis: Melodrama and Male Nudity in the Films of the 90s," in *Masculinity: Bodies, Movies, Culture*, ed. Peter Lehman (New York: Routledge, 2001), 27.

52   Balderston, "Excluded Middle?," 195.

53   Jeffrey R. Guss, "Men, Anal Sex, and Desire: Who Wants What?," *Psychoanalysis, Culture, and Society* 12 (2007): 39.

54   Jeffrey R. Guss, "The Danger of Desire: Anal Sex and the Homo/Masculine Subject," *Studies in Gender and Sexuality* 11, 3 (2010): 125.

55   Octavio Paz, *El laberinto de la soledad*, ed. Enrico Maro Santí (Madrid: Cátedra, 2003), 214. Translation from Octavio Paz, *The Labyrinth of Solitude and Other Writings*, trans. Lysander Kemp, Yara Milos, and Rachel Phillips Belash (New York: Grove Press, 1985), 77.

56   Paz, *El laberinto de la soledad*, 214. Translation from Paz, *The Labyrinth of Solitude and Other Writings*, 77.

57   Tomás Almaguer, "Chicano Men: A Cartography of Homosexual Identity and Behavior," in *The Lesbian and Gay Studies Reader*, ed. Henry Abelove, Michèle Aina Barale, and David M. Halperin (New York: Routledge, 1993), 259.

58   Alex Carballo-Diéguez et al., "Looking for a Tall, Dark, Macho man ... Sexual-Role Behavior Variations in Latino Gay and Bisexual Men," *Culture, Health, and Sexuality* 6, 2 (2004): 160.

59   Paz, *El laberinto de la soledad*, 214.

60   Ibid. Translation from Paz, *The Labyrinth of Solitude and Other Writings*, 77.

61   Barthes, *Camera Lucida*, 53.

62   Russo, *The Celluloid Closet*, 314.

63   James Miller, *The Passion of Michel Foucault* (New York: Simon and Schuster, 1993), 267.

64   Sigmund Freud, *The Standard Edition of the Complete Psychological Works of Sigmund Freud*, ed. and trans. J. Strachey, 24 vols. (London: Hogarth Press, 1953–74), 7: 152–53.

65   Sedgwick, *Tendencies*, 98.

66   Halperin, *How to Be Gay*, 307.

67   Leo Bersani, *Is the Rectum a Grave? And Other Essays* (Chicago: University of Chicago Press, 2010), 19.

68   Leo Bersani, *Homos* (Cambridge, MA: Harvard University Press, 1995), 121–22.

69   Guss, "Men, Anal Sex, and Desire," 42.

70   Bersani, *Is the Rectum a Grave?*, 29.

71   Sedgwick, *Tendencies*, 157.

72   Halperin, *How to Be Gay*, 306–07.

CHAPTER 8—Vengeful Vidal

1   John Carlevale, "The Dionysian Revival in American Fiction in the Sixties," *International Journal of the Classical Tradition* 12, 3 (2006): 384.

2   Gore Vidal, *Myra Breckinridge and Myron* (London: Abacus, 1986), 3.

3   Ibid., 6.

4   Michael Mewshaw, "Vidal and Mailer," *South Central Review* 19, 1 (2002): 4–5.

5   Purvis E. Boyette, "*Myra Breckinridge* and Imitative Form," *Modern Fiction Studies* 17, 2 (1971): 229.

6   Ibid.

7   Northrop Frye, *Collected Works of Northrop Frye*, gen. ed. Alvin A. Lee, 30 vols. (Toronto: University of Toronto Press, 1996–2012), 21: 27.

8   Ibid., 31–32.

9   Carlevale, "The Dionysian Revival in American Fiction in the Sixties," 384.

10   Ibid., 364.

11   Boyette, "*Myra Breckinridge* and Imitative Form," 269.

12   *Time*, February 16, 1968, 111, http://content.time.com/time/subscriber/article/0,33009,837914,00.html.

13   Harold Bloom, "The Central Man," *New York Review of Books*, July 19, 1984, http://www.nybooks.com/articles/archives/1984/jul/19/the-central-man.

14   Harold Bloom, *The Western Canon: The Books and School of the Ages* (New York: Riverhead Books, 1994), 20.

15   John F. Wilhelm and Mary Ann Wilhelm, "*Myra Breckinridge*: A Study in Identity," *Journal of Popular Culture* 3, 3 (1969): 599.

16   Ibid.

17   Charles Berryman, "Satire in Gore Vidal's Kalki," *Critique* 22, 2 (1980): 89.

18   Neville Hoad, "Queer Theory Addiction," in *After Sex: On Writing since Queer Theory*, ed. Janet Halley and Andrew Parker (Durham: Duke University Press, 2011), 135.

19   Dennis Altman, "Gore Vidal, Gay Hero in Spite of Himself," *Gay and Lesbian Review* 19, 6 (2012): 10.

20   Joanne Meyerowitz, *How Sex Changed: A History of Transsexuality in the United States* (Cambridge, MA: Harvard University Press, 2002), 203.

21   Ibid., 204.

22   Ibid., 203.

23   Cited in ibid., 204.

24   Eve Kosofsky Sedgwick, *Epistemology of the Closet* (Berkeley: University of California Press, 1990), 220.

25   Boyette, "*Myra Breckinridge* and Imitative Form," 236.

26   Oswald Spengler, *The Decline of the West* (1918; reprinted, Oxford: Oxford University Press, 1991); Allan Bloom, *The Closing of the American Mind: Education and the Crisis of Reason* (New York: Simon and Schuster, 1987).

27   Boyette, "*Myra Breckinridge* and Imitative Form." 230. Irony and the ironic are all deployed in the following considerations of the novel and/or its

film adaptation: Wilhelm and Wilhelm, "*Myra Breckinridge*"; Catharine R. Stimpson, "My O My O Myra," *New England Review* 14, 1 (1990): 102–15; and David Scott Diffrient, "'Hard to Handle': Camp Criticism, Trash-Film Reception, and the Transgressive Pleasures of *Myra Breckinridge*," *Cinema Journal* 52, 2 (2013): 46–70.

28 Vidal, *Myra Breckinridge and Myron*, 81.

29 Boyette, "*Myra Breckinridge* and Imitative Form," 236.

30 Wilhelm and Wilhelm, "*Myra Breckinridge*," 595.

31 Stimpson, "My O My O Myra," 110.

32 Douglas Eisner, "*Myra Breckinridge* and the Pathology of Heterosexuality," in *The Queer Sixties*, ed. Patricia Juliana Smith (New York: Routledge, 1999), 262.

33 Rape appears in a number of Almodóvar's films: ¡*Átame!* (1990), *Kika* (1993), *Hable con ella* (2002), *La piel que habito* (2011), and *Los amantes pasajeros* (2013).

34 Diffrient, "'Hard to Handle,'" 48.

35 Brent Ledger, "Fucking Straight Guys Is the Best Revenge," *Xtra* 544 (2005): 15.

36 Vidal, *Myra Breckinridge and Myron*, 141.

37 Calvin Thomas, "Must Desire Be Taken Literally?," *Parallax* 8, 4 (2002): 47.

38 Brian Pronger, "Outta My Endzone: Sport and the Territorial Anus," *Journal of Sport and Social Issues* 23, 4 (1999): 380–81.

39 Leo Bersani, *Is the Rectum a Grave? And Other Essays* (Chicago: University of Chicago Press, 2010), 29.

40 Catherine Waldby, "Destruction: Boundary Erotics and the Refiguration of the Heterosexual Male Body," in *Sexy Bodies: The Strange Carnalities of Feminism*, ed. Elizabeth Grosz and Elspeth Probyn (New York: Routledge, 1995), 275.

41 Brian Pronger, "On Your Knees: Carnal Knowledge, Masculine Dissolution, Doing Feminism," in *Men Doing Feminism*, ed. Tom Digby (New York: Routledge, 1998), 69–80.

42 Wayne Koestenbaum, "The Rape of Rusty," in *My 1980s and Other Essays* (New York: Farrar, Straus and Giroux, 2013), 153.

43 Vidal, *Myra Breckinridge and Myron*, 58.

44 Ibid., 59.

45 Ibid., 61.

46 Ibid.

47 Ibid., 62.

48 Ibid.

49 Ibid., 63.

50 Ibid., 64.

51 Giorgio Agamben, "Nudity," in *Nudities*, trans. David Kishick and Stefan Pedatella (Stanford: Stanford University Press, 2011), 65.

52 Vidal, *Myra Breckinridge and Myron*, 64.

53 Ibid., 65.

54 Agamben, "Nudity," 65.

55 Vidal, *Myra Breckinridge and Myron*, 75.

56 Leo Bersani, *Homos* (Cambridge, MA: Harvard University Press, 1995), 101.

57 W. B. Yeats, "The Second Coming," in *The Major Works*, ed. Edward Larissy (Oxford: Oxford University Press, 1997), 91 (ll. 3–8).

58 Bersani, *Homos*, 97.

59 See Wilhelm and Wilhelm, "*Myra Breckinridge*," 594.

60 Leo Bersani, "Genital Chastity," in *Homosexuality and Psychoanalysis*, ed. Tim Dean and Christopher Lane (Chicago: University of Chicago Press, 2001), 357.

61 Bersani, *Homos*, 102.

62 David M. Halperin, *Saint Foucault: Towards a Gay Hagiography* (New York: Oxford University Press), 88.

63 Vidal, *Myra Breckinridge and Myron*, 78.

64 Ibid., 136.

65 Ibid., 140.

66 Ibid., 139.

67 Ibid., 140.

68 Ibid.

69 Ibid., 140–41.

70 Ibid., 141.

71 Ibid., 142.

72 Guy Hocquenghem, *Homosexual Desire*, trans. Daniella Dangoor (Durham: Duke University Press, 1993), 101.

73 Ibid., 99.

74 Camille Paglia, *Sexual Personae: Art and Decadence from Nefertiti to Emily Dickinson* (New York: Vintage Books, 1991), 13.

75 Ibid.

76 Ibid., 14.

77 Vidal, *Myra Breckinridge and Myron*, 143.

78 Ibid., 149.

79 Ibid., 151.

80 Ibid., 151–52.

81 Ibid., 155.

82 Ibid.

83 Ibid., 156.

84 Bersani, *Is the Rectum a Grave?*, 18.

85 Vidal, *Myra Breckinridge and Myron*, 156–57.

86 Ibid., 157.

87 Ibid.

88 Ibid.

89 Ibid., 156.
90 Ibid., 158.
91 Ibid., 224.
92 Wayne Koestenbaum, *The Anatomy of Harpo Marx* (Berkeley: University of California Press, 2012), 47.

References

Abraham, Hilda C., and Ernst L. Freud, eds. *A Psycho-Analytic Dialogue: The Letters of Sigmund Freud and Karl Abraham, 1907–1926*. Translated by Bernard Marsh and Hilda C. Abraham. New York: Basic Books, 1965.

Acuña, Manuel. "Nocturno." http://www.los-poetas.com/acuna/nocturno.htm.

Agamben, Giorgio. "Nudity." In *Nudities*, translated by David Kishick and Stefan Pedatella, 55–90. Stanford: Stanford University Press, 2011.

Agustini, Delmira. "El Intruso." In *Poesías completas*, 143. Barcelona: Editorial Labor, 1971.

Akiwenzie-Damm, Kateri. "Red Hot to the Touch: wRi(gh)ting Indigenous Erotica." In *Me Sexy: An Exploration of Native Sex and Sexuality*, edited by Drew Hayden Taylor, 109–23. Vancouver: Douglas and McIntyre, 2008.

Alberti, John. "'I Love You, Man': Bromances, the Construction of Masculinity, and the Continuing Evolution of Romantic Comedy." *Quarterly Review of Film and Video* 30, 2 (2013): 159–72.

Allan, George, and Merle Allshouse. "Current Issues in Process Theology: Some Reflections." *Christian Scholar* 50, 3 (1967): 167–76.

Allan, Jonathan A. "Reading from Behind: Anal Eroticism in Delmira Agustini's 'El Intruso.'" *Chasqui: Revista de literatura latinoamericana* 43, 2 (2014): 60–69.

———. "Theorising Male Virginity in Popular Romance." *Journal of Popular Romance Studies* 2, 1 (2011). http://jprstudies.org/2011/10/theorising-male-virginity/.

——. "Theorising the Monstrous and the Virginal in Popular Romance Novels." In *Monsters and the Monstrous: Myths and Metaphors of Enduring Evil*, edited by Jonathan A. Allan and Elizabeth Nelson, 67–76. Oxford: Inter-Disciplinary Press, 2012.

Allan, Jonathan A., Cristina Santos, and Adriana Spahr, eds. *Virgin Envy: Beyond the Hymen*. Regina: University of Regina Press, forthcoming.

Almaguer, Tomás. "Chicano Men: A Cartography of Homosexual Identity and Behavior." In *The Lesbian and Gay Studies Reader*, edited by Henry Abelove, Michèle Aina Barale, and David M. Halperin, 255–73. New York: Routledge, 1993.

Altman, Dennis. "Gore Vidal, Gay Hero in Spite of Himself." *Gay and Lesbian Review* 19, 6 (2012): 10–11.

Amico, Michael. "Gay Youths as 'Whorified Virgins.'" *Gay and Lesbian Review* 12, 4 (2005): 34–36.

Amory, Richard. *Song of the Loon*. Vancouver: Arsenal Pulp Press, 2005.

Anderson, Eric. "Adolescent Masculinity in an Age of Decreased Homohysteria." *Thymos: Journal of Boyhood Studies* 7, 1 (2013): 79–93.

——. *Inclusive Masculinity: The Changing Nature of Masculinities*. New York: Routledge, 2009.

Anonymous. Review of *Love and Death in the American Novel*, by Leslie Fiedler. *Daedalus* 92, 1 (1963): 167–72.

Arvin, Newton. *Herman Melville*. New York: Sloan, 1950.

——. *Whitman*. New York: Russell and Russell, 1969.

Atwood, Margaret. *Survival: A Thematic Guide to Canadian Literature*. Toronto: McClelland and Stewart, 2004.

Balderston, Daniel. "Excluded Middle? Bisexuality in *Doña Herlinda y su hijo*." In *Sex and Sexuality in Latin America*, edited by Daniel Balderston and Donna J. Guy, 190–99. New York: New York University Press, 1997.

Barthes, Roland. *Camera Lucida: Reflections on Photography*. Translated by Richard Howard. New York: Hill and Wang, 1981.

——. "The Death of the Author." In *Image-Music-Text*, 142–48. Translated by Stephen Heath. New York: Hill and Wang, 1977.

——. *A Lover's Discourse: Fragments*. Translated by Richard Howard. New York: Hill and Wang, 1978.

——. *Mourning Diary*. Translated by Richard Howard. New York: Hill and Wang, 2010.

——. *Mythologies*. Translated by Richard Howard and Annette Lavers. New York: Hill and Wang, 2012.

——. *The Neutral*. Translated by Rosalind E. Krauss and Denis Hollier. New York: Columbia University Press, 2005.

——. *The Pleasure of the Text*. Translated by Richard Miller. New York: Hill and Wang, 1975.

——. *The Preparation of the Novel.* Translated by Kate Briggs. New York: Columbia University Press, 2011.

——. *Roland Barthes by Roland Barthes.* Translated by Richard Howard. New York: Hill and Wang, 1977.

Beattie, Peter M. "Measures of Manhood: Honor, Enlisted Army Service, and Slavery's Decline in Brazil, 1850–90." In *Changing Men and Masculinities in Latin America,* edited by Matthew C. Gutmann, 233–55. Durham: Duke University Press, 2003.

Berger, David G., and Morton G. Wenger. "The Ideology of Virginity." *Journal of Marriage and Family* 35, 4 (1973): 666–76.

Berkeley-Hill, Owen. "The Psychology of the Anus." *Indian Medical Gazette* 48 (1913): 301–03.

Berlant, Lauren. *Cruel Optimism.* Durham: Duke University Press, 2011.

Berlant, Lauren, and Lee Edelman. *Sex, or the Unbearable.* Durham: Duke University Press, 2014.

Berlant, Lauren, and Michael Warner. "Sex in Public." *Critical Inquiry* 24, 2 (1998): 547–66.

Bermasin, Melina M., et al. "Defining Virginity and Abstinence: Adolescents' Interpretations of Sexual Behaviors." *Journal of Adolescent Health* 41 (2007): 182–88.

Bernau, Anke. *Virgins: A Cultural History.* London: Granta Books, 2007.

Berryman, Charles. "Satire in Gore Vidal's *Kalki.*" *Critique* 22, 2 (1980): 88–96.

Bersani, Leo. *The Culture of Redemption.* Cambridge, MA: Harvard University Press, 1990.

——. "Genital Chastity." In *Homosexuality and Psychoanalysis,* edited by Tim Dean and Christopher Lane, 351–66. Chicago: University of Chicago Press, 2001.

——. *Homos.* Cambridge, MA: Harvard University Press, 1995.

——. *Is the Rectum a Grave? And Other Essays.* Chicago: University of Chicago Press, 2010.

Bhattacharjee, Mala. "It's Raining Men: Tackling the Torrents of Male/Male Romantic Fiction Flooding the Market." RT *Book Reviews* (2012): 22–26. http://www.rtbookreviews.com/magazine-article/its-raining-men-tackling-torrents-malemale-romantic-fiction-flooding-market.

Blank, Hanne. *Virgin: The Untouched History.* New York: Bloomsbury, 2007.

Blechner, Mark J. "The Darkest Continent." *Studies in Gender and Sexuality* 11, 3 (2010): 146–50.

Bloom, Allan. *The Closing of the American Mind: Education and the Crisis of Reason.* New York: Simon and Schuster, 1987.

Bloom, Harold. *The Anxiety of Influence: A Theory of Poetry.* 2nd ed. New York: Oxford University Press, 1997.

——. "The Central Man." *New York Review of Books,* July 19, 1984: 5–8. http://www.nybooks.com/articles/archives/1984/jul/19/the-central-man.

———. *The Western Canon: The Books and School of the Ages.* New York: Riverhead Books, 1994.

Bolton, Matthew. "The Ethics of Alterity: Adapting Queerness in *Brokeback Mountain*." *Adaptation* 5, 1 (2011): 35–56.

Botticelli, Steven. "Thinking the Unthinkable: Anal Sex in Theory and Practice." *Studies in Gender and Sexuality* 11, 3 (2010): 112–23.

Boucher, Leigh, and Sarah Pinto. "'I Ain't Queer': Love, Masculinity, and History in *Brokeback Mountain*." *Journal of Men's Studies* 15, 3 (2007): 311–30.

Boyette, Purvis E. "*Myra Breckinridge* and Imitative Form." *Modern Fiction Studies* 17, 2 (1971): 229–38.

Branfman, Jonathan, and Susan Ekberg Stiritz. "Teaching Men's Anal Pleasure: Challenging Gender Norms with 'Prostage' Education." *American Journal of Sexuality Education* 7, 4 (2012): 404–28.

Brill, A. A. "Anal Eroticism and Character." *Journal of Abnormal Psychology* 7, 3 (1912): 196–203.

Brod, Harry. "They're Bi Shepherds, Not Gay Cowboys: The Misframing of *Brokeback Mountain*." *Journal of Men's Studies* 14, 2 (2006): 252–53.

Brown, Dan. *Angels and Demons.* New York: Washington Square Press, 2000.

Brown, J. Andrew. "Feminine Anxiety of Influence Revisited: Alfonsina Storni and Delmira Agustini." *Revista canadiense de estudios hispánicos* 23, 2 (1999): 191–203.

Butler, John. *This Gay Utopia.* Herndon, VA: Starbooks Press, 2004.

Butler, Judith. *Bodies that Matter: On the Discursive Limits of Sex.* New York: Routledge, 1993.

———. *Gender Trouble: Feminism and the Subversion of Identity.* New York: Routledge, 2000.

Calin, William. *The Twentieth-Century Humanist Critics: From Spitzer to Frye.* Toronto: University of Toronto Press, 2007.

Carballo-Diéguez, Alex, et al. "Looking for a Tall, Dark, Macho Man … Sexual-Role Behavior Variations in Latino Gay and Bisexual Men." *Culture, Health, and Sexuality* 6, 2 (2004): 159–71.

Carlevale, John. "The Dionysian Revival in American Fiction of the Sixties." *International Journal of the Classical Tradition* 12, 3 (2006): 364–91.

Caron, Sandra L., and Sarah P. Hinman. "'I Took His V-Card': An Exploratory Analysis of College Student Stories Involving Male Virginity Loss." *Sexuality and Culture* 17, 4 (2012): 525–39.

Carpenter, Laura M. "Virginity Loss in Reel/Real Life: Using Popular Movies to Navigate Sexual Initiation." *Sociological Forum* 24, 2 (2009): 804–27.

———. *Virginity Lost: An Intimate Portrait of First Sexual Experiences.* New York: New York University Press, 2005.

Carrington, Tori. *Private Sessions.* Don Mills, ON: Harlequin, 2010.

Castiglia, Chris. "'A Democratic and Fraternal Humanism': The Cant of Pessimism and Newton Arvin's Queer Socialism." *American Literary History* 21, 1 (2009): 159–82.

Chase, Richard. "Leslie Fiedler and American Culture." *Chicago Review* 14, 3 (1960): 8–18.

Chen, Elizabeth J. "Caught in a Bad Bromance." *Texas Journal of Women and Law* 21, 2 (2012): 241–66.

Cheyfitz, Eric. "Matthiessen's American Renaissance: Circumscribing the Revolution." *American Quarterly* 41, 2 (1989): 341–61.

Cixous, Hélène. "The Laugh of Medusa." In *Feminisms: An Anthology of Literary Theory and Criticism,* , edited by Robyn R. Hall and Diane Price Herndl, 347–62. New Brunswick, NJ: Rutgers University Press, 1997.

Clement, Ulrich. "Surveys of Heterosexual Behaviour." *Annual Review of Sex Research* 1, 1 (1990): 45–74.

Clover, Joshua, and Christopher Nealon. "Don't Ask, Don't Tell Me." *Film Quarterly* 60, 3 (2007): 62–67.

Cobb, Michael. "God Hates Cowboys (Kind of)." *GLQ: A Journal of Lesbian and Gay Studies* 13, 1 (2006): 102–05.

Connell, R. W. *Gender and Power.* Stanford: Stanford University Press, 1987.

Crimp, Douglas. "Mario Montez, for Shame." In *Gay Shame,* , edited by David M. Halperin and Valerie Traub, 63–75. Chicago: University of Chicago Press, 2009.

Cullinan, Heidi. *Dirty Laundry.* Hillsborough, NJ: Riptide Publishing, 2013. Kindle.

Cusset, François. *The Inverted Gaze: Queering the French Literary Classics in America.* Translated by David Homel. Vancouver: Arsenal Pulp Press, 2011.

Cvetkovich, Ann. *An Archive of Feelings: Trauma, Sexuality, and Lesbian Public Cultures.* Durham: Duke University Press, 2003.

——. *Depression: A Public Feeling.* Durham: Duke University Press, 2012.

——. "Public Feelings." *South Atlantic Quarterly* 106, 3 (2007): 459–68.

Darling, Carol A., and J. Kenneth Davidson. "The Relationship of Sexual Satisfaction to Coital Involvement: The Concept of Technical Virginity Revisited." *Deviant Behavior* 8, 1 (1987): 27–46.

Dean, Tim. "Bareback Time." In *Queer Times, Queer Becomings*, edited by E. L. McCallum and Mikko Tuhkanen, 75–100. Albany: SUNY Press, 2011.

——. *Unlimited Intimacy: Reflections on the Subculture of Barebacking.* Chicago: University of Chicago Press, 2009.

De Botton, Alain. *Essays in Love.* London: Picador, 2006.

Díaz Mediburo, Aaraón. *Los hijos homoeróticos de Jaime Humberto Hermosillo.* Mexico: Plaza y Valdés, 2004.

Diffrient, David Scott. "'Hard to Handle': Camp Criticism, Trash-Film Reception, and the Transgressive Pleasures of *Myra Breckinridge.*" *Cinema Journal* 52, 2 (2013): 46–70.

DiMarco, Hayley. *Technical Virgin: How Far Is Too Far?* Grand Rapids: Revell, Baker Publishing Group, 2006.

Dominguez, Ivo. *Beneath the Skins: The New Spirit and Politics of Kink Community*. Los Angeles: Daedalus, 1994.

Döpp, Hans-Jürgen. *In Praise of the Backside*. New York: Parkstone Press, 2011.

Duggan, Lisa. *The Twilight of Equality? Neoliberalism, Cultural Politics, and the Attack on Democracy*. Boston: Beacon Press, 2003.

Edelman, Lee. *No Future: Queer Theory and the Death Drive*. Durham: Duke University Press, 2004.

Edwards, Jason. *Eve Kosofsky Sedgwick*. London: Routledge, 2009.

Eisner, Douglas. "*Myra Breckinridge* and the Pathology of Heterosexuality." In *The Queer Sixties*, edited by Patricia Juliana Smith, 255–70. New York: Routledge, 1999.

Fiedler, Leslie A. "Come Back to the Raft Ag'in, Huck Honey!" In *Leslie Fiedler and American Culture*, edited by Steven G. Kellman and Irving Malin, 26–34. Cranbury, NJ: Associated University Press, 1999.

——. *Love and Death in the American Novel*. New York: Stein and Day, 1966.

——. "On Becoming a Pop Critic: A Memoir and a Meditation." *New England Review and Bread Loaf Quarterly* 5, 1–2 (1982): 195–207.

——. "Reestablishing Innocence: A Conservation with Leslie A. Fiedler." With Geoffrey Green. *Interdisciplinary Humanities* 20, 1 (2003): 93–105.

Fink, Bruce. *A Clinical Introduction to Lacanian Psychological Theory and Technique*. Cambridge, MA: Harvard University Press, 1997.

Firestone, Amanda. "'I Was with Edward in My Happy Place': The Romance of the *Twilight* Saga as an Aca-Fan." *Monsters and the Monstrous* 2, 2 (2012): 71–77.

Fletcher, Lisa. *Historical Romance Fiction: Heterosexuality and Performativity*. Hampshire: Ashgate, 2008.

Foster, David William. "Of Gay Caballeros and Other Noble Heroes." *Bilingual Review* 29, 2–3 (2008).

——. *Queer Issues in Contemporary Latin American Cinema*. Austin: University of Texas Press, 2003.

——. "Queering the Patriarchy in Hermosillo's *Doña Herlinda y su hijo*." In *Sexual Textualities: Essays on Queer/ing Latin American* Writing, 64–72. Austin: University of Texas Press, 1997.

——. *Sexual Textualities: Essays on Queer/ing Latin American Writing*. Austin: University of Texas Press, 1997.

Foster, Travis M. "Matthiessen's Public Privates: Homosexual Expression and the Aesthetics of Sexual Inversion." *American Literature* 78, 2 (2006): 235–62.

Foucault, M. *The History of Sexuality*. 3 vols. Translated by R. Hurley. New York: Vintage Books, 1978–86.

Francis, Margot. *Creative Subversions: Whiteness, Indigeneity, and the National Imaginary*. Vancouver: UBC Press, 2011.

Frantz, Sarah S. G. "'How We Love Is Our Soul': Joey W. Hill's BDSM Romance Holding the Cards." In *New Approaches to Popular Romance Fiction: Critical Essays*, edited by Sarah S. G. Frantz and Eric Murphy Selinger, 48–59. Jefferson, NC: McFarland, 2012.

———. Review of *Frat Boy and Toppy*, by Anne Tenino. *Dear Author: A Romance Review Blog for Readers by Readers*, March 28, 2012. http://dearauthor.com/book-reviews/overall-b-reviews/b-plus-reviews/review-frat-boy-and-toppy-by-anne-tenino/.

Freeman, Elizabeth. *Time Binds: Queer Temporalities, Queer Histories*. Durham: Duke University Press, 2010.

Freud, Sigmund. *The Standard Edition of the Complete Psychological Works of Sigmund Freud*. Edited and translated by J. Strachey. 24 vols. London: Hogarth Press, 1953–74.

Friedman, David M. *A Mind of Its Own: A Cultural History of the Penis*. New York: Penguin Books, 2001.

Frye, Northrop. *Collected Works of Northrop Frye*. General editor Alvin A. Lee. Toronto: University of Toronto Press, 1996–2012.

Fung, Richard. "Looking for My Penis: The Eroticized Asian in Gay Video Porn." In *Men's Lives*, 6th ed., edited by Michael Kimmel and Michael A. Messner, 543–52. Boston: Pearson, 2004.

Furtado, Ken. "Between the Covers." Review of *Song of the Loon*, by Richard Amory. *Echo Magazine* 16, 21 (2005): 68.

Gallop, Jane. *Anecdotal Theory*. Durham: Duke University Press, 2002.

———. *The Deaths of the Author: Reading and Writing in Time*. Durham: Duke University Press, 2011.

———. "Precocious Jouissance: Roland Barthes, Amatory Maladjustment, and Emotion." *New Literary History* 43, 2 (2012): 565–82.

Garber, Marjorie. "Translating F. O. Matthiessen." *Raritan* 30, 3 (2011): 94–106.

García Márquez, Gabriel. *The Autumn of the Patriarch*. Translated by Gregory Rabassa. New York: Harper Perennial, 1999.

Garibaldi, Christina. "Jennifer Lopez on the Year of the Booty: 'It's about Time.'" MTV *News*, October 1, 2014. http://www.mtv.com/news/1949743/jennifer-lopez-year-of-booty/.

Gay, Peter. *Freud: A Life for Our Time*. New York: W. W. Norton and Company, 1988.

Gilbert, Sandra M., and Susan Gubar. *The Madwoman in the Attic: The Woman Writer and the Nineteenth-Century Literary Imagination*. 2nd ed. New Haven: Yale University Press, 2000.

———. *No Man's Land: The Place of the Woman Writer in the Twentieth Century*. New Haven: Yale University Press, 1988.

Glover, K. C. "Males, Melville, and *Moby-Dick*: A New Male Studies Approach to Teaching Literature to College Men." *New Male Studies: An International Journal* 2 (2013): 62–67.

Goldberg, Jonathan. "Introduction." In *The Weather in Proust*, by Eve Kosofsky Sedgwick, xiii–xvi. Durham: Duke University Press, 2011.

———. *Sodometries: Renaissance Texts, Modern Sexualities.* Stanford: Stanford University Press, 1992.

Gonzalez, Octavio R. Review of *Unlimited Intimacy: Reflections on the Subculture of Barebacking*, by Tim Dean. *Cultural Critique* 81 (2012): 125–32.

Grossman, Jay. "The Canon in the Closet: Matthiessen's Whitman, Whitman's Matthiessen." *American Literature* 70, 4 (1998): 799–832.

Guss, Jeffrey R. "The Danger of Desire: Anal Sex and the Homo/Masculine Subject." *Studies in Gender and Sexuality* 11, 3 (2010): 124–40.

———. "Men, Anal Sex, and Desire: Who Wants What?" *Psychoanalysis, Culture, and Society* 12 (2007): 38–43.

Halberstam, Jack. "Queer Betrayals." In *Queer Futures: Reconsidering Ethics, Activism, and the Political*, edited by Elahe Haschemi Yekani, Eveline Kilian, and Beatrice Michaelis, 177–89. Burlington: Ashgate, 2013.

Halberstam, Judith. *Female Masculinity.* Durham: Duke University Press, 1998.

———. *The Queer Art of Failure.* Durham: Duke University Press, 2011.

———. "Shame and White Gay Masculinity." *Social Text* 84–85/23, 3–4 (2005): 219–33.

Halperin, David M. *How to Be Gay.* Cambridge, MA: Harvard University Press, 2012.

———. *Saint Foucault: Towards a Gay Hagiography.* New York: Oxford University Press, 1995.

———. *What Do Gay Men Want? An Essay on Sex, Risk, and Subjectivity.* Ann Arbor: University of Michigan Press, 2007.

Halperin, David M., and Valerie Traub. "Beyond Gay Pride." In *Gay Shame*, edited by David M. Halperin and Valerie Traub, 3–40. Chicago: University of Chicago Press, 2009.

Hamilton, A. C. *Northrop Frye: Anatomy of His Criticism.* Toronto: University of Toronto Press, 1990.

Hanson, Dian, ed. *Bikers.* Vol. 2 of *Tom of Finland.* Cologne: Taschen, 2012.

Harders, Robin. "Borderlands of Desire: Captivity, Romance, and the Revolutionary Power of Love." In *New Approaches to Popular Romance Fiction: Critical Essays*, edited by Sarah S. G. Frantz and Eric Murphy Selinger, 133–52. Jefferson, NC: McFarland, 2012.

Hattersley, Michael. "Men in Exciting Positions." Review of *Gay Men and Anal Eroticism: Tops, Bottoms, and Versatiles*, by Steven G. Underwood. *Gay and Lesbian Review* 10, 4 (2003): 44–45.

Hazard, Lucy Lockwood. *The Frontier in American Literature.* New York: Thomas Y. Crowell Company, 1927.

Hermosillo, Jaime Humberto, dir. *Doña Herlinda and Her Son* (DVD). Condor Media, 2002.

Hoad, Neville. "Queer Theory Addiction." In *After Sex? On Writing since Queer Theory*, edited by Janet Halley and Andrew Parker, 130–41. Durham: Duke University Press, 2011.

Hoang, Nguyen Tan. *A View from the Bottom: Asian American Masculinity and Sexual Representation*. Durham: Duke University Press, 2014.

Hocquenghem, Guy. *Homosexual Desire*. Translated by Daniella Dangoor. Durham: Duke University Press, 1993.

Hoppe, Trevor. "Loaded Meaning." *Journal of Sex Research* 48, 5 (2011): 506–08.

Horswell, Michael J. *Decolonizing the Sodomite: Queer Tropes of Sexuality in Colonial Andean Culture*. Austin: University of Texas Press, 2005.

Hutcheon, Linda. *A Theory of Adaptation*. New York: Routledge, 2006.

Iannacci, Elio. "What Women Want: Gay Male Romance Novels." *Globe and Mail*, February 11, 2011. http://www.theglobeandmail.com/life/relation-ships/what-women-want-gay-male-romance-novels/article565992/.

Iser, Wolfgang. *The Implied Reader: Patterns of Communication in Prose Fiction from Bunyan to Beckett*. Baltimore: Johns Hopkins University Press, 1974.

Isola, Mark John. "Disciplining Desire: The Fluid Textuality of Annie Proulx's *Brokeback Mountain*." *Nordic Journal of English Studies* 7, 1 (2008): 33–47.

James, Aaron. *Assholes: A Theory*. New York: Doubleday, 2012.

Jameson, Fredric. *The Political Unconscious: Narrative as a Socially Symbolic Act*. Ithaca: Cornell University Press, 1981.

Jones, Ann Rosalind. "Writing the Body: Toward an Understanding of l'Écriture féminine." In *The New Feminist Criticism: Essays on Women, Literature, and Theory*, edited by Elaine Showalter, 361–78. New York: Pantheon, 1985.

Jones, Ernest. "Anal-Erotic Character Traits." In *Papers on Psycho-Analysis*, 413–37. London: Maresfield Reprints, 1977.

———. *The Life and Work of Sigmund Freud*. 3 vols. New York: Basic Books, 1953–57.

Jones, Ginger. "Proulx's Pastoral: *Brokeback Mountain* as Sacred Space." In *Reading* Brokeback Mountain: *Essays on the Story and the Film*, edited by Jim Stacy, 19–28. Jefferson, NC: McFarland Press, 2007.

Joyce, James. *A Portrait of the Artist as a Young Man*. Edited by Seamus Deane. London: Penguin Books, 1992.

Justice, Daniel Heath, Bethany Schneider, and Mark Rifkin. "Heaven and Earth: From the Guest Editors." *GLQ: A Journal of Lesbian and Gay Studies* 16, 1–2 (2010): 1–3.

Kamblé, Jayashree. *Making Meaning in Popular Romance Fiction: An Epistemology*. New York: Palgrave Macmillan, 2014.

Kent, Kathryn R. "'Surprising Recognition': Genre, Poetic Form, and Erotics from Sedgwick's '1001 Seances' to *A Dialogue on Love*." *GLQ: A Journal of Lesbian and Gay Studies* 17, 4 (2011): 497–510.

Kimmel, Michael. "Homophobia as Masculinity: Fear, Shame, and Silence in the Construction of Gender Identity." In *Theorizing Masculinities*, edited by Harry Brod and Michael Kaufman, 119–41. Thousand Oaks, CA: Sage, 1994.

Kippax, Susan, and Gary Smith. "Anal Intercourse and Power in Sex between Men." *Sexualities* 4, 4 (2001): 413–34.

Koedt, Anne. "The Myth of the Vaginal Orgasm." In *Feminism and Sexuality: A Reader*, edited by Stevi Jackson and Sue Scott, 111–16. New York: Columbia University Press, 1996.

Koestenbaum, Wayne. *The Anatomy of Harpo Marx*. Berkeley: University of California Press, 2012.

——. "Foreword: In Defence of Nuance." In *A Lover's Discourse*, by Roland Barthes, ix–xx. New York: Hill and Wang, 2010.

——. *Humiliation*. New York: Picador, 2011.

——. *The Queen's Throat: Opera, Homosexuality, and the Mystery of Desire*. New York: Da Capo Press, 1993.

——. "The Rape of Rusty." In *My 1980s and Other* Essays, 143–54. New York: Farrar, Straus and Giroux, 2013.

Komisaruk, Barry R., and Beverly Whipple. "Non-Genital Orgasms." *Sexual and Relationship Therapy* 26, 4 (2011): 356–72.

Krentz, Jayne Ann. "Introduction." In *Dangerous Men and Adventurous Women: Romance Writers on the Appeal of the Romance*, 1–10. Philadelphia: University of Pennsylvania Press, 1992.

Kristeva, Julia. "Stabat Mother." In *Tales of Love*, translated by Leon S. Roudiez, 234–64. New York: Columbia University Press, 1987.

Krondorfer, Björn. *Male Confessions: Intimate Revelations and the Religious Imagination*. Stanford: Stanford University Press, 2010.

Lacan, Jacques. *Encore: On Feminine Sexuality, the Limits of Love, and Knowledge, 1972–1973*. Edited by Jacques-Alain Miller. Translated by Bruce Fink. New York: W. W. Norton and Company, 1988.

——. *The Other Side of Psychoanalysis*. Translated by Russell Grigg. New York: W. W. Norton and Company, 2007.

La Fountain-Stokes, Lawrence. "Gay Shame, Latina- and Latino-Style: A Critique of White Queer Performativity." In *Gay Latino Studies: A Critical Reader*, edited by Michael Hames-García and Ernesto Javier Martínez, 55–80. Durham: Duke University Press, 2011.

Lamos, Colleen. "James Joyce and the English Vice." *Novel: A Forum on Fiction* 29, 1 (1995): 19–31.

Lassen, Christian. *Camp Comforts: Reparative Gay Literature in Times of* AIDS. Bielefeld: Transcript Verlag, 2011.

Ledger, Brent. "Fucking Straight Guys Is the Best Revenge." *Xtra*, September 1, 2005, 15.

Lee, Joon Oluchi. "The Joy of the Castrated Boy." *Social Text* 23, 3–4 (2005): 35–56.

Lehman, Peter. "Crying over the Melodramatic Penis: Melodrama and Male Nudity in the Films of the 90s." In *Masculinity: Bodies, Movies, Culture*, edited by Peter Lehman, 25–44. New York: Routledge, 2001.

Looby, Christopher. "'Innocent Homosexuality': The Fiedler Thesis in Retrospection." In Adventures of Huckleberry Finn: *A Case Study in Critical Controversy*, edited by Gerald Graff and James Phelan, 535–50. Boston: Bedford–St. Martin's Press, 1995.

Loving, Jerome. *Walt Whitman: The Song of Himself*. Berkeley: University of California Press, 1999.

Madill, Shirley J. "Intelligent Mischief: The Paintings of Kent Monkman." In *The Triumph of Mischief*, edited by David Liss and Shirley J. Madill, 25–30. Hamilton: Art Gallery of Hamilton, 2008.

Márquez, Gabriel García. *Autumn of the Patriarch*. Translated by Gregory Rabassa. New York: Harper Perennial, 1999.

Martin, Robert K. "Newton Arvin: Literary Critic and Lewd Person." *American Literary History* 16, 2 (2004): 290–317.

Matthiessen, F. O. *American Renaissance: Art and Expression in the Age of Emerson and Whitman*. London: Oxford University Press, 1941.

Mavor, Carol. *Black and Blue: The Bruising Passion of* Camera Lucida, La jetée, Sans soleil, *and* Hiroshima mon amour. Durham: Duke University Press, 2012.

———. "Black and Blue: The Shadows of *Camera Lucida*." In *Photography Degree Zero: Reflections on Roland Barthes's* Camera Lucida, edited by Geoffrey Batchen, 211–41. Cambridge, MA: MIT Press, 2009.

———. *Reading Boyishly: Roland Barthes, J. M. Barrie, Jacques Henri Lartigue, Marcel Proust, and D. W. Winnicott*. Durham: Duke University Press, 2007.

McAlister, Jodi. "The Origins, Historical Evolution, and Representations of the Virgin Heroine in English Literature." PhD diss., Macquarie University, forthcoming.

———. "True Tales of the First Time: An Introduction to the Virginity Loss Confessional Genre." *Colloquy* forthcoming. Presented at the Confessional Culture conference, Monash University, July 5–6, 2012.

McCormack, Mark. *The Declining Significance of Homophobia: How Teenage Boys Are Redefining Masculinity and Heterosexuality*. Oxford: Oxford University Press, 2012.

McCune, Jeffrey Q., Jr., *Sexual Discretion: Black Masculinity and the Politics of Passing*. Chicago: University of Chicago Press, 2014.

Medley-Rath, Stephanie R. "'Am I Still a Virgin?': What Counts as Sex in 20 Years of *Seventeen*." *Sexuality and Culture* 11, 2 (2007): 24–38.

Meltzer, Donald. "The Relation of Anal Masturbation to Projective Identification." *International Journal of Psychoanalysis* 47 (1966): 335–42.

Melville, Herman. *Moby-Dick or, The Whale*. New York: Penguin, 1992.

Merino-Salas, Sergio, Miguel Angel Arrabal-Polo, and Miguel Arrabal-Martin. "Vaginal Vibrator in the Rectum of a Young Man." *Archive of Sexual Behaviour* 38 (2009): 457.

Mewshaw, Michael. "Vidal and Mailer." *South Central Review* 19, 1 (2002): 4–14.

Meyerowitz, Joanne. *How Sex Changed: A History of Transsexuality in the United States*. Cambridge, MA: Harvard University Press, 2002.

Miller, D. A. "On the Universality of *Brokeback*." *Film Quarterly* 60, 3 (2007): 50–60.

——. *Place for Us: Essay on the Broadway Musical*. Cambridge, MA: Harvard University Press, 1998.

Miller, James. *The Passion of Michel Foucault*. New York: Simon and Schuster, 1993.

Miller, Merle. *On Being Different: What It Means to Be a Homosexual*. London: Penguin, 2012.

Modleski, Tania. *Loving with a Vengeance: Mass-Produced Fantasies for Women*. 2nd ed. New York: Routledge, 2008.

Monkman, Kent. "Kent Monkman: The Canadian Artist Who Is Exploding the Mythology of the West—One Brushstroke at a Time." Interview with David Furnish. *Interview* 36, 2 (2006): 136–37.

Monro, Kate. *The First Time: True Tales of Virginity Lost and Found (Including My Own)*. London: Icon Books, 2011.

Moody, Sarah T. "Radical Metrics and Feminist Modernism: Agustini Rewrites Darío's *Prosas Profanas*." *Chasqui: Revista de literatura latinoamericana* 43, 1 (2014): 57–67.

Moon, Michael. *Darger's Resources*. Durham: Duke University Press, 2012.

——. "New Introduction." In *Homosexual Desire*, by Guy Hocquenghem, 9–21. Durham: Duke University Press, 1993.

Morin, Jack. *Anal Pleasure and Health: A Guide for Men, Women, and Couples*. San Francisco: Down There Press, 2010.

Mozdzen, Ian. "Reflections on *Song of the Loon* at Forty." *Gay and Lesbian Review* 13, 2 (2006): 40.

Mullaney, Jamie. "Like a Virgin: Temptation, Resistance, and the Construction of Identities Based on 'Not Doings.'" *Qualitative Sociology* 24, 1 (2001): 3–24.

Muñoz, José Esteban. *Cruising Utopia: The Then and There of Queer Futurity*. New York: New York University Press, 2009.

——. *Disidentifications: Queers of Color and the Performance of Politics*. New York: New York University Press, 1999.

——. "Feeling Brown, Feeling Down: Latina Affect, the Performativity of Race, and the Depressive Position." *Signs* 31, 3 (2006): 675–88.

——. "Thinking beyond Antirelationality and Antiutopianism in Queer Critique." *PMLA* 121, 3 (2006): 825–26.

Murphy, Erin, and J. Keith Vincent. "Introduction." *Criticism* 52, 2 (2010): 159–76.

"Myra the Messiah." *Time*, February 16, 1968, 111.

Nair, Drishya. "Pippa Middleton Catches Attention of Plastic Surgery Lovers." *International Business Times*, July 30, 2011. http://www.ibtimes.com/pippa-middleton-catches-attention-plastic-surgery-lovers-photos-820119.

Nayar, Sheila J. "A Good Man Is Impossible to Find: *Brokeback Mountain* as Heteronormative Tragedy." *Sexualities* 14, 2 (2011): 235–55.

Ngai, Sianne. *Ugly Feelings*. Cambridge, MA: Harvard University Press, 2005.

Nordling, Niklas, et al. "Differences and Similarities between Gay and Straight Individuals Involved in the Sadomasochistic Subculture." *Journal of Homosexuality* 50, 2–3 (2006): 41–57.

O'Grady, Jean. "Re-Valuing Value." In *Northrop Frye: New Directions from Old*, edited by David Rampton, 226–46. Ottawa: University of Ottawa Press, 2009.

Paglia, Camille. *Sexual Personae: Art and Decadence from Nefertiti to Emily Dickinson*. New York: Vintage Books, 1991.

Paradis, Kenneth. *Sex, Paranoia, and Modern Masculinity*. Albany: SUNY Press, 2007.

Parker, Richard. "Changing Sexualities: Masculinity and Male Homosexuality in Brazil." In *Changing Men and Masculinities in Latin America*, edited by Matthew C. Gutmann, 307–32. Durham: Duke University Press, 2003.

"The Parking Spot Escalation." Episode 9, Season 6, *The Big Bang Theory*.

Paz, Octavio. *El laberinto de la soledad*. Edited by Enrico Mario Santí. Madrid: Cátedra, 2003.

———. *The Labyrinth of Solitude and Other Writings*. Translated by Lysander Kemp, Yara Milos, and Rachel Phillips Belash. New York: Grove Press, 1985.

Peluffo, Ana. "'De todas las cabezas quiero tu cabeza': Figuraciones de la 'Femme Fatale' en Delmira Agustini." *Chasqui: Revista de literatura latinoamericana* 34, 2 (2005): 131–44.

Pérez, Hiram. "You Can Have My Brown Body and Eat It, Too!" *Social Text* 84–85/23, 3–4 (2005): 171–91.

Petersheim, Steven. "'Naked as a Pair of Tongs': Twain's Philosophy of Clothes." *Papers on Language and Literature: A Journal for Scholars and Critics of Language and Literature* 48, 2 (2012): 172–96.

Phillips, Adam. *The Beast in the Nursery: On Curiosity and Other Appetites*. New York: Vintage Books, 1998.

———. *Monogamy*. London: Faber and Faber, 1996.

———. *On Balance*. New York: Farrar, Straus and Giroux, 2010.

———. *On Flirtation: Psychoanalytic Essays on the Uncommitted Life*. Cambridge, MA: Harvard University Press, 1994.

Pitt, Richard N. "Downlow Mountain? De/Stigmatizing Bisexuality through Pitying and Pejorative Discourses in Media." *Journal of Men's Studies* 14, 2 (2006): 254–58.

Plante, Rebecca F. "Sexual Spanking, the Self, and the Construction of Deviance." *Journal of Homosexuality* 50, 2–3 (2006): 59–79.

Potts, Annie. "'The Essence of the Hard On': Hegemonic Masculinity and the Cultural Construction of 'Erectile Dysfunction.'" *Men and Masculinities* 3 (2000): 85–103.

Pronger, Brian. "On Your Knees: Carnal Knowledge, Masculine Dissolution, Doing Feminism." In *Men Doing Feminism*, edited by Tom Digby, 69–80. New York: Routledge, 1998.

——. "Outta My Endzone: Sport and the Territorial Anus." *Journal of Sport and Social Issues* 23, 4 (1999): 373–89.

Proulx, Annie. *Brokeback Mountain*. New York: Scribner, 1997.

Quiroga, José. *Tropics of Desire: Interventions from Queer Latino America*. New York: New York University Press, 2000.

Radway, Janice. *Reading the Romance: Women, Patriarchy, and Popular Literature*. Chapel Hill: University of North Carolina Press, 1991.

Ramakers, Micha. *Dirty Pictures: Tom of Finland, Masculinity, and Homosexuality*. New York: St. Martin's Press, 2000.

Redding, Arthur. "Closet, Coup, and Cold War: F. O. Matthiessen's *From the Heart of Europe*." *Boundary 2* 33, 1 (2006): 171–201.

Reid, Jennifer. *Louis Riel and the Creation of Modern Canada: Mythic Discourse and the Postcolonial State*. Albuquerque: University of New Mexico Press, 2008.

Regis, Pamela. "What Do Critics Owe the Romance?" *Journal of Popular Romance Studies* 2, 1 (2011). http://jprstudies.org/2011/10/"what-do-critics-owe-the-romance-keynote-address-at-the-second-annual-conference-of-the-international-association-for-the-study-of-popular-romance"-by-pamela-regis/.

Regnerus, Mark, and Jeremy Uecker. *Premarital Sex in America: How Young Americans Meet, Mate, and Think about Marrying*. Oxford: Oxford University Press, 2011.

Rich, B. Ruby. "Ang Lee's Lonesome Cowboys." In *New Queer Cinema: The Director's Cut*, 185–201. Durham: Duke University Press, 2013.

Rohy, Valerie. "In the Queer Archive: Fun Home." *GLQ: A Journal of Lesbian and Gay Studies* 16, 3 (2010): 341–61.

Ruiz-Pérez, Ignacio. "Contra-escrituras: Delmira Agustini, Alfonsina Storni, y la subversión del modernismo." *Revista hispánica moderna* 61, 2 (2008): 183–96.

Russo, Vito. *The Celluloid Closet: Homosexuality in the Movies*. New York: Quality Paperback Book Club, 1987.

Sagarin, Edward. "Typologies of Sexual Behavior." *Journal of Sex Research* 7, 4 (1971): 282–88.

Saint-Amand, Pierre. "The Secretive Body: Roland Barthes's Gay Erotics." Translated by Charles A. Porter and Noah Guynn. *Yale French Studies* 90 (1996): 153–71.

Santos, Cristina. *Bending the Rules in the Quest for an Authentic Female Identity: Clarice Lispector and Carmen Boullosa*. New York: Peter Lang, 2004.

Santos, Cristina, and Adriana Spahr, eds. *Defiant Deviance: The Irreality of Reality in the Cultural Imaginary*. New York: Peter Lang, 2006.

Savage, Dan. "No Homo." *Savage Love*, October 1, 2009. http://www.thestranger.com/seattle/SavageLove?oid=2358429.

Savin-Williams, Ritch C. *The New Gay Teenager*. Cambridge, MA: Harvard University Press, 2005.

Savoy, Eric. "Arvin's Melville, Martin's Arvin." *GLQ: A Journal of Lesbian and Gay Studies* 14, 4 (2008): 609–15.

Schehr, Lawrence R. *The Shock of Men: Homosexual Hermeneutics in French Writing*. Stanford: Stanford University Press, 1995.

Schuessler, Michael. "'Vestidas, Locas, Mayates,' and 'Machos': History and Homosexuality in Mexican Cinema." *Cinematic and Literary Representations of Spanish and Latin American Themes*, special issue of *Chasqui: Revista de literatura latinoamericana* 34, 2(2005): 132–44.

Sedgwick, Eve Kosofsky. *Between Men: English Literature and Male Homosocial Desire*. New York: Columbia University Press, 1985.

——. *Epistemology of the Closet*. Berkeley: University of California Press, 1990.

——. "Queerer than Fiction." *Studies in the Novel* 28, 3 (1996): 277–80.

——. "Shame, Theatricality, and Queer Performativity: Henry James's *The Art of the Novel*." In *Gay Shame*, edited by David M. Halperin and Valerie Traub, 49–62. Chicago: University of Chicago Press, 2009.

——. *Tendencies*. Durham: Duke University Press, 1993.

——. *Touching Feeling: Affect, Pedagogy, Performativity*. Durham: Duke University Press, 2003.

——. *The Weather in Proust*. Edited by Jonathan Goldberg. Durham: Duke University Press, 2011.

Selinger, Eric Murphy, and Sarah S. G. Frantz. "Introduction." In *New Approaches to Popular Romance Fiction*, edited by Sarah S. G. Frantz and Eric Murphy Selinger, 1–19. Jefferson, NC: McFarland Press, 2012.

Shahani, Nishant. *Queer Retrosexualities: The Politics of Reparative Return*. Lanham: Lehigh University Press, 2012.

Shand-Tucci, Douglass. *The Crimson Letter: Harvard, Homosexuality, and the Shaping of American Culture*. New York: St. Martin's Press, 2003.

Shengold, Leonard. *Halo in the Sky: Observations on Anality and Defense*. New Haven: Yale University Press, 1988.

Showalter, Elaine. "Feminist Criticism in the Wilderness." In *The New Feminist Criticism: Essays on Women, Literature, and Theory*, edited by Elaine Showalter, 243–70. New York: Pantheon, 1985.

———. *A Jury of Her Peers: Celebrating American Women Writers from Anne Bradstreet to Annie Proulx*. New York: Vintage, 2010.

Simonet, Madeleine. "Delmira Agustini." *Hispania: A Journal Devoted to the Teaching of Spanish and Portuguese* 39, 4 (1956): 397–402.

Snediker, Michael D. *Queer Optimism: Lyric Personhood and Other Felicitous Persuasions*. Minneapolis: University of Minnesota Press, 2009.

Snider, Clifton. "Queer Persona and the Gay Gaze in *Brokeback Mountain*: Story and Film." *Psychological Perspectives: A Quarterly Journal of Jungian Thought* 51, 1 (2008): 54–69.

Snitow, Ann. "Mass Market Romance: Pornography for Women Is Different." In *Women and Romance: A Reader*, edited by Susan Ostrov Weisser, 307–22. New York: New York University Press, 2001.

Solnit, Rebecca. *Men Explain Things to Me*. Chicago: Haymarket Books, 2014.

Spengler, Oswald. *The Decline of the West*. 1918; reprinted, Oxford: Oxford University Press, 1991.

Spohrer, Erika. "Not a Gay Cowboy Movie? *Brokeback Mountain* and the Importance of Genre." *Journal of Popular Film and Television* 37, 1 (2009): 26–33.

Stacey, Jackie. "Wishing Away Ambivalence." *Feminist Theory* 15, 1 (2014): 39–49.

Stavans, Ilan. "The Latin Phallus." In *Muy Macho: Latino Men Confront Their Manhood*, edited by Ray González, 143–64. New York: Random House, 1996.

Stimpson, Catharine R. "My O My O Myra." *New England Review* 14, 1 (1990): 102–15.

Stockton, Kathryn Bond. *Beautiful Bottom, Beautiful Shame: Where "Black" Meets "Queer."* Durham: Duke University Press, 2006.

Stopes, Marie C. "The Technique of Contraception: The Principles and Practice of Anti-Conceptional Methods." *Eugenics Review* 21, 2 (1929): 136–38.

Tebor, Irving B. "Male Virgins: Conflicts and Group Support in American Culture." *Family Life Coordinator* 9, 3–4 (1961): 40–42.

Tenino, Anne. *Frat Boy and Toppy*. Hillsborough, NJ: Riptide Publishing, 2012.

Thomas, Calvin. "Must Desire Be Taken Literally?" *Parallax* 8, 4 (2002): 46–56.

Thomas, Kate. "Post Sex: On Being Too Slow, Too Stupid, Too Soon." In *After Sex? On Writing since Queer Theory*, edited by Janet Halley and Andrew Parker, 66–75. Durham: Duke University Press, 2011.

Todd, Ian Scott. "Outside/In: Abjection, Space, and Landscape in *Brokeback Mountain*." *Scope* 13 (2009). http://www.scope.nottingham.ac.uk/article.php?issue=13&id=1098.

Tomkins, Silvan. *Shame and Its Sisters: A Silvan Tomkins Reader*. Edited by Eve Kosofsky Sedgwick and Adam Frank. Durham: Duke University Press, 1995.

Twain, Mark. *Adventures of Huckleberry Finn*. Edited by Emory Elliot. Oxford: Oxford University Press, 1999.

———. *The Adventures of Tom Sawyer*. New York: Modern Library, 2001.

Uecker, Jeremy E., Nicole Angotti, and Mark D. Regnerus. "Going Most of the Way: 'Technical Virginity' among American Adolescents." *Social Science Research* 37 (2008): 1200–15.

Underwood, Steven G. *Gay Men and Anal Eroticism: Tops, Bottoms, and Versatiles*. Binghamton, NY: Harrington Park Press, 2003.

Valdés, Mario J. *World-Making: The Literary Truth-Claim and the Interpretation of Texts*. Toronto: University of Toronto Press, 1992.

Valenti, Jessica. *The Purity Myth: How America's Obsession with Virginity Is Hurting Young Women*. Berkeley: Seal Press, 2010.

van Driel, Mels. *Manhood: The Rise and Fall of the Penis*. London: Reaktion Books, 2009.

Vidal, Gore. *The City and the Pillar*. 1948; reprinted, New York: Vintage, 1995.

———. *Myra Breckinridge and Myron*. 1968; reprinted, London: Abacus, 1986.

Waldby, Catherine. "Destruction: Boundary Erotics and the Refiguration of the Heterosexual Male Body." In *Sexy Bodies: The Strange Carnalities of Feminism*, edited by Elizabeth Grosz and Elspeth Probyn, 266–77. New York: Routledge, 1995.

Warner, Michael. *Fear of a Queer Planet: Queer Politics and Social Theory*. Minneapolis: University of Minnesota Press, 1993.

———. *The Trouble with Normal: Sex, Politics, and the Ethics of Queer Life*. Cambridge, MA: Harvard University Press, 1999.

Weeks, Jeffrey. "Introduction." In *Homosexual Desire*, by Guy Hocquenghem, 23–47. Durham: Duke University Press, 1993.

Weiss, Margot. *Techniques of Pleasure: BDSM and the Circuits of Sexuality*. Durham: Duke University Press, 2011.

Wendell, Sarah, and Candy Tan. *Beyond Heaving Bosoms: The Smart Bitches' Guide to Romance Novels*. New York: Simon and Schuster, 2009.

Werth, Barry. *The Scarlet Professor: Newton Arvin, a Literary Life Shattered by Scandal*. New York: Talese, 2001.

White, Hayden. *Tropics of Discourse: Essays in Cultural Criticism*. Baltimore: Johns Hopkins University Press, 1978.

Whitehead, Stephen M. *Men and Masculinities*. London: Polity, 2002.

Whitman, Walt. *Leaves of Grass: The First (1855) Edition*. Edited by Malcolm Cowley. New York: Penguin, 1959.

Wiegman, Robyn. "The Times We're In: Queer Feminist Criticism and the Reparative 'Turn.'" *Feminist Theory* 15, 1 (2014): 4–25.

Wieland, Christina. "Human Longings and Masculine Terrors: Masculinity and Separatism from the Mother." *British Journal of Psychotherapy* 22, 1 (2005): 71–86.

Wilbern, David. "Like Two Skins, One inside the Other: Dual Unity in *Broke-back Mountain*." *PsyArt: An Online Journal for the Psychological Study of the Arts* (2008). http://www.psyartjournal.com/article/show/willbern-like_two_skins_one_inside_the_other_dual.

Wilhelm, John F., and Mary Ann Wilhelm. "*Myra Breckinridge*: A Study in Identity." *Journal of Popular Culture* 3, 3 (1969): 590–99.

Wilkinson, Margaret. "His Mother-Tongue: From Stuttering to Separation, a Case History." *Journal of Analytical Psychology* 46 (2001): 257–73.

Winnicott, D. W. *The Child, the Family, and the Outside World*. Cambridge, MA: Perseus Publishing, 1987.

———. *Playing and Reality*. London: Routledge, 2005.

Wright, William. *Harvard's Secret Court: The Savage 1920 Purge of Campus Homosexuals*. New York: St. Martin's Press, 2005.

Yeats, W. B. "The Second Coming." In *The Major Works*, edited by Edward Larissy, 91–92. Oxford: Oxford University Press, 1997.

Index

241

JONATHAN A. ALLAN IS CANADA RESEARCH Chair in Queer Theory and Assistant Professor in Gender and Women's Studies and English and Creative Writing at Brandon University. He is an editor of and contributing author to *Virgin Envy: The Cultural (In)Significance of the Hymen*, forthcoming from the University of Regina Press. He is currently writing two books: *Uncut: The Foreskin Archive*, a cultural study of the foreskin that brings together literary criticism, religious studies, the biomedical sciences, and critical theory; and *Happily Ever After? Affect, Futurity, and Popular Romance*, a critical study of the phrase "happily ever after."

Allan sits on the editorial/advisory boards of *Feral Feminisms*, *Journal of Popular Romance Studies*, *Journal of Men's Studies*, *Chasqui: Revista de literatura latinoamericana*, *Masculinities: A Journal of Identity and Culture* and is the book series editor of *The Exquisite Corpse*, published by University of Regina Press.